HINDU VIEW OF CHRIST

By the same author

MODERN PROBLEMS AND RELIGION
SPIRITUAL PRACTICES
MENTAL HEALTH AND HINDU PSYCHOLOGY
HINDU PSYCHOLOGY
HINDU VIEW OF CHRIST

SWAMI AKHILANANDA

Hindu View of Christ

By

SWAMI AKHILANANDA

Introduction by Dr. Walter G. Muelder
Dean, Boston University, School of Theology

BOSTON
BRANDEN PRESS
PUBLISHERS

Standard Book Number 8283-1355-5
Library of Congress Catalog Card Number 72-77209
Printed in the United States of America

CONTENTS

Chapter *Page*

Introduction 5
Preface 11
I. Christ, An Incarnation 15
II. Christ, An Oriental 45
III. Christ, A Yogi 72
IV. Christ and Spiritual Practices 100
V. Christ and Everyday Problems 128
VI. Christ and Power 152
VII. Christ and the Cross 179
VIII. Spirit of Easter 198
IX. Teaching and Preaching 219
X. Christian Missions 245
Bibliography 285
Index 289

To my beloved Master

SRIMAT SWAMI BRAHMANANDAJI MAHARAJ

spiritual son of Sri Ramakrishna
with loving devotion and humble salutations

INTRODUCTION

The dialogue between the living world religions and Christianity has developed greatly in the twenty years since Swami Akhilananda published his *Hindu View of Christ*.

The study of history of non-Christian religions has grown markedly in the U. S. A. In such a context the serious study of persons and symbols like Jesus Christ by the maturest personalities like Swami Akhilananda must not go unnoticed. His deep appreciation for Christ does not compromise his Vedantist faith that loyalty to Christ is consistent at the practical dualistic level with non-dualistic ultimate monism.

November, 1971

WALTER G. MUELDER
Dean, Boston University,
School of Theology

INTRODUCTION

In his book, *Hindu Psychology*, Swami Akhilananda introduced Western minds to the principles of psychology which dominate Hindu thought. This book has performed a significant service for general psychology, for students of the psychology of religion, and for the cause of intercultural understanding. By the use of many Western illustrations and ideas drawn from the Scriptures of Christianity and the writings of the mystics, he showed not only the meaning of unfamiliar Hindu concepts but also a wide grasp of the classics of the Church. His many references to Christ's experiences and teachings revealed an intimate knowledge of Christ's psychological and spiritual insights. In *Hindu Psychology* the interest in Jesus is primarily for purposes of illustration. The purpose is to show its meaning for the West. In the present volume, however, the author makes the personality of Christ central. This book extends the mutuality of understanding from the general perspectives of psychology to the practical religious problems of humility, obedience, conversion and love to God incarnate in Christ. There is much of the spirit of the *Theologia Germanica* in its pages:

> He who knoweth and understandeth Christ's life, knoweth and understandeth Christ Himself; and in like manner, he who understandeth not His life, doth not understand Christ Himself. And he who believeth on Christ, believeth that His life is the best and noblest life that can be, and if a man believe not this, neither doth he believe on Christ Himself. And in so far as a man's life is according to Christ, Christ Himself dwelleth in him. . . . And whatever may bring about that new birth which maketh alive in Christ, to that let us cleave with all our might and to nought else; and let us forswear and flee all that may hinder it.

It is natural for Hindus to affirm unity in religion. A Hindu view of Christ turns easily to such passages in the Johannine literature as "I and my Father are one." This, like the famous expression, "That art thou," is regarded as the last word on religion. But there are other expressions in the Synoptic tradition of the teachings of Jesus which Hindus eagerly adopt: "Lay up for yourselves treasures in heaven, where neither moth nor rust doth corrupt and where thieves do not break through nor steal"; "For you always have the poor with you, but you will not always have me"; "You cannot serve God and mammon"; "My Father, . . . not as I will, but as thou wilt." Since these and many other sayings commend themselves to Christians and Hindus alike, it is significant to have a full length statement of a Hindu view of Christ. This book speaks not only of the words of Jesus but of Christ, the incarnation of God. Swami Akhilananda unites East and West in a moving appreciation of Jesus Christ and his significance for the whole world.

The religious significance of Christ is here explored from within and in such a way that the daily relevance of his life and instruction are clearly delineated. This appreciative method stands in sharp contrast to the predominantly external type of criticism generally employed by Western scholars and Christians in approaching Hinduism, Buddhism and other great religions. Thus, while it is important at the present time to consider Christ through oriental perspectives, it is even more important to appropriate him from an inclusive standpoint. Hindu loyalty to Christ and the New Testament are more important in the long run than expedient Indian policy regarding Christian missions in the short run.

Throughout this book the main outlines of Hindu philosophy and psychology of religion are apparent. Handling the source material about Christ within such an outline brings out the affinities between his way of life and religion and that of Hinduism. Such a treatment is culturally illuminating in both directions, giving the Christian equivalents of Hindu thought and the Hindu equivalents of Synoptic and Johannine teachings. Inevitably, in such a discussion, the "Hindu view of Christ" stands in especially marked contrast to some forms of Western theology. It raises the stimulating question as to whether some aspects of Eastern philosophy of religion may not be closer to earliest Christianity than some forms of it born amid the despair of Western society. Swami Akhilananda's criticism of certain theologians is interesting because he thinks they violate essential Christianity, not simply that they contradict Hinduism. He raises here a vital issue. Philosophical and theological issues are not raised or debated as such, however. One of the great contributions of the book, is its genuinely practical method. What is at stake is the religious life itself. It is this religious life which everywhere in the world today is threatened by secularism and the new paganisms. The spiritual disciplines by which human experience must be redirected have much in common the world over in their work of overcoming egocentricity and converting men to God-centered lives of obedience and sharing love. Swami Akhilananda is not baffled by the Christian thought of conversion to which we have just referred. Jesus' word to Nicodemus, "You must be born anew" is fully acceptable. The author comes to terms not only with Christian teaching but with Christ himself.

It has long been recognized that the Johannine Christ is a figure congenial to Eastern modes of thought and experience. Hindus have pointed out the similarities of the Bhagavad Gita and the Gospel of John. But Christian leaders, especially among the Younger Churches, have no less focused attention on the appeal which the Johannine literature has to Buddhists and Taoists as well as to Hindus. One of the papers dealing with the International Missionary Council held at Tambaram in 1938 is entitled "The Johannine Approach." In this paper Karl Ludwig Reichelt, after expressing his conviction of the essential harmony between the synoptic Gospels and the Fourth Gospel and after expressing the conviction also that there is full harmony between St. Paul and St. John states: "I think that St. Paul goes a long way in his work and his writings to put into practice the Johannine principles and methods of approach." It is especially the problem of John's relevance for practical missionary work that

Professor Reichelt has in mind. From a world-wide perspective this conviction outweighs strict exegetical considerations, for what is felt is the force of John's Gospel, "with its ringing and special emphasis on the fact that Christ Jesus is the Kyrios (Lord) also in the sense of the all-embracing and all-pervading creative Word of God." Even officially the Tambaram Conference pointed out that Christianity must overcome the demand of expressing itself in terms acceptable to a Western Theologian alone. Swami Akhilananda's sympathetic use of John and the Synoptic Gospels indicates how strong the inclusive approach can be. Although Hindus believe in universal conceptions, Christians also seek the all-embracing fellowship of God's all-including love. It is significant that today the Fourth Gospel has a renewed status among the Western Christian scholars as well as among Eastern Christian thinkers and missionaries.

The practical approach employed in this book enriches the older methods of comparative religion which were primarily intellectualistic and which therefore handled the riches of Eastern religious Scriptures almost exclusively from the doctrinal side. There is urgent need that this procedure be corrected in at least two ways, both of them growing out of the practical approach. In the first place, religion is primarily an experiential affair, and a religious adjustment to life can hardly be fully understood apart from a sincere personal quest. Thus the practical method is deeply functional and invites the seeker to enter seriously and with empathy into a religion with which he may not be thoroughly at home. Spiritual truth must be spiritually appropriated In the second place, the older studies of Hinduism have left a thick deposit of error in the West. This deposit of error needs desperately to be removed. Through the comparison of doctrines as if the religions were but barren intellectual algebras, many valued judgments have been passed on about terms which have not been intimately lived with or accurately understood from within. The present study adds to that growing literature of efforts to bring corrected understanding to the attention of the religious public. Hindus and Christians alike should enter into a deeper appreciation of each others' analogous and often identical insights into the spiritual life. Long experience on the part of many persons who have intermingled and shared their religious life both in the East and West testifies to the existence of a common spiritual brotherhood which goes deeper than language, artifacts, and cultural institutions. Significant differences have also been brought out by the practical inner approach. In any event, here is a method which provides data which philosophers of religion and theologians must take seriously. Thus the functional method may prove much more rewarding than many who now defend Eastern or Western perspectives alone surmise.

Whether the functional approach is finally the best method of handling comparative problems or not, there can be little doubt that it makes for mutuality and intercultural harmony. Whether many agree with what is said of Christ or not, it remains true that Swami Akhilananda's writing will enrich the spiritual life of any one who takes the book seriously, and seriously it must be taken. The spiritual life is finally one. In these days it is not so important any longer what the East thinks about Western civilization or the West about Eastern civilization. More basic is the struggle of the religious life against its enemies in all cultures. Excessive nationalism and false notions of national sovereignty, scientism, materialism, secularism, positivism, religious fanaticism, reliance on power and violence, the love of creature comforts and transient good have eaten corrosively into all cultures. All the great religions of the world have a common task in combatting these evils. This is an era in which the creative interaction of the world's universal religions should bring unity for a world weary of war but too distracted, confused, and anxious to find peace. Swami Akhilananda shows how Christ can overcome violence and bring peace.

Finally, this book deals specifically with many questions of interest to Christians: Was Jesus Christ an incarnation? What is Yoga? Did Jesus practice spiritual exercises? Whence were they derived? Is Hinduism interested in practical service? Was Christ a mystic? What is the meaning of the Cross? How shall we think of Easter? Is Hinduism merely negative in its attitude toward life? What is the function of preaching, of teaching?

HINDU VIEW OF CHRIST

What is the basic Hindu attitude toward missions? What is the meaning of Christ for the power struggle in the world? On all of these points Swami Akhilananda writes with clarity and with persuasive religious appeal.

Walter G. Muelder
Dean, School of Theology
Boston University

PREFACE

Nearly thirty-five years ago we had the privilege of attending the Christmas celebration in the headquarters of the Ramakrishna Order, a Hindu monastery situated on the bank of the Ganges in Belur, a suburb of Calcutta, India. Swami Brahmananda, our great master, and a few other disciples of Sri Ramakrishna, were celebrating the occasion. It made a deep impression on our youthful minds, and we observed with what reverence and devotion they worshipped Jesus, the Christ, as an incarnation of God. This and successive celebrations of Christmas were so elevating that even now the effect remains with us.

It is impossible for the human mind to comprehend fully the advent, nature, and life of an incarnation of God. Philosophically or rationally speaking, it is difficult to understand how the Infinite can become finite in the form of a man. The very problem of incarnation baffles the greatest philosophers and thinkers. So we feel that it is audacious to attempt to discuss the life and purpose of an incarnation. Yet, the human mind often tries to grasp what is ever beyond its comprehension. There is a saying in India: "What a pity that this ignorant mind wants to fathom the unfathomable (Infinite) which is beyond the comprehension of the greatest saints." We fully realize our inability to discuss the various implications of the life and teachings of Jesus, the Christ. We are only trying to share with the readers a few reflective thoughts regarding this personality, whom we, as well as most Christians, view as divine.

Christianity and Hinduism are the two great religions which maintain that God incarnates Himself as a human being to establish the spirit of religion in the world. But for the advent of divine incarnations, man would grope blindly for the experience of God. They are connecting links between God and man. As such, they advise us to contemplate them and mold our lives according to the model which they demonstrate. They are also taken as redeemers and saviours of the human soul through their infinite love and grace.

This humble attempt will seek to present the similarities and differences in the views of the Christians and the Hindus. In brief, orthodox Christians conceive that God has been incarnated only once, as Jesus, the Christ, while Hindus believe that God incarnates Himself at different times to fulfill a particular mission and to re-establish the spirit of religion, whenever religion declines and irreligion prevails. We are fully aware that many orthodox Christians will consider that our views are not acceptable to them and that many liberal Christians will regard our views as far too orthodox, as we look upon Jesus as an incarnation of God rather than merely as a "good man." We hope that both the groups will consider that we are attempting to present a Hindu conception of Jesus. We also hope that the readers will try sympathetically to understand our viewpoint.

In later chapters, considerable attention is given to social problems in present day Christian communities, in the light of what we understand as the life and teachings of Jesus. We have also tried to make clear from the Hindu point of view what religious teachings and missionary activities should be. We know that there will be a difference of opinion; yet we are compelled by the desire for dispassionate understanding of spiritual ideals and their implication in social and individual life to present the views that seem to be in accordance with the words of this great Master, Jesus. As we are going through a critical juncture of the world's history, it is worth while for all of us to evaluate our activities in the light of great personalities. Christians in the Western world have been active for several centuries. We hope that they will consider the evaluation of their activities, which are discussed in the later chapters, in the spirit in which it is given. We are offering the ideas as sympathetic and loving co-workers for a future civilization rather than as critics.

It goes without saying that sincere thinkers all over the world are seeking a solution to current conflicts and tensions. It is needless to say that we cannot remove tensions and other disturbances without basic understanding of the different cultures and religious groups. If we really want to preserve modern civilization, we must go to its foundation. The main purpose of this presentation is to establish harmony and understanding among religious groups and to show the common background of the various religious ideals imparted by the founders of the different religions. It is a humble attempt to establish harmony of religious ideals.

That harmony can be established was demonstrated in the life of Sri Ramakrishna of Calcutta, India, in the last century, when He practiced the methods prescribed by various religions. It was He who verified not only the Hindu methods of realization of God but also those of the Christians, Mohammedans, and others. It was also He who, while remaining a Hindu, experienced God through the Christian way in His spiritual experiences. His disciples, like Swami Vivekananda, Swami Brahmananda, Swami Saradananda, Swami Ramakrishnananda, and others, also had exalted experiences of Jesus and the Christian ideals. These disciples made a tremendous impression on the Hindu mind. So a Hindu may worship Jesus as an incarnation of God, as shown in this book.

One may question whether this liberalism in the Hindu group was introduced by Sri Ramakrishna and His disciples among themselves and their followers or whether it is a tendency of the Hindu teachings in general. We must make it clear that Hindu scriptures teach universality of religion all over India. Yet it was indeed Sri Ramakrishna who actually first demonstrated the full universality of religion. He was the elaborator and demonstrator of the harmony of religion. He introduced the worship of Jesus as an incarnation, as the Hindus worship other incarnations of God. So the ideas that are humbly expressed in the book are in accordance with the ancient Hindu teachings, as carried further by Sri Ramakrishna.

If there is any value in this book, the credit goes to Sri Ramakrishna and His great disciples. The teachings of our great leaders, Swami Vivekananda and Swami Brahmananda, are the inspiring power behind this attempt; and whatever worth there may be in it is due to their blessed influence and that of the other disciples of the great Master.

The twelve chapters were originally extemporaneous lectures delivered in Boston and Providence and recorded by stenographers or by recording machine. For this reason, it may seem that some of the chapters are a little less formal than one might expect in a book. However, the material has undergone considerable revision.

Most of the Swamis of the Ramakrishna Order in America read the manuscript partly or wholly. We gratefully aknowledge thanks to them for their valuable suggestions.

Professor Edgar S. Brightman of Boston University, Dean Walter Muelder of the Boston University School of Theology, Professor Paul E. Johnson, Professor L. Harold DeWolf, and Professor Robert P. Benedict of Boston University, Professor Joachim Wach of the University of Chicago, Professor Pitirim A. Sorokin of Harvard University, Professor Henry Cadbury of the Harvard University Divinity School, and Dr. Allen E. Claxton of New York City, were kind enough to read the manuscript. All of them gave very important suggestions. We gratefully acknowledge their contributions to the book. Professor Brightman and Dean Muelder especially deserve our affectionate gratitude. We are thankful to Dean Muelder for his valuable Introduction. We thank some of our students who helped in typing the manuscript and reading the proofs. We also acknowledge and thank the authors and publishers, for permission to quote from books published by them.

May the fruit of this work be acceptable to the All-Loving Being.

Akhilananda

Vedanta Society
Boston, Massachusetts
November 24, 1948.

CHAPTER I

CHRIST, AN INCARNATION

> In the beginning was the Word, and the Word was with God and the Word was God.
>
> The same was in the beginning with God.
>
> All things were made by him; and without him was not anything made that was made.
>
> In him was life; and the life was the light of men.
>
> And the light shineth in darkness; and the darkness comprehended it not.[1]

Jesus is recognized by orthodox Christians as God incarnate. Christians usually view Him as the "only begotten son," the only incarnation of God. "For God so loved the world, that he gave his only begotten Son, that whosoever believeth in him should not perish, but have everlasting life."[2] This makes it clear that Jesus was the life and the light of man, even though "his own received him not."[3] It is a fact that the advent of an incarnation is not comprehended by his contemporaries or even by some of his followers. As a result, there have been considerable confusion and misunderstanding in the minds of the people throughout the ages. Man also faces pertinent questions about the very advent of an incarnation. Why was Jesus born? Is there any basic difference between Jesus and other human beings in their lives and activities? Did He come to the world as others have come, seemingly impelled by longings, desires, and other such tendencies? These questions often baffle even the most brilliant thinkers.

We want to know if Jesus came to this world with all the ordinary human requirements and tendencies. St. John tells us that "The Word was made flesh and dwelt among us."[4] There seems to be a marked difference between the personalities known as divine incarnations and other, ordinary people. We are dragged by longings and desires, while the incarnations are free of all earthly inclinations and attachments. They know the purpose for which they came to the world. We are unaware of our purpose in life and do not understand why we were born. We are unsteady like little children when they begin to walk; and we go to and fro, first taking one thing as the goal of life, and the next moment another. However intellectual we may be, we still seem to lack understanding of our purpose in life. Although we are seeking satisfaction in the sense realm, we do not know exactly how to get it, as the various objects of the senses constantly stimulate our desires for more and more gratification. Because of instability of mind, we cannot find satisfaction and we are frustrated time and again. We repeatedly seek new pleasures, thinking that they will satisfy our inner nature. A keen analytical mind easily realizes that our purpose is often defeated by the mad rush for enjoyments of the objective world. We seem to be oblivious of what will really satisfy our inner nature and fulfill the purpose of our lives. Most people are like this. Even great personalities, leaders of human destiny, are disappointed and frustrated toward the end of life.

On the other hand, incarnations of God are fully aware of their purpose, goal, and method of life. They are also fully aware of the opposition they are likely to face as well as the success they will achieve. They give their message and go away peacefully. Jesus likewise came to the world with a definite purpose. From the Hindu point of view, He was fully conscious of His mission as an incarnation and clearly understood the objective of His life and the method that He and His followers must use, whether or not the world accepted His message at that time. He knew that it was bound to be accepted eventually. There was no faltering in His consciousness. He definitely expressed the ideal and left the world cheerfully like a great hero. Swami Vivekananda says:

> But, in the history of mankind, you will find that there come these Messengers, and that from their very birth their mission is found and formed. The whole plan is there, laid down, and you see them swerving not one inch from that. Because, they come with a mission, they come with a message.
>
> . . . .
>
> Do you not remember in your own scriptures the authority with which Jesus speaks: "Go ye, therefore, and teach all nations . . . Teaching them to observe all things whatsoever I have commanded you."

> It runs through all His utterances, that tremendous faith in His own message.[5]

Divine incarnations come to fulfill the crying need of the age. It is true that the people of that age do not understand how to stabilize their lives and reach the objective of life. Ordinary people naturally falter as to the goal, as well as to the means of reaching that goal. Even religious personalities often falter in their leadership and guidance of the people. They do not directly follow the method which would lead the human race to a stable society. One of the most important factors in the life of incarnations is that they have a clear vision of the path the mass must follow, even though the mass may remain absolutely ignorant of and indifferent to it. It often happens that their contemporaries misunderstand their motives and criticize and condemn them, even though the incarnations come for the good and happiness of the people. As St. John says: "And the light shineth in darkness; and the darkness comprehended it not."[6] The light is undaunted in administering its luminous power for the removal of darkness from the world. So the incarnations are undaunted and unperturbed by the antagonistic activities of the people for whom they come.

During the last century about a half dozen books have been written by some psychiatrists and other scholars emphasizing that Jesus was definitely a mental case, that He was a paranoiac with other symptoms of mental disorder.[7] In his book, the *Psychiatric Study of Jesus,* Dr. Albert Schweitzer gives an answer to the charges levelled against the personality of Jesus.[8] It is not unusual for psychiatrists to evalute Him from that point of view. They often criticize the religious tendencies of man as disintegrating forces. Freud and others claim that the religious element creates censorship and consequent tension in the mind. Little do they understand that there is a world of difference between the paranoiac and schizophrenic cases and the divine incarnations. Dr. Schweitzer tried to defend Jesus by telling the public that the Fourth Gospel, which is quoted so much by these psychiatrists, is not authentic historically. This seems to us a very weak argument. His arguments regarding the experiences of Jesus do not seem to penetrate to the spiritual depths. However, he rightly establishes the fact that the behavior of Jesus proves that He is not a mental case. It is our contention that divine incarnations are unusual personalities and they are fully aware of their mission, as we shall explain further on in this chapter. Even though occasionally they may use the term "I" in a very exalted sense, below this "I" is the consciousness of "Thou," or the Father, or the Absolute. Their behavior pattern is beyond and above all normality that we can conceive. They are really supernormal beings. In fact, they can transform even subnormal persons to normality and supernormality, as we shall discuss later. It seems that the minds of many psychiatrists are so entangled with abnormal states that they cannot imagine that there is a possibility of a supernormal state. These incarnations soar so high that people who deal with pathological cases cannot even breath the rarified atmosphere of these heights. It is suffocating to them. We beg to submit to these psychiatrists as well as to Dr. Schweitzer, that a study of the activities of Jesus will clearly reveal that He was a dynamic personality.

One of the most important and unusual characteristics in the lives of all divine incarnations is that they are not only fully conscious of their mission but they are also perfectly satisfied and peaceful. Being aware of the goal of life, they go directly to it without faltering. They reveal joy and bliss in their lives. A survey of their lives shows that their joy knows no bounds. The attraction that the average man and woman feels toward them is due to the joyous atmosphere in them. The blissful nature of God can easily be understood through contact with them. They radiate so much joy that even a disturbed and disgruntled person becomes peaceful and restful after the contact. People are attracted to them like iron to the magnet because of this blissful nature that is revealed in and through their very presence. They have no internal or external conflicts, like ordinary people who have to struggle to overcome their conflicts, even though they are great personalities. The emotions of incarnations are harmoniously integrated; moreover, any person who is trained by them becomes integrated and dynamic. It is apparent that they possess a power which singles them out from the race in which they were born. Thus it is said that they are the "special manifestations of God." Sri Ramakrishna says:

> . . . They are human beings with extraordinary, original powers and entrusted with a Divine commission. Being heirs of Divine powers and glories, they form a class of their own. To this class belong the Incarnations of God like Christ, Krishna, Buddha, and Chaitanya and their devotees of the highest order.[9]

Why was Jesus born? There is an interesting and ennobling statement in the teachings of Sri Krishna:

"Whenever . . . there is decline of Dharma (religion), and rise of Adharma (evil), then I body Myself forth."[10] Christianity and Hinduism are the two great religions which accept the fact that God incarnates Himself as man. However, the Hindus believe that there have been numerous incarnations (*Avataras*) in the history of the world, of whom Jesus was one, while the Christians take Jesus to be the only one. Here we have a basic resemblance and a basic difference between Hinduism and Christianity. It seems to us that, in spite of the difference, there is a similar attitude toward an incarnation in both the religions, as we shall see in the following pages.

The declaration of the *Gita* has been fulfilled time and again, ever since man began to live on this planet. At critical periods in the history of India, when men and women were extremely materialistic and forgot the spirit of religion, such personalities have made their appearance every five hundred or thousand years and saved the soul of man from utter degradation and disintegration. It is amazing to note that there is a peculiar sequence in the events of history in which divine incarnations appear. Study of their lives will reveal the selfsame historical reason for every one of them. After observing the facts of history, it seems as if the advent of an incarnation can almost be predicted.

Jesus, the Christ, came to the world to re-establish the spirit of religion in the Jews and other people who then existed in that part of the world. The Jews were extremely ritualistic and many of them had lost the spirit of religion completely. Some Jews twisted the texts of the scriptures to suit their materialistic desires. Temples became business centers for commerce and trade and money changers. It is also an historical fact that the Roman Empire was at the height of its material success, with all the vices of imperialism. The powerful men and women of the empire dominated and exploited the subject groups, keeping them in a state of insecurity, while they, themselves, were addicted to all sorts of vices. Their whole attitude was one of seeking the greatest amount of sense enjoyment and power, and their intellect and other human resources were used for these expressions. The religious side of their lives was completely negated. What little religion they had was used for material success and enjoyment. Although the stoic philosophers like Cicero, Seneca, Epictetus, and Marcus Aurelius were outstanding personalities in the Roman tradition, the major trend in Roman society was not influenced at that time by these great philosophers and religious personalities. It was the most propitious time for the advent of an incarnation to show the then world the way of religion. It is needless to say that the condition of Jewish and Roman life necessitated the coming of an incarnation.

When there are such changes in religious life, the Divine Being out of love and mercy manifests Himself as man to inspire our spiritual ideals and demonstrate that man can realize God. God is not limited to scriptures and philosophies. He is not limited to pulpits and discourses by priests, rabbis, ministers, and swamis. God is a fact of direct and immediate experience. He is a reality. The reality of God is to be demonstrated to mankind by actual verification in life. By His illumination of the soul, He is its redeemer.

Divine incarnations also show us how to be aware of the presence of God and our true nature. As Jesus says: "All things are delivered unto me of my Father: and no man knoweth the Son, but the Father; neither knoweth any man the Father, save the Son, and he to whomsoever the Son will reveal him."[11] They lead a life which is in itself a demonstration. Human beings require examples and evidence to show the way; otherwise, they cannot understand the abstract ideas and ideals. Incarnations are the very embodiment of the ideals so that we can witness their expression. But for the divine incarnations, human beings could not have understood the real purpose of life and the method of its fulfillment; nor could we have understood the nature of God and the fact that He can be experienced by man. As Sri Ramakrishna tells us, they are the connecting link between God and man.

> The saviours of humanity are those who see God, and being at the same time anxious to share their happiness of divine vision with others . . . willingly undergo the troubles of rebirth in the world in order to teach and lead on struggling humanity to its goal.
>
> An Avatara (incarnation) is a human messenger of God. He is like a viceroy of the mighty Monarch. As when there is any disturbance in some far off province, the king sends the viceroy to quell it, so whenever there is any waning of religion in any part of the world, God sends His Avatara there to guard virtue and foster its growth.
>
> . . . .
>
> When a mighty log of wood floats down the stream, it carries on it hundreds of birds and does

> not sink. . . So when a Saviour incarnates, innumerable are the men who find salvation by taking refuge in him.
>
> . . . .
>
> Nothing is problematic to the Avatara. He solves the most difficult and intricate problems of life and the soul as the simplest things in the world, and his expositions are such as even a child can follow. He is the sun of Divine knowledge, whose light dispels the accumulated ignorance of ages.[12]

A question may arise in some minds that if an incarnation is fully illumined and is fully aware of his divine nature and if he has no human desires whatsoever, then how can he come again to this world? There may also be a question whether or not an incarnation is completely in God while he is in this world as a human being. Krishna, in the *Bhagavad-Gita*, and Sri Ramakrishna, in His *Sayings*, explain this clearly when they declare that an incarnation willingly imposes on himself some of the human tendencies. St. Paul also says: "Who, being in the form of God, thought it not robbery to be equal with God; But made himself of no reputation, and took upon him the form of a servant, and was made in the likeness of men."[13] Consequently, an incarnation has the power to remove at will this imposition of human nature on Himself. He is always aware of his divine nature; consequently, he is not bound by any limitations whatsoever.

There is a wonderful blending in a divine incarnation of the human and divine. There is a little trace of human characteristics in them, and at the same time their divinity shines forth like the midday sun. The sun is never affected by darkness, even though darkness may be present. Similarly, even though divine incarnations assume human form and live in the midst of human beings who are steeped in ignorance and darkness, who are not aware of their true nature and their relationship with God, they are fully aware of their divinity from the time of their birth. They know that they have a definite purpose to accomplish and that regardless of world conditions it will be fulfilled, no matter what the people do to them or their message. There is no darkness in their consciousness.

As incarnations have no longing or consciousness of permanent multiplicity, people may wonder why they come to this world to help others. Our answer is that, although they are fully aware of the divine presence in all, they know that in the relative state of existence human beings are unaware of their true nature. Most human beings are aware only of diversity; consequently, they are entangled in the consciousness of multiplicity so they act and react emotionally on the basis of their understanding of differences. They become attracted and repelled by others. They seek pleasure and satisfaction in this state of plurality and become more and more entangled in gross worldly desires and their fulfillment, forgetting completely the divine presence within them. In the attempt to satisfy their desires, they become slaves to their passions and adopt means which actually defeat their own purpose. Sri Ramakrishna gives a beautiful example to illustrate this. "Camels are very fond of thorny shrubs: the more they eat them, the more do their mouths bleed, yet they do not refrain from making them their food."[14]

Herein lies the necessity for the advent of a divine incarnation. He comes to show the people that their methods of obtaining joy and satisfaction are wrong and he reveals ways to get them directly by becoming aware of God. This does not mean, however, that divine incarnations prohibit enjoyment of the objective world. They show us that the background of the world is divine, as the eternal subject of experience is also divine. In other words, the subject and object of experience are basically one. They also demonstrate how to live on the basis of this knowledge.

It should be emphasized here that even though ordinary people are born as slaves of ignorance and consequent longings, they have the possibility of becoming free from attachment and bondage. According to the Hindu tradition, ordinary people realize God through their devotional exercises, spiritual practices, and the blessings of divine incarnations of God and great illumined souls. They have to struggle to overcome their inordinate desires through self-discipline. The lives of Christian mystics will illustrate these statements.[15] Sri Krishna also says:

> The turbulent senses . . . do violently snatch away the mind of even a wise man, striving after perfection.
>
> The steadfast, having controlled them all, sits focused on Me as the Supreme. His wisdom is steady, whose senses are under control.[16]

When they realize God, these aspirants are illumined and become centers of inspiration and enlightenment. Herein lies the difference between ordinary saints and divine incarnations. Saints are at first bound souls and then they become illumined, while incarnations are the veritable embodiment of divine light and power from the very beginning of their lives. The illumined souls are grouped in five classes:

(1) The *Swapna-Siddhas* are those who attain perfection by means of dream-inspiration.

(2) The *Mantra-Siddhas* are those who attain perfection by means of a sacred *mantra* (name of God, by repeating which, God is realized).

(3) The *Hathat-Siddhas* are those who attain perfection suddenly, like a poor man who at once becomes rich by finding a hidden treasure.

(4) The *Kripa-Siddhas* are those who attain perfection through the grace of God. As a man in clearing a forest may discover some ancient tank or house and need not construct one himself . . . so some fortunately become perfect with very little effort on their own part.

(5) The *Nitya-Siddhas* are those who are ever perfect. As in the gourd or pumpkin creeper, the petals of the flower come out after the appearance of the fruit, so the ever perfect soul is already born a *Siddha*, and all his seeming exertions after perfection are merely for the sake of setting an example to humanity.[17]

India has had the privilege of nurturing various illumined souls at different periods in her history. Many people have pondered over their lives and observed the expression of their power in reforming others, helping and guiding those around them, and lifting them to the divine plane. Some of the illumined souls inspired a few, while others transformed innumerable persons, giving them higher spiritual realization and transporting them to the consciousness of the presence of God. These are the eternally free souls who come to the world with an incarnation to fulfill his mission.

Divine incarnations are, of course, eternally free and they not only transform human beings by giving them illumination but they also start new civilizations. Spiritual power of the greatest magnitude is expressed in their lives through their consciousness of the unity of existence and God; and it is transferred to individuals or even entire groups at the same time. It has been observed that ordinary saints and seers can lift only a few persons, but the eternally free souls and incarnations can transform a whole group of persons simultaneously to a higher plane of existence.

Incarnations live an intense life of God-consciousness without any struggle or effort. Their very lives are proof that the superconscious state is to them a normal experience, while the ordinary plane of existence is unnatural. It is an effort for them to bring their minds down to this plane and teach others to reach superconsciousness. It is indeed a struggle for them to force their minds into this realm to help and bless us. Yet willingly and lovingly they sacrifice their consciousness of oneness to re-establish the spirit of religion in human society.

One of the most astounding factors in the lives of these personalities is that they do not utter a word that is not lived by them or that cannot be applied to the lives of all people. That is the very reason that the teachings of divine incarnations are so powerful and enlightening. Whoever hears or reads their words cannot help being inspired and remolded because their words are the dynamics of life. Force is instilled in what they say by the power of their lives. Their words become living; their ideals are translated into action. That is the very reason there is a world of difference between the words of a divine incarnation or illumined soul and the philosopher or theologian. One has dynamic power while the other has only intellectual conception. One has the backing of illumination and the other has only conceptual postulation. One has living force while the other has placid argumentation. One transforms the personality while the other satisfies intellectual curiosity.

The question may arise: If that be the case, then why does not everyone follow the teachings of the incarnations immediately? The reason, according to Hinduism, is that men are steeped in ignorance, inordinate affections and longings, when the incarnations make their appearances. We know what happened to the Roman Empire; it sank to the lowest stage of human existence. The Romans lived such a hedonistic life, it seems that they cared not whether any other man existed. They exploited everyone for their own enjoyment. It takes a long time for spiritual teachings to penetrate the thick veil of ignorance. However, those who are inspired and remolded by the teachings of the incarnations gradually influence the lives of others; and in this way a new dawn of civilization takes place.

It is often considered by some thinkers, who interpret the words of Jesus, that incarnations come merely to destroy the old ways.

> Think not that I am come to send peace on earth: I came not to send peace, but a sword.
>
> For I am come to set a man at variance against

> his father, and the daughter against her mother, and the daughter in law against her mother in law.[18]

It is our understanding that when divine incarnations come to the world, people who are engrossed in ignorance and the activities thereof become extremely antagonistic to the higher ideals of life which are taught by the incarnations. As the spiritual attitude basically requires self-control and self-discipline, those who are at the lowest ebb of spiritual culture are unwilling to undergo the necessary restraint, fearing they will lose the pleasures of life. They not only dislike any teaching that will require discipline for themselves but they also object to anyone else taking up this method. They seem to suffer from a sense of inferiority in the presence of such persons. This is the very reason that when incarnations come, antagonism and disharmony can be observed in families. When one of the members of a family follows the higher philosophy of life, the other members oppose him because of their selfish attitude of life. They can hardly stand it as they are still in ignorance and consequently do not understand higher values or the primary objective of life. They not only want to give first place to the secondary phases but they want others to do the same. Even well-meaning parents and other relatives, such as husbands or wives, cannot help acting in this manner as they know no better. When incarnations make an appearance in the world, there is discord and dissension and a chaotic condition in society in general.

Unfortunately, the vast majority of the people are used to the hedonistic attitude of life, seeking pleasures in every field of activity. Even scholars and intellectuals use their intellectual achievements for the same purpose. Consequently, contemporary brilliant minds do not understand the higher values which the incarnations come to establish and they are antagonistic and condemn them. Apart from that, well-meaning humanistic persons do not seem to understand the real purpose of incarnations. They seem to criticize them and their immediate followers as otherworldly persons who emphasize the mystic realizations of God and ignore this world. According to Albert Schweitzer, who is a great man and a very practical follower of the social gospel:

> And Christianity also brought European thought into relationship with world and life negation. World and life negation is found in the thought of Jesus in so far as He did not assume that the Kingdom of God would be realised in this natural world. He expected that this natural world would very speedily come to an end and be superseded by a supernatural world in which all that is imperfect and evil would be overcome by the power of God.[19]

Then he confuses the reader by saying that the idea of world and life negation in the teachings of Jesus is different from that found in the Orient. However, he admits that:

> It is characteristic of the unique type of the world and life negation of Jesus that His ethics are not confined within the bounds of that conception. He does not preach the inactive ethic of perfecting the self alone, but active, enthusiastic love of one's neighbor. It is because His ethic contains the principle of ac-

> tivity that it has affinity with world and life affirmation.[20]

So it is that different members of society, the intellectualists, and, unfortunately, even the humanists, misunderstand divine incarnations. Consequently, there arise various types of conflicts at the time of their advent, even though they come to establish harmony in the world. "... I am not come to destroy, but to fulfill."[21]

Their only desire, if it can be called desire, is to establish a spirit of religion and rescue the souls of men from utter degradation. They do not come to create any confusion in the existing conception of religion; on the contrary, they give a new spirit and power to the existing real religious attitude. From a study of their lives it is evident that their practices and words are meant to push the people forward from where they stand in spiritual development. In the reconstruction of human life and society they always use constructive and evolutionary methods rather than those which are destructive and dissipative. No doubt their message is meant to a great extent for the stabilization of individuals; yet this very process on an individual basis leads to the reconstruction of society at large. The influence of the incarnations is felt like the dewdrops of a tropical spring which nourish the blossoms of the flowers. Likewise society feels their influence in the reconstruction and stabilization of the new structure. That is the very reason all incarnations express practically the sentiment of Jesus: "... I am not come to destroy, but to fulfill." Sri Krishna says: "... for the establishment of Dharma (religion), I come into being in every age."[22] The same idea is expressed in the *Bhagavatam.*

This again brings up the question of whether or not divine incarnations have desire as we understand it. True, there is a kind of desire or longing in them, because of what we have already mentioned, the little touch of the human element. But at any moment they can give it up as they are not bound by it, being free souls. Of their own volition they assume the desire to alleviate the sufferings of humanity.

On the other hand, how much we human beings suffer if we cannot fulfill our objectives and desires! How restless and miserable we are! For such desires are based on an egocentric attitude of life. Divine incarnations have no such attitude. They are not selfish. On the contrary, they are completely established in the higher self; and, consequently, their desire is only for the good of the world.

When they depart from the world, they feel no pain or agony because they are leaving it; there is no feeling of separation. They are free from attachment to the world and are established in their divine nature. According to Indian or Hindu philosophy, they are called the rulers of *maya* (*mayadhisa*), while we are the slaves of *maya* (*mayadhina*). In other words, incarnations are masters of ignorance, while human beings are its slaves.

Many persons question whether or not Jesus fulfilled His purpose during His lifetime. If He did not, then we would assume that He must have been disappointed. We feel disappointed when we do not obtain the objects of our desires. When we suffer misfortune, we are extremely disturbed and many times go to pieces. Observe human life and you will find that most people behave in that way. They act recklessly when threatened with failure or disappointment. Therefore, we naturally suppose that Jesus was disappointed in His mission, as it did not seem at that time that He established the Kingdom of God as He professed. If it can be accepted as true that He was disappointed, it is logical to assume that He was on the same plane as any other human being. Under such conditions, He would have had noble ideas of doing good to the world but would think that He could not give the world the Kingdom of God. So He would have been disappointed just as any ordinary man would be.

There is, however, actually a vast difference between an incarnation and the ordinary person whose expectations are defeated when he cannot do something for himself, his family, or society. Take, for instance, political leaders or social reformers; many are pessimistic and heartbroken when they approach the evening of life. Yet divine incarnations, such as Jesus, are not frustrated when they see no immediate results of their work. They understand human nature and realize that time is needed for the world to absorb their message.

A man once went to Sri Ramakrishna for advice concerning his daily life. Sri Ramakrishna talked with him and gave the advice. Afterwards, He told one of His disciples: "This man will not heed my words nor do what I suggested; he will do exactly as he wishes. Just the same, I have told him what is the right thing to do." Now, if we know that a man will not do what we advise, we become furious, even in routine matters. Some of us would say: "I am not going to waste my time; he will not do it anyhow. I intend to sit tight and mind my own business." Others would express hatred and anger. However, Sri

Ramakrishna did not utter a word of disappointment although He well knew that the man would not accept His suggestions. His love impelled him to give advice to erring humanity.

Divine incarnations understand human frailties and the nature of the human mind. They are the real psychologists. Although it takes a long time for the mind to change its pattern and old ways of thinking, Jesus still gave His message of love. He declared: "Thou shalt love thy neighbor. . ."[23] when He knew full well the Jews and Gentiles would not immediately accept that as a principle and method of life. He was also aware that His disciple, Judas, would betray Him for thirty pieces of silver. He knew it during the Last Supper when He said: "He that dippeth his hand with me in the dish, the same shall betray me."[24] Yet He did not withdraw His blessings, His love, or His grace from Judas. Can an ordinary man be found who will behave in this manner when he knows that an avowed friend and follower is going to betray him and be the cause of his crucifixion? Anyone else would have hated and killed Judas. But Jesus allowed him to carry out his destructive plans.

Buddha declared: "Let a man overcome anger by love, let him overcome evil by good . . ."[25] But He knew that the people would not immediately practice the gospel of love. Similarly, Jesus said: "But I say unto you, Love your enemies, bless them that curse you, do good to them that hate you, and pray for them which despitefully use you, and persecute you."[26] As an incarnation of God, Jesus also knew that it would perhaps be a few centuries before His message of love would be accepted, that the

Romans would not assimilate His ideas at once nor would the Jews put them into practice. But it was not His failure when only a handful of Jews and Gentiles became His followers.

As an incarnation, God sees the past, present, and future. In the Indian language, He is called *Trikalajnas*, a knower of time in three periods — past, present, and future. As He is fully enlightened, He knows the whole world's history for centuries. We know from the life of Sri Ramakrishna that He was fully aware of what was going to happen in the world. On one occasion, Swami Vivekananda privately discussed the future of India and definitely stated when the Indian situation would change in an "unprecedented way," years later. Does anyone think that Jesus did not know the world's future? According to the Hindu viewpoint, Jesus as an incarnation must have understood what was going to happen and with this knowledge He gave His message. He was not at all disappointed, as some persons seem to conclude.

Human beings are slow to change habits and ways of life. For instance, we often realize that we have been guilty of anger; we know that hatred is not right; and we are aware that we should not have behaved in certain ways toward our friends and relatives. Yet we repeatedly have the same feelings and express the same behavior; because, in spite of our knowledge, understanding, and historically religious background, we do not take the time to change our thought forms and ways of life. Psychologically speaking, it is evident that when certain emotional reactions are created by persons and objects our conscious as well as unconscious mind retains those impressions. Whenever similar occasions arise, we react almost automatically, due to our previous reactions which are preserved in the unconscious. In order to transform these thought patterns created by inordinate tendencies, disagreeable as they may be from the conscious point of view, considerable time is required to reconstruct new types of reactions. But new sets of unconscious impressions must be built in order to overcome the old impressions.

The divine incarnations intensely love their disciples and followers; love is the connecting link between them. It is this love that attracts the disciples to the incarnations, as the magnet attracts base metal. We have seen time and again in history as well as in our personal experience that illumined souls have intense love for human beings. They can inspire and transform the people because of their love for them. In fact, it is love that becomes the dynamic power in their influence over others. It is very interesting to note that the modern psychoanalysts think in different terms, even though they are often helpful to their patients and clients. Many of their techniques seem to be quite different from what we observe in the lives of divine incarnations and other illumined souls or saints.

The analyst, teacher, or spiritual leader must also have an infinite amount of patience. He is not a true leader if he has not infinite patience, sympathy, and above all, infinite love. The analyst will be a failure in the long run, in spite of technical knowledge, if he has not sympathy for human suffering and patience with man's inability to change himself overnight. An impatient person cannot have the confidence of anyone. On the other hand, a person with patience, who knows human nature as it is, persistently sympathizes with the weaknesses of individuals. This gradually creates confidence in them. This confidence of the client, patient, follower, or disciple is of vital importance in the reconstruction of human personality. Love between the teacher and disciple is the most important factor in the transformation of an individual. Divine incarnations are veritable embodiments of patience and forgiveness, love and sympathy. The love that we find in them cannot be duplicated anywhere else in the world.

I remember a statement which was made by our master, Swami Brahmananda. He said: "What love have we seen in Sri Ramakrishna! If one can have just a little glimpse of that love, one gets intoxicated by it." Then he added: "Do you know, we were boys when we went to Sri Ramakrishna. What fullness of love He had for us! We could not stay away from Him. His love was so intense that we left everything and went to Him."

When we study the lives of other divine incarnations like Sri Krishna and Buddha, we find the same intense love in Them. In fact, the people who went to any of the incarnations were irresistibly drawn to them by their all-consuming love which was showered on all without any differentiation or expectation. It was supremely unselfish.

It seems as if a tidal wave of love flows from them. This is a distinctive mark which separates incarnations from all others. They forgive the weaknesses and inordinate tendencies of human beings. Jesus forgave Judas and blessed him. He forgave those who crucified Him, saying: "Father, forgive them, for they know not what they do," because He had infinite love for human beings and infinite sympathy for their weakness. Ordinary people become disappointed and angry if their friends and relatives misbehave and do not act as they wish. Swami Brahmananda told us one day that "Even if you do all the good things you can for a person all your life and do one thing that is not wished or liked by him, all your good deeds are in vain. You are no good to him. God is just the opposite. You do everything wrong all your life and then one day you think of Him with love and devotion and you do the right thing. At once He forgives your entire past and lifts you to the higher plane." The parable of the prodigal son as told by Jesus is well known, in this connection.[27]

A question may arise in the minds of many thinkers that if God, as the great Swami said, forgives and showers His grace and blessings even on persons of misdeeds, then where is the place of the law of *karma* (cause and effect)? Naturally, one would think that the Hindu-Buddhistic idea of the law of *karma* cannot justify the grace of God. If the law of *karma*, or, as Emerson calls it, the law of compensation and retribution, is exact, then how can the Hindus justify the Christian idea of the grace of God? This idea is not exclusively a Christian idea in the first place. It is accepted by the Hindus, even though they firmly believe in the law of causation. Sri Krishna says in the *Gita*: "Fixing thy mind on Me, thou shalt, by My grace overcome all obstacles. . ."[28]

Sri Ramakrishna says that God is beyond any law although all laws are according to His will. If He chooses, He can wipe away all effect of laws. It may seem arbitrary, yet the lawmaker is greater than the law itself. When anything functions on the relative plane, it is, no doubt, within the realm of the law of causation; but God, as the maker of law, can also suspend its functioning.[29] This is not only the Christian view; it is also accepted by the Hindus.

A divine incarnation, being a manifestation of God, has the power of grace. That is the very reason that our prayers, supplications, and such other devotional practices become effective, provided, however, there is a desire to depend on God. The breeze of God's grace blows constantly, but only the person who is energetic enough to keep his sails unfurled can enjoy it.[30] To use a Christian expression: When a man is "repentant," he gets the grace of God. According to the Hindu view, the divine incarnation has the power of dispensing all limitations and weaknesses of a man and giving direct illumination to a saint as well as a sinner.

It is very interesting to note that Professor Rudolph Otto, a great German thinker, finds the doctrine of redemption and grace fully developed in Hinduism as it is in Christianity. In his book, *India's Religion of Grace and Christianity,* he gives a very clear account of the grace of God, as advocated by the Hindus. He writes:

> Beginning in the profound verses of the pre-Christian *Bhagavad-Gita,* the book most loved and honoured by millions of Hindus, passing through times of obscuration and reformation, as with us, this doctrine of grace rises till it gains at last positions which dumbfound us Protestants by their analogy to our fundamental ideas. . .[31]

When an incarnation comes to the world, the path of religion seems to be very easy. Men and women of every station in life and development and even lower beings and those on other planes of existence are redeemed.[32] His presence makes the path easy and simple. Thus Jesus says:

> Come unto me, all ye that labour and are heavy laden, and I will give you rest.
>
> Take my yoke upon you, and learn of me; for I am meek and lowly in heart: and ye shall find rest unto your souls.
>
> For my yoke is easy, and my burden is light.[33]

Similarly, Sri Krishna tells us: "Relinquishing all Dharmas (laws) take refuge in Me alone, I will liberate thee from all sins; grieve not."[34] And again Sri Ramakrishna says: "As a large and powerful steamer moves swiftly over the waters, towing rafts and barges in its wake — so when a Saviour descends, He easily carries thousands to the haven of safety across the ocean of *Maya*."[35] When we study the lives of divine incarnations, we find an extraordinary display of power of spiritual illumination. It seems they can transform any person instantaneously and lift him to the radiant presence of God, with no personal effort on the part of the individual. This is what Christians call grace and redemption.

Incarnations are never disappointed. Jesus was never disappointed because of the iniquities and weaknesses of human beings, as we know from the many incidents of His life. He came to demonstrate how man can become God-conscious. His purpose was fulfilled when He inspired a few persons, however small the number might be.

He knew that this group would perpetuate and transmit His message through successive links of teachers and disciples, and that the spirit He awakened in the souls of men would operate for centuries until mankind would again become materialistic and selfish. He was also aware that His message would be diluted by His followers in the course of time and that they would act against His ideals; that the reforms He introduced would be misunderstood by them in a few centuries; that they would twist the meaning of His teachings to suit their own desires and ambitions. How beautifully St. John said: "And the light shineth in darkness; and the darkness comprehended it not."[36]

Swami Vivekananda tells us that civilizations move in wavelike motion, up and down.

> The wave rises on the ocean, and there is a hollow. Again another wave rises, perhaps bigger than the former, to fall down again; similarly, again to rise — driving onward . . . . This is the nature of the universe. Whether in the world of our thoughts, the world of our relations in society, or in our spiritual affairs, the same movement of succession, of rises and falls, is going on.[37]

Jesus was aware of this fact. Yet, because of His infinite mercy, His infinite love, He took human beings as they were. He introduced reforms to inspire people.

When an incarnation comes, the world is blessed, even though, as St. John tells us, "He came unto his own, and his own received him not."[38] The souls of many are inspired and they are irresistibly drawn to that center of spiritual and magnetic power. Those who come to the world during the lifetime of an incarnation or a little after are thrice blessed. God is manifested to the fullest extent in Him; nay, He is God. Swami Vivekananda understood this when he said of Christ: "If I, as an Oriental, have to worship Jesus of Nazareth, there is only one way left to me, that is, to worship Him as God and nothing else."[39] This shows how an Oriental spiritual personality considers Jesus. Naturally, a thinking man would like to know if the ideal lived and taught by Jesus is in harmony with the ideals of the so-called Oriental people.

In closing this chapter, we may say that it is evident that the Hindu view is closer to Christian orthodoxy than to "liberalism." The Hindu will agree with the orthodox in regarding Christ as unique in comparison with ordinary men; yet he will differ in holding that there have been and will be numerous incarnations of God. The Hindu would reject the view of those Christian liberals who regard all men as equally divine, Christ no more than anyone else. The Hindu accepts many special revelations and special manifestations in the form of divine incarnations.

---

1. John 1:1-5.
2. Ibid., 3:16.
3. Ibid., 1:10.
4. Ibid., 1:14.
5. **The Complete Works of Swami Vivekananda** (Mayavati, Almora, Himalayas; Advaita Ashrama, 1931-, IV, 118, 120. Hereafter, this source will be listed as **Works.**
6. John 1:5.
7. David Friedrich Strauss, **The Life of Jesus Revised for the German People** (1865); H. J. Holtzmann, **The Messianic Consciousness of Jesus** (1907); Herman Werner, "The Historical Jesus of Liberal Theology, A Psychotic," **The New Ecclesiastical Journal,** XXII (1911), 347-390; Oskar Holtzmann, **Was Jesus an Ecstatic?** (1903); Julius Baumann, **The Character of Jesus** (1908); George de Loosten (Dr. Georg Lomer), **Jesus Christ from the Standpoint of Psychiatry** (Bamberg, 1905); William

Hirsch, **Conclusions of a Psychiatrist** (New York, 1912), pp. 87-164; Charles Binet-Sanglé, **The Insanity of Jesus** (3rd ed., Vols. I, II; 1st ed., Vols. III, IV (Paris, 1911-1915); Emil Rasmussen, **Jesus, A Comparative Study in Psychopathology** (Leipzig, 1905); Walter E. Bundy, **The Psychic Health of Jesus** (New York: The MacMillan Co., 1922).

8. Albert Schweitzer, **The Psychiatric Study of Jesus** (Boston: The Beacon Press, 1948).
9. **The Gospel of Ramakrishna**, revised by Swami Abhedananda (New York: The Vedanta Society, 1947), pp. 300-301.
10. **Srimad-Bhagavad-Gita**, trans. Swami Swarupananda (5th ed.; Mayavati, Almora, Himalayas: Advaita Ashrama, 1933), chap. IV:7.
11. Matt. 11:27.
12. **Sayings of Sri Ramakrishna** (3rd ed.; Mylapore, Madras: Sri Ramakrishna Math, 1925), chap. IV: 135, 136, 140, 144.
13. Phil. 2:6-7.
14. **Sayings of Sri Ramakrishna** XXXV:690.
15. See the works of St. Teresa of Avila, St. John of the Cross, St. Catherine of Siena, and other such Christian mystics.
16. **Srimad-Bhagavad-Gita** II:60-61.
17. **Sayings of Sri Ramakrishna** XXVII:558.
18. Matt. 10:34-35.
19. Albert Schweitzer, **Indian Thought and Its Development** (New York: Henry Holt & Co., 1936), p. 4.
20. Ibid., pp. 4-5.
21. Matt. 5:17.
22. **Srimad-Bhagavad-Gita** IV:8.
23. Matt. 22:39; Mark 12:31; and Luke 10:27.
24. Ibid., 26:23; see also Mark 14:18; Luke 22:21; and John 13:26.
25. **Dhammapada** (Sayings of Buddha) XLVIII:36.
26. Matt. 5:44.
27. Luke 15:11-32.
28. **Srimad-Bhagavad-Gita** XVIII:58.
29. Swami Saradananda, **Sri Ramakrishna Lilaprasanga**, Vol. II. (Calcutta: Udbodhan Office).
30. **Sayings of Sri Ramakrishna** XXVI:538.
31. Rudolph Otto, **India's Religion of Grace and Christianity Compared and Contrasted**, trans. Frank High Foster, D. D. (New York: The Macmillan Co., 1930), p. 18.
32. **Srimad-Bhagavatam.**
33. Matt. 11:28-30.
34. **Srimad-Bhagavad-Gita** XVIII:66.
35. **Sayings of Sri Ramakrishna** IV:138.
36. John 1:5.
37. "Christ the Messenger," **Works**, 134.
38. John 1:11.
39. **Works**, IV, 143.

CHAPTER II

CHRIST, AN ORIENTAL

No man can serve two masters . . . Ye cannot serve God and Mammon.

Therefore I say unto you, take no thought for your life, what ye shall eat, or what ye shall drink; nor yet for your body, what ye shall put on.

. . . .

And why take ye thought for raiment? Consider the lilies of the field, how they grow; they toil not, neither do they spin.

And yet I say unto you, That even Solomon in all his glory was not arrayed like one of these.

. . . .

. . . your heavenly Father knoweth that ye have need of all these things.

But seek ye first the kingdom of God, and his righteousness; and all these things shall be added unto you.[40]

. . . .

. . . Thou shalt love the Lord thy God with all thy heart, and with all thy soul, and with all thy mind.

> This is the first and great commandment.
>
> And the second is like unto it, Thou shalt love thy neighbor as thyself.[41]

In these passages we learn what Jesus thought of life and the ways of life. In a sense His first commandment emphasizes the negative side of religion, and the second commandment emphasizes the positive aspect. In considering the teachings of Jesus as a whole, we find that He was the Oriental of Orientals; He was the ideal of typical Oriental life. In other words, He was the embodiment of the ideals the Oriental people cherished and manifested in their thoughts and actions. (Briefly we can say that we are associating the spiritual ideal with the Orientals and the materialistic Greco-Roman ideal with the modern Occidentals, not merely as geographical differences but rather differences in the outlook of life and cultural emphasis. We do not necessarily mean that Orientals as such are superior and were always spiritual. As Jesus was born in an Oriental country with that background and ideal, we are making this distinction. We hope the readers will understand our spirit. We shall explain this viewpoint later). The texts of the teachings of Jesus cannot fit in the philosophy of life found in modern Occidental countries, where persons superimpose their own ideas on His and interpret them in His name. This statement may seem to be extremely harsh and one-sided; yet critical analysis of cultural activities of different countries will justify this impression. We do not believe that any real admirer, follower, or worshipper of Jesus would question the veracity of this statement.

In the civilizations of the world there have been two distinct ideals. "One thing is the good and (quite) different indeed is the pleasant. . . Good befalls him who follows the good, but loses he the goal, who chooses the pleasant."[42] "He that findeth his life shall lose it: and he that loseth his life for my sake shall find it."[43] For better or for worse, the Orient has chosen to follow the path of good for thousands of years. Ever since the dawn of civilization, Orientals — especially the Hindus, Chinese, and early Christians — followed the path of religion which emphasized the attainment of knowledge or realization of God or feeling the presence and grace of God. Everything else has been subordinated to that ideal.

The Greek or Roman civilization, on the other hand, emphasized the path of pleasure as the solution to the problems of man. We admit that Socrates, Plato, Plotinus, and others of Greek tradition, and Marcus Aurelius and others of Roman tradition differed from this viewpoint, yet the general tendency of the Greek or Roman civilization was to make life on the sense plane happy and pleasant by overcoming the onslaughts of nature. When we make a distinction between Oriental and Occidental civilizations, we really mean the difference between the civilization based on the spiritual ideal and that which is based on sense pleasure. In *The Crisis of Our Age*, Professor Pitirim A. Sorokin classifies these two civilizations as idealistic and sensate. It is evident from historical facts that the post-Renaissance civilization of the modern West has deviated from the early Christian trends of thought and has become a descendant of the Greco-Roman civilization.

The true type of sensate civilization has been manifested in the West for the last few centuries.

It is evident that the Hindu and early Christian and other such cultures subordinated all their activities to the spiritual ideal. This does not mean that they became otherworldly or negated "world and life"; on the contrary, they developed an all-round culture. We like to make it clear that Orientals also lost that ideal at different periods of their history, yet they emphasized the attainment of supreme knowledge or God-realization as the goal of life and the guiding spirit of other activities. In other words, religion became the main theme of their civilization. Oriental cultures, including true Christian civilization, are theocentric while the Greco-Roman and modern Western civilizations are geocentric.

By *religion* is not meant the narrow viewpoint so often advocated by some custodians of religion in many countries. In a conference attended by many philosophers, religious leaders, and outstanding neo-orthodox theologians, the causes of original sin were discussed. According to one of the theologians, the primary cause of sin, or of original sin, is the desire to know God, as they interpreted Genesis. Few persons, whether Oriental or Occidental, would naturally give this interpretation of religion. If the desire to know God is "sinful," then Jesus Himself was not a religious man; in fact, all the distinguished followers of Jesus from St. Peter to John Wesley and George Fox were irreligious. The whole ideal that Jesus taught would fall through completely if the desire to know God is the cause of our degradation. According to these neo-orthodox theologians and neo-Calvinists, one must not have any desire to know God, if we understand them rightly.

It is very encouraging to note that many American and European thinkers wholly differ from this viewpoint. Professor Brightman expresses a representative view of the outstanding thinkers in America. He says:

> The outstanding feature of this somewhat confused trend is a sense of despair about everything human. Man's original and hereditary sin poisons every human understanding. Man's will is corrupt and no goodness is in him. His reason is proud, rebellious against God, unable to find God. Only faith can save man in such a plight, but faith itself is a gift of God and not an act of sinful man. Only revelation can give divine truth, but no human interpretation can grasp the contents of revelation . . . . And if we are to take seriously the utterances of the neo-orthodox, the teachings of Jesus in the Synoptics and in John are, by themselves, inadequate and misleading.[44]

Albert Schweitzer writes:

> Renunciation of thinking is a declaration of spiritual bankruptcy. Where there is no longer a conviction that men can get to know the truth by their own thinking, scepticism begins. Those who work to make our age sceptical in this way, do so in the expectation that, as a result of renouncing all hope of self-discovered truth, men will end by accepting as truth what is forced upon them with authority and by propaganda.[45]

The neo-orthodox viewpoint thoroughly undermines the commandment of Jesus that we should love God, as a

Hindu sees it. Psychologically speaking, a man cannot love anyone whom he does not know. Love presupposes a certain form of knowledge of the object of love, otherwise it becomes an impossibility. In the face of a psychological understanding of love, then, this very viewpoint is meaningless.

It may be argued by these theologians that God should reveal Himself to us out of His infinite mercy. As human beings are "sinful," they cannot aspire of themselves to the knowledge of God. This point also seems baseless. It is true that human beings are finite and incapable of comprehending the Infinite, but at the same time there is something noble and divine in them as St. Paul says. ". . . We are the children of God: and if children, then heirs; heirs of God, and joint heirs with Christ; . . ."[46] This shows that however "sinful" and weak human beings may be, they still possess possibilities of divine realization. From the Hindu point of view, the soul of man is inherently divine; therefore, he can aspire to divine realization and divine love. This divine love can be manifested by the human soul because there is potential divine love inherent in it. When a devotee craves realization of God and manifestation of divine love, he fully knows his limitations in the search for it but he makes himself a proper instrument for it.

According to some neo-orthodox and crisis theologians, reason should not be applied to religion as religion is not based on reason. The only way one can have any idea or understanding of God is through faith or through His grace. Of this Dean Hough says:

> You cannot construct an argument without assum-

> ing the essential validity of the knowing process. Karl Barth and all the psychopathic theologians founder on this rock. For the purpose of a very noble sense of man's dependence on God, they discredit the very power without which all argument — and especially their own — is made invalid. The major premise of all thought is the essential validity of the knowing process.[47]

And Dean Knudson comments:

> He (Barth) regards God as so absolutely sovereign that no real human initiative is possible. The only good thing possible to man is faith, and faith is a divine not a human act. So far as man is concerned faith denotes pure passivity, emptiness, a vacuum. Man himself has no capacity for God. . .
>
> . . . .
>
> Not even faith attains security. It has no anchor; it swings free. . . . This view of faith and of reason has no doubt its challenging feature, but it is hardly a view that in the long run can be said to be conducive to mental or spiritual health. . . A unity, in which both head and heart can find anchorage, must be the goal of all serious intellectual and religious endeavor.[48]

They imply that if God so chooses, He will reveal Himself. We do not know how they can have a place for morality, for their prayers, or for the teachings of Jesus regarding the love of God. We do not understand how they can utilize ethical principles or spiritual practices (which they often do), if there is nothing to be done to obtain God-realization or the grace of God. Why should we practice meditation or prayer if human efforts have no place in religious evolution? This point of view would take away all incentive for spiritual practices. The neo-orthodox conclusions seem to be absurd in the face of the teachings of Jesus and His great followers and devotees who prescribed distinct types of mystical practices and spiritual exercises and who had direct and immediate knowledge of God and His love. Is it not an indication that they are considerably confused in the aim and methods of religious attainment in the light of the life of Jesus and His great mystic followers?

Talking about the scriptures or writing a few books on religion does not make a man religious. A religious man is he who has direct experience of God or awareness of the divine Presence, not just conceptual or philosophical interpretation. Religion is second-hand, a matter of theories, philosophies, and theologies, so long as we have no experience of God, no direct and immediate knowledge of God. There is no conviction of the existence of God. If Bertrand Russell or Sigmund Freud or John B. Watson claims that there is no God, that you and I are mere external appearances in the blind activities of material forces, we have no basis on which to refute the challenge. How do we know that God exists if we have not experienced Him? Just as we are convinced of the existence of a person when we see him, so real conviction of the existence of God comes only with the experience of Reality. Intellectual conceptions and theories are not sufficiently powerful to give the dynamics of religion. A man of religious experience not only has conviction, his whole life is changed by that experience. From this effect we judge the cause, namely from the transformation we understand the power of immediate religious realization (*Pratyaksha*). This is the convincing proof of the validity of religious experiences. "Wherefore by their fruits ye shall know them."[49]

Both Hindu and Christian mystics, Oriental or Occidental, emphasize direct realization of God as the goal of religion. Swami Brahmananda used to tell us, his disciples, that real religion begins with superconscious realization. It is emphasized in the teachings and mystical writings of St. Teresa of Avila, St. John of the Cross, author of *The Cloud of the Unknowing*, and other Christian leaders. Swami Brahmananda says in his Teachings: "God you must realize, now in this very life you must see Him. In vain is your being, in vain your mind, in vain your life, everything is in vain, if you cannot realize Him here in this very life."[50] Swami Vivekananda, too, lays stress on this in his writings.

> Religion is realization; not talk, nor doctrine, nor theories, however beautiful they may be. It is being and becoming, not hearing or acknowledging; it is the whole soul becoming changed into what it believes. That is religion.[51]

The conviction of these two great Hindu personalities and their understanding of reality came not from books nor theology nor philosophy but from the depths of their spiritual realization. How beautifully St. Teresa expresses her conviction:

> But our Lord made such haste to bestow this grace upon me, and to declare the reality of it, that all doubts of the vision being a fancy on my part were

> quickly taken away, . . . For if I were to spend many years in devising how to picture to myself anything so beautiful, I should never be able, nor even know how to do it; for it is beyond the reach of any possible imagination here below; the whiteness and brilliancy alone are inconceivable. . . . It is a light so different from any light here below that the very brightness of the sun we see, in comparison with the brightness and light before our eyes, seems to be something so obscure, that no one would ever wish to open his eyes again.[52]

Some theologians or materialistic psychologists may say that spiritual experiences are mere fabrications of the mind and the creative imagination, but we cannot accept their statements because spiritual experiences transform our lives; consequently, we find that no human being can dissuade us from our conviction of the reality of God.

Jesus emphasized spiritual life, differing in this from his contemporaries and the ideals of the Greco-Roman civilizations. It is not possible to have spiritual experiences or the experience of God unless the lower propensities or inordinate tendencies are negated. Thomas à Kempis, in his wonderful book, *The Imitation of Christ*, tells us that unless we overcome inordinate affections there is no possibility of realizing God.

> Whensoever a man desireth anything inordinately, he is presently disquieted within himself.
>
> He that is weak in spirit, and in a manner yet carnal and inclined to sensible things, can hardly withdraw himself wholly from earthly desires.
>
> It is then by resisting our passions, that we are to

> find true peace of heart, and not by being slaves to them.[53]

This is the negative approach to spiritual life. Unless many of the things that we enjoy and love and experience are negated, there is no possibility of entering into the Kingdom of God. Jesus tells us that we cannot serve both God and Mammon.[54] If we treasure Mammon, or pleasures of the world, we cannot think of God or the desirability of realizing God. We cannot then establish the Kingdom of Heaven within. This may seem too difficult or otherworldly. We hear some Occidental religious leaders express that Orientals are otherworldly. But what was Jesus? Was He not an Oriental in saying that we cannot serve God and Mammon? Was He not an Oriental in saying: "But seek ye first the kingdom of God, and his righteousness; and all these things shall be added unto you."[55] In this and such other passages, Jesus emphasized the supreme goal of life as the attainment of the Kingdom of Heaven or, as the Hindus say, realization of God.

Dr. Albert Schweitzer seems to think that Oriental religions, including the teachings of Jesus, emphasize "world and life negation."[56] He and some others stress that religion should affirm the world and life. However, Hinduism and Christianity, for instance, do not negate the world and life; they rather give proper valuation to them with worldly pleasures as secondary, while the supreme objective of religion is regarded as the understanding and realization of God — the attainment of the Kingdom of Heaven. Some thinkers seem to feel that this very idea of Jesus and other great Oriental personalities, that God and Mammon cannot be served simultaneously, is "negative mysticism." What the critics mean by this is that Oriental religious leaders emphasize negation of the pleasures of the world. When Jesus says: "For what is a man profited, if he shall gain the whole world, and lose his own soul?";[57] "Thou shalt love the Lord thy God...";[58] and "Seek ye first the kingdom of God...";[59] He gives the greatest emphasis on the highest value of life, namely the Kingdom of God — the realization of God. All religious leaders, Occidental or Oriental, emphasize the same value. If we consider the Hindu view of life, the Hindu evaluations and objectives, we find that the teachings of Jesus are completely in harmony with those of other Orientals.

Let us clarify the Hindu attitude of life. According to the Hindus, there are four objectives in human effort. They are: (1) attainment of eternal life or realization of God, (2) following of moral principles or ethical living, (3) pursuit of happiness in the world, and (4) proper training and discipline for the attainment of happiness on this plane. Attainment of eternal life or God-realization is regarded as the supreme goal. The other three values are subordinated to that goal so that man can pursue happiness in the world in a way that will lead him to the ultimate objective. Pursuit of happiness in the world is not regarded as an end in itself. Therefore, as a Hindu understands Jesus, he finds Him a thorough Oriental in His emphasis on the attainment of "the Kingdom of God" or "perfection." The rest will be added unto us.

If we place emphasis on things of the world, we, too, will develop that kind of philosophy, whether we are Hindus, Christians, Mohammedans, or Jews. On the other hand, if we understand that the primary duty of religion is to know God, we necessarily come to the conclusion that the standards and pleasures of the world must be subordinated to the realization of God. We may be called otherworldly or pessimistic; it makes no difference. It stands to reason that psychologically we cannot do otherwise. No person can think of two things simultaneously or have the same intense interest in diverse objectives. The path of good leads one to God; the path of pleasure takes one away from God. Whenever man gives his attention to the path of pleasure, unfortunately he forgets God. So when we direct our energy to creature comforts or worldly pleasures as the primary objective of life, we do not have time for, nor interest in higher aspirations, higher thoughts, or spiritual experiences. Do we not observe that the people who are giving so much attention to things of the world have no interest in God? Can any trace of religious idealism be found in any system of thought or organization where sense pleasure is emphasized as the primary objective of life? True religion is not related to the hedonistic outlook of life. "And Jesus said unto him, No man, having put his hand to the plough, and looking back, is fit for the kingdom of God."[60] Often religion is used for the accumulation of money or for the attainment of health, position, prestige, and power. It is inevitable that God is used for such purposes if emphasis is placed on worldly comforts; man will invariably subordinate religion and God to the ideal of pleasure. Religion will not be sought for its own sake but rather for the fulfillment of pleasure and the expression of power.

What is happening in most of the countries in these

modern times? According to Hindu observation, people first seek everything else thinking that God will be added unto them. But it does not happen this way. God is not added unto them because they have money, power, position, and domination of empires. On the contrary, God is far, far away.

Do the educational institutions have a place for God? Some do, but not many. A prominent professor and his wife were having a discussion with me not long ago. He is a fine person and one of the greatest intellectualists in this part of the country. While we were talking, he turned to his wife and said: "Do you find religious persons in— University?" He was laughing because he knew that men with experience of God were not to be found there. The reason for this is that the educational ideal is not necessarily religious. The secular ideal is to control nature and enjoy the creature comforts. Consequently, the educational system is organized to develop technical knowledge, chemical engineering, electrical engineering, or some other engineering, so that nature can be controlled and enjoyed. Even social organizations are developed so that all the social institutions can help us to reach that goal of pleasure, rather than God.

In the countries where the religious ideal is emphasized, the educational, social, and political institutions are organized to lead one to the truth. The Orient understands, too, the utility of social principles, applied sciences, and creature comforts, yet everything should be subordinated to the realization of God. In other words, the objective is knowledge of God, as Jesus emphasizes. Now, was He otherworldly in that sense? It is our answer that

He was neither otherworldly nor thisworldly; He was a realist in the highest sense of the term. He did not deny the existence of this world, nor do the Hindu and other Oriental teachers deny its existence. A realist in spiritual life takes God as a fact of experience, not as a distant ideal which is to be kept seperate from us. A realist in the highest sense of the term understands religion as an actuality. As such, he will use the means that will be conducive to the realization of God. The early Christians were realsts in the spiritual sense and they developed a civilization n which the religious ideal was held as the supreme objective of life; all other activities were subordinated to hat ideal. Dr. Pitirim A. Sorokin says of Christianity:

> Take, for instance, Western medieval culture. Its major principle or value was God, the true-reality value. All the important sectors of medieval culture articulated this fundamental principle-value as formulated in the Christian Credo .... In brief, the integrated part of medieval culture was not a conglomeration of various cultural objects, phenomena, and values, but a unified system—a whole whose parts articulated the same supreme principle of true reality and value: an infinite, supersensory, and superrational God ....[61]

nd of other cultures he writes:

> A basically similar major premise respecting the superrational and supersensory reality of God, though differently perceived in its properties, underlay also the integrated culture of Brahmanic India, the Buddhist and Taoist cultures, Greek culture from

the eighth to the end of the sixth century B.C., and some other cultures.[62]

In this respect, the teachings of Jesus are purely religious. Now let us consider whether, as Oriental, they were pessimistic. Jesus was neither a pessimist nor an optimist in the sense that people apply the terms. A pessimist sees the dark side of life and gets into a kind of helpless condition. He seems to think that there is no way out of the sufferings of life. He almost comes to the conclusion that suicide is practically the only solution. Some of the pessimists who are stoics advocate that people should endure their sufferings or close their eyes to them, and somehow go through this hard, painful life as graciously as possible. This attitude gives us no solution to the problems of life.

It is true that there are various problems and sufferings in the world because the world itself is changeable. The word that is used in India for the world is *jagat*, meaning that which changes constantly. The young man with his hopes and aspirations enters the world, thinking he can fulfill all the desires of life. After a few years, he realizes that his body is deteriorating. His friends who were promising so many joys have changed. His own mind has changed. He used to like certain things which he does not like today. There is change in both the outside and inside world. Consequently, things are not as they used to appear in the course of life. It is very different. Financial and social conditions change. Today you are a prince and tomorrow you are a beggar. When we consider the contemporary history of Europe, we find that the people who were wielding tremendous power in Germany and Italy are nowhere. The victorious nations treated them a criminals and consequently inflicted punishment on them. When these men were in power, no one would dare to call them criminals. The same was true when the Czar, Nicholas II, was in power. He was the absolute ruler of Russia. After the Revolution, he, his family, and many of his supporters and admirers vanished completely into oblivion. The same thing can happen to anyone who has power and position. If similar revolutions take place in the present victorious nations, the people in power will also share the same fate, however painful it may be.

These radical changes are observed not only in political circles but also in other spheres of life. Today a man is financially powerful. Then certain changes take place in his mind and he commits suicide. One man is president of his country, then another takes his place. He becomes insane and other unfortunate changes take place. Again, a man is a ruler and aspires to dictatorship. Cruel death claims him, and there is a radical change in the circle of his family and friends. Think of the people who tried to determine the destinies of mankind about seven or eight years ago. Where are they now? Mr. Hitler was a great leader. Nobody knows where he is today. Mr. Mussolini was also a powerful leader. He is dead. Mr. Churchill told the world that he was not appointed Prime Minister to preside over the liquidation of the British Empire. Where is he today? Perhaps in a few months you will not find any trace of that vigorous man who was determined to maintain British power. Where is Mr. Roosevelt? He shared the fate of his contemporaries, Mr. Hitler and Mr. Mussolini. It will not take very long, either, for Mr. Stalin to share the fate of his contemporaries, Mr. Roosevelt, Mr. Hitler, and Mr. Mussolini. It is inevitable. Already, then, some of the leaders who were bent on power have departed and are despised and forgotten. This is the condition of life. All worldly power and position are transient. We may be puffed up because of our success, but it is all "vanity of vanities," according to the writer of Ecclesiastes and Thomas à Kempis.

A realist like Jesus takes the world as it is and finds a solution to the problems of life. Buddha also lived in the world a few centuries before Christ. He was often regarded and is still regarded as a pessimist. This is far from the truth. If Buddha was a pessimist then Jesus is equally a pessimist. On the other hand, if Buddha was an optimist, Jesus is equally an optimist. In our opinion, neither one can be called a pessimist. Both of them were optimists and realists in the sense that they found a way out of the sufferings of the world. Buddha declared that there is sorrow in the world, that there is a cause for sorrow, and that it will cease to exist. The fourth truth of Buddha is the greatest optimistic expression a man can have: that there is a way to overcome suffering; there is a path which leads to the cessation of sorrow.[63]

Jesus declares this truth when he says: "Be ye therefore perfect, even as your Father which is in heaven is perfect."[64] He definitely comes to the conclusion that there is a possibility in every man to become perfect as the "Father in heaven." There is an opportunity, a way to enter into perfection. He shows the way to perfection. Is that not optimism? In this we find the positive aspect of the teachings of Jesus. When He says that we must love God with all our heart, soul, strength, and mind,[65] He means that in loving God with everything we have, we attain to that perfection or establish the Kingdom of God within us. Without love for God, it cannot be done. How encouraging and inspiring are His words!

This love can be understood in different ways. It does not mean merely emotional relationship with God. A person may not be emotional by nature. Take, for instance, Sir Arthur Keith, the Scotch scientist. In his work, *What I Believe In,* he tells us that he was born in a very pious Christian family. However, he could not subscribe to the views of the Scotch Presbyterian Church; it was almost impossible for him to accept those ideas and apply them in his life. Consequently, he left that church. He says that if he had to take up a religion it would be Buddhism. The reason for this was that he was not primarily an emotional man. It was not that Christianity was wrong or anything of the kind, but rather because the emotional method was not suitable for his temperament, according to our understanding of the statements of this man. He wanted an intellectual approach to God or truth; he wanted to know the truth primarily through the intellect and not through the emotions.

There are a number of persons in the Eastern and Western worlds who are intensely intellectual; therefore, their approach to problems is intellectual. So when Jesus says to love God with heart, soul, strength, and mind, He does not mean merely an emotional relationship but also intense thought about God. What is the expression of love? The expression of love is the continual flow of thought to the beloved. When a man loves another, he constantly thinks of him. When we think of God with heart, soul, strength, and mind, we find that our interest in other things subsides as our interest in Him grows. So the method for the intellectual type of person is to think of God.

"But seek ye first the kingdom of God, . . ."[66] It does not matter in what way a person seeks Him, whether it is through the emotions, intellect, active service, or meditation. It does not make any difference whether external nature and lower passions are conquered through devotion, reasoning, work, or meditation. The primary objective is to conquer nature, know the truth, and realize God. How beautifully Swami Vivekananda tells us:

> Each soul is potentially divine.
>
> The goal is to manifest this divine within, by controlling nature, external and internal.
>
> Do this either by work or worship, or psychic control, or philosophy, by one, or more, or all of these—and be free.
>
> This is the whole of religion. Doctrines, or dogmas, or rituals, or books, or temples, or forms, are but secondary details.[67]

The positive side of Jesus is seen in His teaching the people to seek the Kingdom of God first. He teaches a method by which we can reach the state of "perfection" in which there will be no pain. The troubles of the world cease to exist. To quote the Hindu idea, there will be "abiding peace (*alatashanti*) that passeth all understanding." By realizing it, as we read in the *Bhagavad-Gita,* everything else becomes known to us. "This is to have one's being in Brahman (God) . . . None, attaining to this, becomes deluded. Being established therein, even at the end of life, a man attains to oneness with Brahman."[68] Similarly, Jesus tells His disciples: "These things I have spoken unto you, that in me ye might have peace. In the world ye shall have tribulation: but be of good cheer; I have overcome the world."[69] That realization, that knowledge of God, gives us abiding joy, a peace that has no cessation, a peace that goes beyond all understanding of the relative world.

Another aspect of the spiritual ideal found in Jesus is His religious attitude toward life. He was a practical rather than a theoretical man. He was not a philosopher in the same sense as the modern philosophers of Europe and America. Nor was He a theologian of the modern type. He was a realist in His practical application of religion in everyday life. He teaches us to live the life, not to theorize about God. When Jesus came to His people, there were scholars and intellectuals at that time as well as those who observed rituals and ceremonies; but they did not practice or apply the spirit of religion to their everyday life.

Jesus practiced religion in two ways. First, He practiced what most Christians call prayer, and what Hindus call meditation, and other Hindus call *yoga* practices. He spent a number of years in seclusion; and although we do not know the details of that period of His life, we do feel that He must have intensified His spiritual life.

Jesus advocated prayer. He Himself prayed, as we know from the Gospel, and He taught the people how to pray. He did not say that the grace of God will come down from the sky and all we have to do is to sit tight. He said we must direct our prayers to God. His followers, who were inspired by Him, also intensified their prayers, meditation, and other devotional exercises. Those who understood Jesus lived according to His model and they reached God-consciousness through their devotional exercises. Jesus set a living example of spiritual practices.

The second way in which Jesus practiced religion was in His application of spiritual ideals in everyday life. The second part of His commandment, ". . . love thy neighbor as thyself,"[70] showed Him again to be practical. He was an Oriental in religious matters in that one must first have realization of God and then apply that knowledge practically in everyday life. As Sri Ramakrishna explains it: "With the divine knowledge of *Advaita* (union with God) in thy pocket, dost thou whatever thou wishest, for then no evil can ever come out of thee."[71] St. Augustine says also, "Love God and do as you will." Jesus not only had divine knowledge but He also applied it in His everyday life. As a practical religious man, He placed emphasis on God. This is the pragmatic value of religion. It is sometimes argued that Orientals are dreamers and philosophers; they are not practical. Jesus as an Oriental applied religion in a practical manner, and His methods are giving peace to those who practice them as well as improving society, as we shall see in the chapter on "Christ and Everyday Problems."

He inspired His disciples to serve and love man, not as a sentimental expression but as dynamic force. He sent them out to serve man with spiritual teachings and succor. "And as ye go, preach, saying, the kingdom of Heaven is at hand. Heal the sick, cleanse the lepers, raise the dead, cast out devils; freely ye have received, freely give."[72]

Similarly, the outstanding spiritual personalities of the Orient, from Sri Krishna to Swami Vivekananda, all emphasized service to man, based on divine realization. What Sri Krishna says in the *Bhagavad-Gita* means nothing but service of man.

> Being steadfast in *Yoga*, . . . perform actions, abandoning attachment, remaining unconcerned as regards success and failure. This evenness of mind (in regard to success and failure) is known as *Yoga*.[73]
>
> . . . .
>
> Therefore, do thou always perform actions which are obligatory, without attachment;—by performing action without attachment, one attains to the highest.[74]

We are to serve man as a veritable manifestation of God. The *Gita* teaches us how to live in the world, how to do our duties in a spirit of service and consecration without being attached to them. Later teachers, like Swami Vivekananda, emphasized the teachings of the *Gita*.

But let us not forget that Jesus did not speak merely of the service of man. The first part of His commandment was "Thou shalt love the Lord thy God . . ." Many Occidentals jump to the conclusion that we can serve man without serving God. Humanists and many of the progressive liberals and religious leaders advocate the service of man, but this is not possible in the best sense without service of God. Jesus first emphasized the love of God. Man cannot properly serve man unless he establishes a relation between himself and God and then between himself and man. This idea may create a little disturbance in the minds of some noble individuals who are inspired by love of neighbor or humanistic ideals. Our answer to them is that pure social gospel or philanthropic activities are noble indeed but they must be used for the main purpose of religion—awareness of God. It has been found that if the primary objective of religion is not kept brightly in view, our minds gradually become entangled in the meshes of egoism and our sense of superiority. Psychologically speaking, it becomes very difficult indeed to keep up the true spirit of a social gospel and of humanistic philanthropy, unless our minds are strengthened by the thought of God. This is emphasized by St. Paul: "And though I bestow all my goods to feed the poor, and though I give my body to be burned, and have not charity, it profiteth me nothing."[75]

Time and again we have seen many attempts made by different types of humanists to serve man. Invariably they lost the higher ideal and failed to achieve what they proposed to do. They fell short of the ideal because they forgot the first part of the commandment of Jesus. There are individuals here and there who are altruistic, though they claim they do not have any real conviction about God. But such persons are few and far between and their influence is generally not felt in society. Man cannot really succeed in loving his neighbor until he learns to love God, in fulfillment of the first part of the commandment. Here again we find the expression of an Oriental in Jesus; in fact, His whole life was an expression of the Oriental ideal—the religious ideal.

A criticism generally levelled against what are termed "Oriental" religions is that they put too much stress on renunciation. Did Jesus emphasize renunciation? His words manifest clearly that His teachings were particularly based on the spirit of renunciation. Some of His followers may try to find worldliness and power politics in Him, but unless they impose their ideas on His teachings, they will not succeed. As we explained before, the spirit of renunciation is not negation of the world; it is only negation of false values, a change of emphasis from worldly pursuits to the understanding of God. It is not giving up life. So what the Hindus understand from the teachings of Christ is the positive side of the knowledge of God, giving secondary value to other activities of life. Swami Vivekananda says in *Christ the Messenger*:

> Therefore the one work his whole life showed, was calling upon them (the people) to realize their own spiritual nature . . . He never talks of this world and of this life. He has nothing to do with it; except that he wants to get hold of the world as it is, give it a push and drive it forward and onward until the the whole world has reached to the effulgent Light of God; until everyone has realised his spiritual nature; until death is vanquished and misery banished.[76]

Naturally, we want to know how to integrate the personality and how to make the highest religious ideal actual in life. It is obvious that Jesus, as an incarnation of God and the embodiment of the religious ideal, must have shown ways of religious fulfillment. According to the Hindu viewpoint, religious or *yoga* practices are essential for this purpose. Jesus as the teacher of mankind demonstrated the ideal in His life through actual spiritual practices.

---

40. Matt. 6:24, 25, 28, 29, 32, 33.
41. Ibid., 22:37-39; Mark 12:30-31; Luke 10:27.
42. **Katha Upanishad**, trans. Swami Sharvananda (3rd ed.; Mylapore, Madras: Sri Ramakrishna Math, 1932), chap. II:1.
43. Matt. 10:39; Mark 8:35.
44. Edgar Sheffield Brightman, "The Neo-Orthodox Trend," **The Journal of Bible and Religion**, XIV, No. 3 (August, 1946), 129-130.
45. Albert Schweitzer, **Out of My Life and Thought**, trans. C. T. Campion, M. A. (New York: Henry Holt & Co., 1933), p. 258.
46. Rom. 8:16-17.
47. Lynn Harold Hough, **The Meaning of Human Experience** (New York: Abingdon-Cokesbury Press, 1945), p. 26.
48. Albert C. Knudson, "The Theology of Crisis," **The Sixth Biennial Meeting of the Conference of Theological Seminaries and Colleges in the United States and Canada**, Bulletin 6, September, 1928, pp. 72 and 76.
49. Matt. 7:20.
50. **Spiritual Teachings of Swami Brahmananda** (2nd ed.; Mylapore, Madras: Sri Ramakrishna Math, 1933), p. 129.
51. **Works**, II, 394.
52. **The Life of St. Teresa of Jesus**, trans. David Lewis (London: Thomas Baker, 1924), p. 248.
53. Thomas á Kempis, **Following of Christ** (New York: Catholic Publishing Co.), Book I, chap. VI.
54. Matt. 6:24.
55. Ibid., 6:33.
56. Schweitzer, **Indian Thought and Its Development**, passim.
57. Matt. 16:26; Mark 8:35-37.
58. Ibid., 22:37; Mark 12:30; Luke 10:27.
59. Matt. 6:33.
60. Luke 9:62.
61. Pitirim A. Sorokin, **The Crisis of Our Age** (New York: E. P. Dutton & Co., Inc., 1942), pp. 17-19.
62. Ibid., p. 19.
63. **Dhammapada** (Sayings of Buddha), XII.
64. Matt. 5:48.
65. Ibid., 22:37; Mark 12:30; Luke 10:27.
66. Matt. 6:33.
67. **Works**, I, 119.
68. **Srimad-Bhagavad-Gita** II:72.

69. John 16:33.
70. Matt. 22:39; Mark 12:31; Luke 10:27.
71. Sayings of Sri Ramakrishna I:11.
72. Matt. 10:7-8; see also Luke 9:2.
73. Srimad-Bhagavad-Gita II:48.
74. Ibid., III:19.
75. I Cor. 13:3.
76. Works, IV, 142.

CHAPTER III

CHRIST, A YOGI

> Thus always keeping the mind steadfast, the Yogi of subdued mind attains the peace residing in Me, — the peace which culminates in Nirvana (moksha) (freedom).
>
> Verily, the supreme bliss comes to that Yogi, of perfectly tranquil mind, with passions quieted, Brahman-become, and freed from taint.[77]

A *yogi* is he who can declare: "I am the Self," or "I am *Brahman*," just as Jesus says: "I and the Father are one." In considering the descriptions of *yoga* and its nature, the question would naturally arise whether or not Jesus, the Christ, was a *yogi* in this sense. Orientals can understand whether or not He was a *yogi* because they understand the import of the word *yoga*. On the other hand, there is considerable misunderstanding of it in the West, as it is associated with rope tricks, fortune telling, burial alive, thought reading, thought transference, etc. When a man can display such extraordinary powers, he is regarded as a *yogi* in the West. Therefore, it is natural that Occidentals are sceptical about the idea that Jesus was a *yogi*. They say that He was not a *yogi* but He was the Son of God. It is true He was not a trickster or fortune teller, although it is reported that He controlled some of the laws of nature and displayed extraordinary power such as healing the sick, raising the dead, and stopping the wind and storm. However, Occidental devotees and followers of Christ would certainly not think of Him as a trickster, so they say that the display of His extraordinary powers constituted miracles rather than tricks.

When we understand the proper meaning of the word *yoga*, we can really evaluate Jesus as a *yogi*. Again, if we know the correct meaning of the word, there cannot be any confusion. But it must be admitted that Western people have sufficient reason to misunderstand its import, as it is a foreign term. Some of the Hindus are greatly responsible for creating confusion in the minds of Westerners, as they have taken advantage of Western curiosity about some of the extraordinary powers of *yoga*. They often call themselves *yogis* when they tell fortunes or display spiritualistic mediumship. Some Occidental people are also responsible, as they deliberately try to confuse Western minds regarding the practice of *yoga*, intimating that it is a mysterious, shady affair.

The word *yoga* is derived from the Sanskrit root of *yuj* which means to yoke. In India it means union with God, as we read in the teachings of Sri Ramakrishna. Patanjali, the founder of *yoga* systems, defines it in his *Aphorisms*: "Yoga is restraining the mind-stuff (Chitta) from taking various forms (Vrittis)."[78] Sri Krishna says:

> When the mind, absolutely restrained by the practice of concentration, attains quietude, and when seeing the Self by the self, one is satisfied in

> his own Self; when he feels that infinite bliss—which is perceived by the (purified) intellect and which transcends the senses, and established wherein he never departs from his real state; and having obtained which, regards no other acquisition superior to that, and where established, he is not moved even by heavy sorrow;—let that be known as the state called by the name of Yoga,—a state of severance from the contact of pain. . . .[79]

And according to Swami Vivekananda: "*Yoga* is the science of restraining the *chitta* (mind) from breaking into *vrittis* (modifications)."[80] When a man is thoroughly established in the knowledge of God, when he is united with Him, when there is no longing but for Him, when he realizes the source of all existence, when he is established in abiding bliss, then alone he is a *yogi*. This joy which knows no bounds can be attained only by knowing and realizing God and God alone. In order to have that peace "which passeth all understanding,"[81] he must have thorough control of his mind and his emotions must be integrated. So long as the mind is disturbed by inordinate tendencies and conflicting urges, there is no possibility of *yoga*. According to the *Katha Upanishad*:

> That firm control of the senses is known as Yoga. Then the Yogi must be free from all vagaries of the mind; for the Yoga can be acquired and lost.
>
> When all the desires that dwell in the heart are destroyed, then the mortal becomes immortal, and here one attains Brahman (God).[82]

Patanjali describes the eightfold path of *yoga.*[83] The first two are *yama* and *niyama. Yama* is ethical observation and mental control; *niyama* is physical purification, dietetic restrictions, and the like, as well as certain mental training. Non-killing, truthfulness, non-stealing, continence, internal and external purification, contentment, and self-control constitute *yama* and *niyama.*[84] At first, the body and mind should be cleansed by proper purificatory processes. Stimulants or drugs should be avoided and nutritious and wholesome food and liquid taken to sooth and quiet the whole body. A moderate amount of regulation of food and drink is helpful in the early stages of spiritual practices. Mental cleansing is even more important than physical cleansing. Primitive urges and inordinate emotions are extremely disturbing to the mind and cause it to remain restless. In his *Yoga Aphorisms,* Patanjali therefore prescribes the cultivation of contentment, and such other qualities.[85] He also advocates that a person deliberately cultivate higher ethical qualities when he is given to expressions of extreme suspicion, jealousy, or hatred. Nothing ruins human peace and happiness more thoroughly than ill-directed emotions. According to Patanjali, anyone who is swayed by them should aggressively cultivate friendliness, generosity, and affection toward any individual against whom he has ill feelings. "Friendship, mercy, gladness and indifference, being thought of in regard to subjects, happy, unhappy, good and evil respectively, pacify the Chitta (mind)."[86] Therefore, in order to reach union with God, one must be thoroughly established in the first two steps of *yoga,* namely *yama* and *niyama.* Without these purificatory processes for mind and body, the state of *yoga* cannot be attained.

No man can have abiding peace and undisturbed tranquillity and serenity unless he is thoroughly established in the Reality. Desires vanish when a man is established in unity. Jesus had something like this in mind when He said: "For where your treasure is, there will your heart be also."[87] One who treasures God has no reason for inordinate desires, as there is nothing outside him or beyond him. People become jealous, envious, and disturbed because their desired and beloved objects may be taken away by somebody else. The root of these weaknesses is destroyed by the removal of ignorance of their true nature. In the words of Jesus to His disciples: "Peace I leave with you, my peace I give unto you: not as the world giveth, give I unto you. Let not your heart be troubled, neither let it be afraid."[88] When a man understands his own relationship with God, he also understands the relationship between his fellow-beings and God. As Jesus again says: "I am the vine, ye are the branches."[89] So when an individual knows that he is inseparably connected with God, he also realizes that the same is true of others. As such he becomes aware of a common divine heritage. Consequently, he cannot have any justification for jealousy, envy, and such other deplorable tendencies. "Finally, brethren," says St. Paul, "Whatsoever things are true, whatsoever things are honest, whatsoever things are just, whatsoever things are pure, whatsoever things are lovely, whatsoever things are of good report; if there be any virtue, and if there be any praise, think on these things."[90] The more a person becomes established in the higher spirit of religion, the less he is subject to mental disturbances. In fact, an illumined soul who is aware of the Divine Presence everywhere is free from mental tension, conflict, and confusion.

There may be a question concerning the utility of *yoga*, if it takes away all incentive for human efforts and activities. A real *yogi* who dispels his ignorance and becomes established in the Reality will find the manifestation of that in every being. He will feel the presence of God everywhere, in whom "we live, and move, and have our being."[91] In fact, he will declare with Swami Vivekananda:

> I should see God in the poor, and it is for my salvation that I go and worship them. The poor and the miserable are for our salvation, so that we may serve the Lord, coming in the shape of the diseased, coming in the shape of the lunatic, the leper, and the sinner! Bold are my words, and let me repeat that it is the greatest privilege in our life that we are allowed to serve the Lord in all these shapes.[92]

This is to be compared with the words of Jesus: " . . . Inasmuch as ye have done it unto one of the least of these my brethren, ye have done it unto me."[93] The real incentive in the service of man lies in understanding and realizing the presence of God in all. All the destructive tendencies and selfish, egocentric attitudes of life are accentuated by the erroneous understanding of the very nature of man. When ordinary people work under the spell of delusion and feel a definite separateness of themselves from others, then they become egocentric, selfish, and greedy. They indulge in the most deplorable and unholy acts because of their selfishness. On the other hand, a real *yogi*, feeling the presence of God everywhere, becomes a true servant of humanity. How beautifully it is stated in the *Gita* that "The knowers of the Self look with an equal eye on a Brahmana endowed with learning and humility, a cow, an elephant, a dog, and a pariah."[94] When a *yogi* looks equally on all persons and feels the presence of God in them, he really understands what Jesus meant when He said: "Thou shalt love thy neighbor as thyself."[95] So a *yogi* is he who is thoroughly established in the real Self. As Sri Krishna tells us, when the Self is seen by the self, one is satisfied in his real Self.[96] A *yogi* is really a center of love because he realizes God who is love itself. "That One who is Self-made is verily the joy. Having attained this joy, man becomes blessed."[97] And again we read in the *Gita*:

> He who hates no creature, and is friendly and compassionate towards all, who is free from the feelings of "I and mine," even-minded in pain and pleasure, forbearing, ever content, steady in meditation, self-controlled, and possessed of firm conviction, with mind and intellect fixed on Me,—he who is thus devoted to Me, is dear to me.[98]

This shows that a *yogi* is not a mere intellectual; he is the veritable embodiment of love.

We can now consider whether or not Jesus was a *yogi* in the light of the teachings of Hindu teachers such as Sri Krishna, Patanjali, Sri Ramakrishna, and others. We cannot find a better *yogi* than Sri Krishna himself or Patanjali, the father of the *yoga* system of thought in India. Sri Krishna has given us the basic ideas of *yoga* and the different methods by which one can attain to the state of union with God. When we survey the incidents in the life of Jesus we are compelled to find indications of *yoga* in Him.

We know from the lives of Krishna, Buddha, Ramakrishna, and others that They transformed innumerable people and transported them to higher planes of consciousness. Nay, they could give direct realization of God, as Jesus did. It will not be out of place to relate an incident in the life of Sri Ramakrishna which will clarify this point and help us understand how Jesus transformed the people and gave the realization of God. It was the first day of January in 1886. A number of lay devotees had gone to visit Sri Ramakrishna, among them being Girish Ghosh, a great dramatist of Bengal. In a moment of devotional fervor he said to Sri Ramakrishna: "Oh Lord, what do I know of you? What can I understand?" This very expression of devotion made Sri Ramakrishna enter a superconscious state and He touched the devotees one after another as they approached Him. All were transported into the highest state of consciousness, beatific vision, and realized the Ultimate Reality in their individual ways.

The incident of the Transfiguration of Jesus in the presence of Peter, James, and John is a similar glorious example of transformation from the human to the divine plane. The effect of this incident on His disciples was tremendous. They had beatific vision and divine realization.[99] The Resurrection of Jesus is also a glorious example of the manifestation of His divine power, when He appeared after the Crucifixion first to Mary Magdalene and then to His other disciples. The effect of this experience in the lives of His disciples cannot be measured in terms of ordinary experiences. Incidents of the Resurrection are no doubt often regarded as miraculous, but there is nothing mysterious about them from the standpoint of an incarnation. They had a profound effect on the disciples whose lives were thoroughly transformed by the direct perception and immediate realization of the divine nature of Jesus. This and many such incidents convince us that Jesus, like other great teachers, had the power of *yoga* to mold human personalities by giving the highest realization of God.

The real power of a *yogi* lies in his ability to transform individuals. There is a world of difference between an ordinary *yogi* and one of the highest type, namely an incarnation of God. An ordinary *yogi*, a man really aware of God, can influence and change the lives of a few persons and help them to try to realize God. He can inspire us and show us the path to the Reality. A *yogi* of the highest type, the incarnation of God, can pick a man from anywhere and lift him to a higher plane. Consider the life of Mary Magdalene. Hers was an immoral life; but by His touch, His blessing, and His love, Jesus transformed that woman and made her a saint. Perhaps some persons may not like to admit this; but if we consider the life of that questionable personality, we will find that she was made whole, pure, and blessed by the magnetic touch of Jesus. A man thoroughly established in the Reality, who is identified with God completely, can alone transform any man or woman. Sri Ramakrishna gives an illustration of these two types of *yogis*:

> A *Siddha-Purusha* (perfected soul) is like an archaeologist who removes the superimcumbent earth and dust, and lays open an old well which had been covered up owing to ages of disuse. The *Avatara* or the Incarnation is like a great engineer who sinks a new well even in a place where there was no water before. Whereas the former can give salvation only to those men who have the waters of salvation near at hand, the *Avatara* saves him too whose heart is devoid of all love and dry as a desert.[100]

A *yogi* of the highest type can also lift a group of people simultaneously to the higher plane. A number of times we have seen true *yogis* lead hundreds of people simultaneously to the higher plane of consciousness. It is amazing; and unless one has that experience, one can hardly understand or grasp that an ordinary mind hovering around the objects of the senses and interested in all the ordinary things of the world can be lifted to a higher plane at a moment's notice. Did not St. Paul tell us in one of his letters to the Corinthians that: "In a moment, in the twinkling of an eye . . . we shall be changed."[101] Yes, the highest type of *yogi* can transform a person in a moment's time and change the course of his whole life. When Jesus called fishermen or money changers to follow Him, His very words had a tremendous effect on these ordinary people. They were transformed and their lives were changed.[102] When we observe these facts, we are compelled to believe that Jesus was thoroughly established in *yoga*, union with God.

Now what about the display of psychic powers? It is true that they have very little to do with spiritual evolution in the higher state of *yoga*. We find that there are persons who are not really *yogis*, who are not aware of God, and who have no supreme devotion or love for Him; yet they can display extraordinary powers. For instance, a few years ago a man went to London from India and displayed these powers in controlling the burning power of fire. In the presence of the medical association in London, he walked on fire which was burning at a temperature of about eight hundred degrees. He was not even slightly burned. Young medical students, who were present, tried to find out whether it was a trick or a hypnotic spell. So they took off their shoes and socks and just touched the outer edge of the fire with their feet. They were so badly burned that they had to be given medical care. Yet the man from India walked on the intense heat as if it were nothing. He admitted that he had no real spiritual knowledge; yet he had learned how to control the laws of nature in connection with the burning quality of fire. (His name is Khoda Box).

There was another man in India who recently displayed the extraordinary power of controlling the effect of venomous poison, a few drops of which would kill any man. He would pour it in a glass and drink it like water. He could also swallow glass, nails, and other such objects. These displays were carried on in the presence of the highest government officials and medical authorities in India and Burma. Unfortunately, the man died because of his carelessness. During a performance, he drank poison but soon realized that he had made a blunder. He left the stage at once and said to those who were with him: "I am finished. You cannot save me.

I made a mistake. Before I went to the stage I did not go through certain practices. No one can save me now." By the time he had spoken these words, he was dead. Many English medical men were there with him and examined what he had been drinking. It was real poison. They tried to do what they could for him, but death was practically instantaneous.

Such *yogis* immunize themselves from the effect of the usual laws of nature by certain processes. There are phenomena which can be manifested by a person when he goes through certain psychophysical exercises. He thereby develops subtle mental powers through which he controls ordinary natural laws and the subtle particles and forces of matter. A few years ago, a man in India allowed himself to be buried alive and he remained there for nearly six weeks. Sentinels were posted to watch the place. He was able to remain alive so long because he suspended his animation through control of the breath. We personally saw two persons who could suspend animation through control of the respiratory system. They could also control ordinary elementary and involuntary functions of the human body. It was evident that they did not have supreme knowledge of God nor intimate love for Him. Hence their "miracles" were worthless.

Patanjali, in his *Aphorisms*, describes various methods of developing extraordinary powers for controlling the so-called exact laws of nature through mental exercises. He elaborately gives the methods of concentration through which one can manifest extraordinary psychic powers; but then he categorically says that such powers are obstacles to spiritual realization. He advocates that a spiritual aspirant or a real *yogi* must not be allured by these extraordinary powers:

> These are obstacles to Samadhi (superconscious realization); but they are powers in the worldly sense.
>
> By giving up even these powers comes the destruction of the very seed of evil, which leads to Kaivalya (complete emancipation).
>
> The Yogi should not feel allured or flattered by the overtures of celestial beings, for fear of evil again.[103]

There are some subtle experiences which come to a true *yogi* in the course of his exercises, even though he may not be seeking extraordinary powers. At times, he involuntarily and indeliberately expresses them in the course of spiritual discipline. We knew persons who happened to develop levitation and emanation of light spontaneously. Some disciples of Sri Ramakrishna developed these powers as a matter of course; yet the great Master advised His disciples to avoid them completely. As a by-product of spiritual practices, people often get the powers of levitation, suspended animation, emanation of light, mind reading, clairvoyance, and other such powers; yet they should be controlled. Sri Ramakrishna says of them:

> These powers . . . are obstacles to the realization of God.
>
> *Siddhis* or miraculous powers are to be avoided like filth. These come of themselves by virtue of *Sadhanas* or religious practices, and *Samyama* or control of the senses. But he who sets his mind on

> *Siddhis*, remains stuck thereto, — he cannot rise higher.[104]

Swami Vivekananda also says:

> The powers acquired by the practice of Yoga are not obstacles for the Yogi who is perfect, but are apt to be so for the beginner, through wonder and pleasure excited by their exercise. . . . The Yogi who has conquered all interest in the powers acquired . . . comes into the "cloud of virtue" (name of one of the states of *Samadhi*) and radiates holiness as a cloud rains water.[105]

Again it is stated by Sri Krishna:

> Various are the occult powers that come to the yogi while practicing concentration . . . No power is beyond the reach of the sage who, self-controlled, poised, and tranquil, has complete command of the prana (vital force) and who concentrates on me.
>
> But great powers though these may be, they are regarded as obstacles by the true yogi, who seeks union with me.[106]

In the course of spiritual development and realization, these powers are sometimes manifested without any effort, as we have already said. Some *yogis* of India have made deliberate efforts to develop their powers to control the laws of nature, such as the burning quality of fire, or to control forms and walk on water or float in the air. But a real *yogi*, a real spiritual man, never makes an attempt to manifest these powers for display. We happen to have known persons who had some of these powers which they never displayed as they were thoroughly established in the highest state of spiritual consciousness. These powers are such in a worldly sense, but in a spiritual sense they are bondages. If a man manifests them, he loses his spiritual consciousness.

In the face of these statements, then, why did Jesus display extraordinary powers? It may be assumed that on the basis of the above conclusions he would have lost His spiritual power. Our answer is that Jesus manifested extraordinary powers in order to convince the undeveloped people of His time that He possessed spiritual power to lift them. Children can understand power when it is manifested. But can a child be taught the nature of electricity, for example, unless its effect is shown in heat, light, or motion? The child understands electricity only when it is displayed. Similarly, the Jews and Gentiles of that period were childish in their spiritual development. Consequently, they needed some signs. "An evil and adulterous generation seeketh after a sign; and there shall no sign be given to it, but the sign of the prophet Jonah."[107] The poor, childish people needed signs and Jesus gave them Jonah's preaching of repentance and His own Resurrection.

An incarnation of God, the highest type of *yogi*, has tremendous compassion. His love knows no bounds. When he sees suffering, particularly of devoted persons who are entirely dependent on him, he does something for them, which is regarded as a miracle. Although he knows that these are not ordinarily to be used without having a baneful effect, the highest type of *yogi* once in a while displays these powers to express his love and do good to humanity. Mary and Martha were devoted to Jesus and to Jesus alone. They knew no one else in the world but Him and they entirely depended on Him. When their only brother was taken away by cruel death, their hearts went to Jesus in their sorrow. Jesus was the veritable embodiment of divine love and He expressed that love in raising the dead.

A number of such incidents are related in the life of Sri Krishna. He also displayed various extraordinary powers which are regarded by common man as miracles. Nevertheless, they were within the laws of the mind, as it was true in the case of Jesus. Where ordinary people lose their balance and high spiritual ideals in the course of the manifestation of such powers, these great *yogis*, the divine incarnations, can express them without being affected by them, as they have the fullest control over themselves and are completely aware of their divine nature. A man who is really established in God, whether he is an incarnation or a lesser personality, has certain strength with which to withstand the temptations of extraordinary power. He has no selfish desires, so these things do not affect his mind. Jesus could remain unaffected by the after-effect of His display of power as His mind constantly soared to the realm of God. He was always aware that "I and my Father are one." The man who has no attachment to his "I" has no other attachments. To whom will he be attached? He sees God and God alone. Consequently, Jesus was not at all affected by the expression of extraordinary power.

In the *Bhagavad-Gita* various types of *yoga* are described and different methods of *yoga* or realization of God are given. Naturally, the question would arise: What type of *yogi* was Jesus? Was He a follower of the path of knowledge, love, meditation, or action? In the first place, we are compelled to believe that He was predominantly a follower of the path of love. He insisted that we love God. ". . . Thou shalt love the Lord thy God with all thy heart, and with all thy soul, and with all thy strength, and with all thy mind; . . ."[108] That was His first commandment. He Himself loved God intensely. The true nature of Jesus is revealed in the Gospel according to St. John, in chapters thirteen through fifteen. He was nothing but love. He not only loved God but also the manifestation of God, the world. He declares: "I am the vine, ye are the branches: He that abideth in me, and I in him, the same bringeth forth much fruit: for without me ye can do nothing."[109] He was inseparably connected with God; nay, He was in God and the devotees were in Him, as He says: "At that day ye shall know that I am in my Father, and ye in me, and I in you."[110] This does not mean thereby that only His disciples were inseparably connected with Him, but all persons were in Him, as a Hindu understands it. "Neither pray I for these alone," He says, "but for them also which shall believe on me through their word."[111] Only a true lover can feel this.

In the *Bhagavatam*, Skandha 10, we read how divine incarnations love all persons irrespective of their position, power, or qualities. Love is not based on consideration of merit or otherwise. Just as the sun cannot withdraw its rays from any person, whether he is good or evil, so the divine incarnation, the Bliss itself, radiates love to all persons irrespective of their good or evil tendencies. "For he maketh his sun to rise on the evil and on the good, and sendeth rain on the just and on the unjust."[112]

Everyone talks of love; but no one has it who possesses the slightest trace of selfishness, arrogance, envy, or jealousy. Selfishness and love cannot exist in the same person simultaneously. They are opposite qualities, just as darkness and light. Where there is light there is no darkness; similarly, where there is love there is no selfishness and its by-products of envy, jealousy, and such tendencies. We observe that in the world there is considerable selfishness and exploitation practiced by the people who talk so much of love. Unfortunately, they do not know its true nature. Swami Vivekananda says in his poem "To A Friend":

> Aye, born heir to the Infinite thou art,
> Within the heart is the ocean of Love,
> "Give," "give away," — whoever asks return,
> His ocean dwindles down to a mere drop."[113]

The great dramatist and spiritual leader, Girish Ghosh of Calcutta, India, has said: "Why does a lover expect love in return? When you have the spirit of give and take in love, the desire and nature of love vanish."

Jesus expressed love for God without expecting anything in return. He had love for love's sake. Ordinary people love God because they want something from Him. Often they want material possessions; they want to get rid of pain and agony; and they want other things, so they think of God. In the life of Jesus we find that there was no want in Him so He did not demand anything from God. In the Gita we read that there are four types of people who seek God. "Four kinds of virtuous men worship Me, . . . the distressed, the seeker of knowledge, the seeker of enjoyments, and the wise, . . ."[114] The two lower types of people, the distressed and seekers of enjoyment, want to get rid of pain or they want to have something. Devotees of the third group think of God because they want to know Him. Those in the fourth category are the blessed people who know God and love Him for His sake alone. When a man loves God with all the strength of his mind and soul, he is capable of loving the manifestations, creatures, or children of God, because he sees God in them. An incarnation of God is established in Him constantly. Consequently, He is the man who can love with no trace of selfishness. It is something that ordinary poople do not know. There is a madness or intoxication in it. If a man has a glimpse of that love, he is indeed blessed. That is the reason Jesus says that we should love God in every way possible and also our neighbors. The philosophical interpretation of that statement is that when we love God wholly, then alone are we capable of loving our neighbors. In complete love of God, all desires, ambitions, love of power, and thought of "I" vanish. There remains only "Thou." As a Hindu poet says: "I have lost myself in Him." When that state comes, then alone is a man capable of loving others. That is the meaning of the statement by Jesus to His disciples: "This is my commandment, That ye love one another, as I have loved you."[115]

It is very nice to hear about that love; it is inspiring to talk about it; it is uplifting to think about it; yet unfortunately, hardly any of us has tasted even a little of it.

Jesus showed us how to cultivate and manifest such love; He never indicated that it is His possession alone. On the contrary, He encouraged His disciples to love one another as He had loved them. Did He not inspire them to love the whole world? He showed a way of loving the world through service. As we observe His relation with God, His disciples, and others, we are compelled to believe that He was a natural *Bhakta* (*yogi* of love). That is to say, He was an exponent of the path of love. He Himself showed how love can make one realize God and thereby He demonstrated to His disciples the true nature of divine love.

The major trend of the teachings of Jesus is indeed directed to the path of love or *Bhakti Yoga*. Even a casual reader would be convinced of this. It is seen in His expression of love for His disciples and for mankind. As He gave great emphasis to the practice of love, the question may arise in the minds of many critical observers: Why did He so strongly emphasize this one tendency of man? From observation of human nature, the answer is evident. Human beings are predominantly emotional; the majority of our activities are governed by emotional drives, even though we have intellectual and active elements in us. With His knowledge of human tendencies, Jesus as a perfect Master tried to show how this noble emotion of love can be directed to God. According to Sri Ramakrishna: "By following this path one comes to God more easily than by following the others."[116] Again Swami Vivekananda declares: "The one great advantage of *bhakti* is that it is the easiest, and the most natural way to reach the great divine end in view; . . ."[117] So Jesus gave a method to the people which they could follow spontaneously and naturally without going through any unusual struggle and effort. Moreover, the people of that period were disorganized and disrupted. Apart from that, they had very little intellectual interest, so it was fitting for them to follow the path of love. We make bold to say that this method is the most effective and it is almost universally applied in every age. It is true that there may be exceptions, but a great teacher gives the greatest emphasis to the most applicable method. It is also true that he gives private instructions to individuals who are suited for other methods, as we find when Jesus gave intimate teachings to His disciples which are related in the Gospel of St. John.

Jesus was also a *Karma Yogi*, a follower of the path of action. The acts performed at the Last Supper prove convincingly that He also taught *Karma Yoga*. He Himself served His disciples by washing their feet and He instructed them to do likewise. "If I then, your Lord and Master, have washed your feet; ye also ought to wash one another's feet."[118] He also healed the sick and raised the dead and performed many such activities. He was ever ready to serve humanity at the cost of His life on this plane of existence. Because He served humanity by teaching the highest principle of spiritual life, the people did not understand Him. They crucified Him. "And the light shineth in darkness; and the darkness comprehended it not."[119] He knew that Judas would betray Him and that the people who glorified Him on Palm Sunday would later condemn Him. Not only did the leading Jews and Gentiles condemn Him, but the whole crowd changed their attitude. They laughed at Him and mocked Him. He knew that they were unstable and unintegrated and could not withstand temptation or tribulation. Yet He never changed His spirit of service. A *Karma Yogi* always works in the spirit of service without attachment.

Swami Vivekananda tells us that a *Karma Yogi* is he who never figures out the result of his action. He works for the sake of work. ". . . Work — work — . . . without looking at results, and always keeping the whole mind and soul steadfast at the lotus feet of the Lord!"[120]

> Karma Yoga teaches us how to work for work's sake, unattached, without caring who is helped, and what for. The Karma Yogi works because it is his nature, because he feels that it is good for him to do so, and has no object beyond that. His position in this world is that of a giver, and he never cares to receive anything.[121]

Sri Krishna says in the *Gita*: "Thy right is to work only; but never to the fruits thereof."[122] He further says:

> Being steadfast in Yoga, . . . perform actions, abandoning attachment, remaining unconcerned as regards success and failure. This evenness of mind (in regard to success and failure) is known as Yoga.[123]

As a *Karma Yogi*, Jesus worked and served the world, even though "He came unto his own, and his own received him not."[124] His only duty was to give them understanding and light. This is the true spirit of *Karma Yoga.* He demonstrated that the man who follows the path of action should never consider the result of his action. He was indifferent to praise or blame in the performance of His service to humanity. The modern social gospel gets its inspiration from this aspect of the life of Jesus.

He was also a *Raja Yogi*, as we know from His display of extraordinary powers, which have already been discussed. A *Raja Yogi* established in meditation can easily express those powers; in fact, they can be expressed by a *yogi* of any type. To seekers of truth they come as a by-product, not as a primary result of *Raja Yoga* practices. *Raja Yoga* is the royal method of God-realization. The followers of this path practice a system of psychophysical exercises to train the mind. There is another system, *Hatha Yoga*, which is mainly a system of physical exercises, but some *Hatha Yogis* go through certain processes of *Raja Yoga* for spiritual development. However, the majority of them give more attention to the development of occult and psychic powers. As we have already mentioned, there are persons who deliberately go through certain forms of *Raja Yoga* and *Hatha Yoga* to manifest these subtle powers. An incarnation does not manifest occult powers for the sake of performing miracles; he does it for the good of the people without any sense of "I." The motive is always spiritual. From our observation of the life of Jesus, we are compelled to believe that He was established in meditation and mental control in His display of mental poise and emotional integration. His whole personality shows the effect of *Raja Yoga*.

The chief aim in *Raja Yoga* is to realize God by control of the mind, so it is called the psychological process of God-realization. In this form of *yoga*, a seeker of truth is advised to control and regulate the emotions and to practice concentration and meditation. When the mind is absolutely concentrated on God, the truth reveals itself and man realizes God. So the main purpose of *Raja Yoga* is realization of God, as it is the objective of other paths of *yoga—Bhakti, Karma,* and *Jnana,* the paths of love, unselfish action, and knowledge.

Jesus was also a follower of the path of knowledge. A follower of this path can alone declare: "I and my Father are one."[125] Devotees can never say that, as they want to remain separate from God and enjoy Him as their object of devotion. As Hindu devotees say, they want to enjoy sugar rather than become sugar. When Jesus says: "I and my Father are one," He establishes unity. The loving relationship culminates in unity; what remains is the Absolute, One, *Sat-chit-ananda*—Existence, Knowledge, Bliss.

A *Jnana Yogi* removes the veil of ignorance and, thereby, the basis of multiplicity or duality. He always fixes his mind on unity. Anything that suggests plurality or duality is negated by a *Jnana Yogi*. His aim is to remove the basic ignorance of cosmic illusion which creates multiplicity. This cosmic illusion, or *Maya*, has two powers. One covers the true nature of the universe; the other creates something instead. *Maya* covers the true nature of oneness and gives rise to multiplicity. In the statements of Jesus that "I and my Father are one" and ". . . I am in my Father, and ye in me, and I in you,"[126] He makes oneness clear. He was indeed a *Jnana Yogi* in the state of superconscious union, being established in that state of unity which obliterates plurality and multiplicity. He removed the twofold power of *Maya* and found that He Himself was one with the Reality. For Him there was nothing else except God or the Absolute; He felt the presence of that Reality in all. From the Hindu point of view, a man of His type had the fullest expression of all the forms of *yoga*. It is not difficult for them to conceive that these paths or *yogas*—devotion, unselfish work, meditation, and knowledge— culminated in Him as they have culminated in other incarnations.

Where did Jesus learn *yoga*? It is not inconceivable that He learned the technique of the *yogas* in the Near East where He lived. We are also told that the followers of Buddha had their monasteries and centers all over the Near East at the time Jesus was born. We also know from history that Egypt, Palestine, and Arabia had definite commercial and cultural contacts with India in those days. Therefore, it is quite possible that some of the Hindu teachers spread their influence in that region. It does not make much difference where He learned *yoga*; the fact remains that the expressions of the four *yogas* were manifested in His personality. In fact, as an incarnation, He knew God directly.

Jesus as an incarnation did not need to learn *yoga* from anyone. As He was a born teacher, He was intimately aware of all ways of spiritual life and development. Spiritual practices become evident in the life of an incarnation. It is true that an incarnation sometimes goes to a teacher to learn certain spiritual practices; but He also proves that without going to a teacher He knows these things directly and immediately. For instance, Jesus went to John the Baptist and evidently had some spiritual instructions from him. His forty days' fasting in the wilderness and such other instances show that He practiced some of the devotional exercises. It is quite conceivable that He knew other methods without being taught. However, it is immaterial whether He learned *yogas* from other teachers or whether He manifested them from within. He was a Master. He was a master *yogi*, as Swami Vivekananda tells us:

> ... The Nazarene himself was an Oriental of Orientals.... All the similes, the imageries, in which the Bible is written... speak to you of the Orient.
>
> . . . .
>
> So, we find Jesus of Nazareth, in the first place, the true son of the Orient, intensely practical. He has no faith in this evanescent world and all its belongings. He had... no other thought except that one, that he was a Spirit.
>
> . . . .
>
> You find that all these three stages (of spiritual development) are taught by the Great Teacher... The Messenger came to show the path: that the spirit is not in forms... This is the great lesson of the Messenger, and another, which is the basis of all religions, is renunciation.[127]

And Swami Abhedananda says of Him:

> ... The powers and works of this meek, gentle, and self-sacrificing Divine man, who is worshipped throughout Christendom as the ideal Incarnation of God and the Saviour of mankind, have proved that

he was a perfect type of one who is called in India a true *Yogi*.[128]

---

77. Srimad-Bhagavad-Gita VI:15, 27.
78. Yoga Aphorisms of Patanjali I:2.
79. Srimad-Bhagavad-Gita VI:20-23.
80. Works, VII:59.
81. "And the peace of God which passeth all understanding, shall keep your hearts and minds through Christ Jesus." Phil 4:7.
82. Katha Upanishad 6:11 and 14.
83. Yoga Aphorisms of Patanjali II:29.
84. Ibid., II:30.
85. Ibid., II:32.
86. Ibid., I:33.
87. Matt. 6:21.
88. John 14:27.
89. Ibid, 15:5.
90. Phil. 4:8.
91. Acts 17:28.
92. Works, III, 246-247.
93. Matt. 25:40; see also verses 31-45.
94. Srimad-Bhagavad-Gita V:18.
95. Matt. 22:39; Mark 12:31; Luke 10:27.
96. Gita VI:20-23.
97. Taittiriya Upanishad, Vol. VII, Brahmananda Valli.
98. Gita XII:13-14.
99. Luke 9:28-36; Matt. 17:1-9; Mark 9:2-9.
100. Sayings of Sri Ramakrishna IV:137.
101. II Cor. 15:52.
102. Matt. 4:18-22 and 9:9; Luke 5:27-28; John 1:43.
103. Yoga Aphorisms of Patanjali III:38, 51-52.
104. Sayings of Sri Ramakrishna XXXVI:701-702.
105. Works, VII, 63-64.
106. Srimad Bhagavatam, The Wisdom of God, trans. Swami Prabhavananda (New York: G. P. Putnam's Sons, 1943), p. 260.
107. Matt. 12.39.
108. Luke 10:27; Matt. 22:37; Mark 12:30.
109. John 15:5.
110. Ibid., 14:20.
111. Ibid., 17:20.
112. Matt. 5:45.
113. Works, IV, 429.
114. Srimad-Bhagavad-Gita VII:16.
115. John 15:12.
116. The Gospel of Sri Ramakrishna, trans. Swami Nikhilananda (New York: Ramakrishna-Vivekananda Center, 1942), p. 468.
117. Works, III, 32.
118. John 13:14.
119. Ibid., 1:5.
120. Works, VII, 272.
121. Ibid., II, 390.

122. **Srimad-Bhagavad-Gita** II:47.
123. Ibid., II:48.
124. John 1:11.
125. Ibid., 10:30.
126. Ibid., 14:20.
127. **Works**, IV, 138-145.
128. Swami Abhedananda, **How to be a Yogi** (San Francisco: The Vedanta Ashrama, 1902), pp. 168-169. See also **Teachings of Swami Shivananda** (Calcutta: Udbodhan Office).

CHAPTER IV

CHRIST AND SPIRITUAL PRACTICES

> Not everyone that saith unto me 'Lord, Lord,' shall enter into the kingdom of heaven; but he that doeth the will of my Father which is in heaven.[129]
>
> . . . .
>
> Watch ye therefore, and pray always, that ye may be accounted worthy to escape all these things that shall come to pass, and to stand before the Son of man.[130]
>
> . . . .
>
> But thou, when thou prayest, enter into thy closet, and when thou hast shut thy door, pray to thy Father which is in secret; and thy Father which seeth in secret shall reward thee openly.[131]

There are often misconceptions regarding the significance of these utterances of Jesus. Different types of minds misconstrue the meaning of the will of God and of spiritual practices. Everyone agrees that we are to express the will of God and that we are to love God as Jesus says in His commandments, but there are persons who think that spiritual practices and discipline are unnecessary in religious life. By practices and discipline we do not mean mere observation of certain ethical principles; one must also know the will of God and carry it out accordingly.

There is considerable misunderstanding of the term "spiritual practices." We are to be careful that they are practices and not imagination. We find that groups in both Oriental and Occidental countries not only perform spiritual exercises but they also advocate some of the occult and psychic methods, the "spooky" and spiritualistic theories. They often come to the conclusion that these habits and exercises are also religious practices. This is far from the truth. Occult, psychic, and spiritualistic methods do not indicate that there is any integration in the emotions of a man. They do not help anyone to develop will power. They do not help in emotional uniformity. On the contrary, we find that people who indulge in such practices go further and further from God. As Sri Krishna says: "Votaries of the Devas (angels) go to the Devas; to the Pitris (departed souls) go their votaries; to the Bhutas (lower than angels), go the Bhuta worshippers; My votaries, too, come unto me."[132] In other words, those who are devoted to departed souls go to their plane; those who are devoted to other subtle-bodied beings, go to their plane; and those who are devoted to God reach Him. So we must think a little carefully that we do not identify spiritual practices with occult habits or psychic experiences. Many a man has fallen into the trap of occult, psychic spiritualism in the name of religion. By driving evil spirits away from the people, Jesus indicated that devotion to them is not meant for real lovers of God.

So let us take a note of warning. Genuine religious exercises are those which lead us to God through integration of the emotions, will, and thought. Any practice that demoralizes or weakens the will, that disintegrates the emotions, that makes us narrow and dogmatic, that makes us irrational, and that does not lead us to God is not spiritual and will not ultimately give us an understanding of the will of God, no matter how attractive and alluring it may be at present. Neither will such practices allow us to carry out the will of God in our everyday life. On the other hand, genuine spiritual practices will enable us not only to understand the will of God but also to carry it out in life and reach the supreme goal.

Some persons advocate that we do good to others. They emphasize "love thy neighbor." They want to do something for the welfare of their fellow beings. As a result, we find there is a sound system of what is called "social gospel." However, some of these people apparently see no necessity for spiritual practices, but at the same time they agree that they must love God and neighbor.

Still others who misconstrue the meaning of spiritual practices seem to have the impression that they are methods of self-hypnosis, and that when we go through certain rituals and ceremonies we hypnotize ourselves. They think that this spirit of "hypnosis" is not only meaningless but also harmful.

Another misconception of some people is that they can go through various devotional exercises and thereby seek salvation for themselves, without consideration for their neighbors. They forget the second commandment of Jesus. Their interpretation of the love of God is vague; they do not explain what they mean by it. Some give a sentimental expression; others do not give any description.

Love of God implies continuous thought of God without cessation. Narada, one of the greatest thinkers and greatest exponents of devotion in India, describes this love of God beautifully:

1. Bhakti is intense love for God.
2. It is the nectar of love;
3. Getting which man becomes perfect, immortal and satisfied forever.
4. Getting which man desires no more, does not become jealous of anything, does not take pleasure in vanities:
5. Knowing which man becomes filled with spirituality, becomes calm and finds pleasure only in God.[133]

Later writers, such as Sri Ramanujacharya and others, elaborate the constant love of God. Swami Vivekananda says:

> When this supreme love once comes into the heart of man, his mind will continuously think of God and remember nothing else. He will give no room in himself to thoughts other than those of God, and his soul will be unconquerably pure, and will alone break all the bonds of mind and matter and become serenely free. He alone can worship the Lord in his heart; . . .[134]

The nature of love does not need explanation. When we love someone, we constantly think of that person in various ways. All of us have experienced, at some time or another, a maddening love, an intoxication of love. It is not a passing fancy, mere appreciation, or just an intellectual understanding of the person. In love, the whole mind, emotions, and thought continually flow to that individual; there is both emotional satisfaction and intellectual understanding in the experience.

Talking about love of God is not enough; we must cultivate continual thought of God and consequent inner satisfaction and complete joy, a joy that cannot be broken by anything and that will not waver in the presence of anything whatsoever in this world. Because of the very nature of God, complete absorption in Him is required in order to love Him. In our ordinary friends we find that love wavers. We feel that something is still lacking. We know that there is a form of love, but there is no fulfillment and complete satisfaction in it. In divine love all the emotional urges of the human mind are satisfied; in fact, the whole being of man is absorbed in the intensity of divine love. It not only culminates in the highest emotional gratification, it also makes one aware of the presence of the divine Being. It makes one realize the highest spiritual consciousness of God. Moreover, the lover is inseparably connected with God. Sri Ramakrishna says:

> Prema (intense divine love) is like a string in the hands of the Bhakta, binding to him that Sachchidananda (Existence—Knowledge—Bliss) which is God. The devotee holds the Lord, so to speak, under his control. God comes to him whenever he calls.[135]

When people talk in sentimental or loose terms of the love of God, it does not seem that they have reached the highest state of love, in spite of their professions. How many persons think of Him and find satisfaction in Him? There are few who have such satisfaction in God and immediate and direct awareness of God. Even though they are associated with religious organizations and churches, they are restless and constantly expressing a want. They are restless because something is lacking in them. If we analyze the outer expressions of divine love, we find that most people are absolutely lacking in those expressions. So we are compelled to believe that they have not that love. Would to God that everyone had that love! Unfortunately, it is not so.

Consequently, all the religious teachers, who know something about divine love, as described by Jesus, advocate certain methods for cultivating it. It can be developed and manifested gradually. Every one of us possesses divine love within us in a potential form. Our very emotional nature implies that we possess it.[136] However, it is so much confused and mixed with selfishness and self-assertion that it almost appears as if it were altogether different. When we seek satisfaction in loving others, we are really impelled by the divine love that is in us. Unfortunately, our lower tendencies step in and change the whole color of the love. This is the very reason that many outstanding thinkers, such as Swami Vivekananda and others, make a distinction between human affection and divine love. They observe the outer expressions of human emotions are toward their worldly objects of love and the expression of divine love is directed to God. The distinction between human affection and divine love can be made on the basis of their characteristics.

There are three types of love. In the lowest form, a person demands something from his beloved. The whole attention is given entirely to himself. His inner emotional reaction stems from egocentricity. The lover becomes the center of attention because of his selfish attitude. He expects that the beloved will conform to his own likes, dislikes, and passions to satisfy him in every way. In the second form of love, there is reciprocity, mutuality. The lover gives affection, thought, and consideration to the beloved, and expects the same in return. He is not satisfied only by getting love from his beloved but he is also anxious to pour out his heart to his beloved. The spirit of demand is considerably modified by the spirit of giving. Egocentricity and selfishness are minimized by selflessness. In the third form of love, the lover is satisfied only by giving love to his beloved. He does not consider himself nor has he any thought of getting something in return; in fact, his heart is full when he is giving to his beloved. He is constantly pouring out love in service of the beloved and is prepared to sacrifice everything for him. There is no sense of envy or jealousy as he is completely unselfish; there is no bargaining. Swami Vivekananda says:

> . . . Love knows no bargaining. Wherever there is any seeking for something in return, there can be no real love; it becomes a mere matter of shopkeeping. . . . Begging is not the language of love . . . Ask not anything in return for your love; let your position be always that of the giver; . . .[137]

These three forms of love can be directed to a friend or relative and also to the fountain of love, God. In fact, these three forms of love are expressed more or less in human relationship, although it is expected that a devotee will have the third type of love. Unfortunately, few have it. Even most of the people who are known as religious persons approach God in their faith and devotion with certain petitions and prayers, constantly asking for this and that. It reminds us of a very interesting story from the life of Akbar, a great seventeenth century Mohammedan emperor of India. It happened that he met a holy man one day in the course of his itinerary and he expressed the desire to present a gift to the holy man. He persuaded him to wait for a few minutes until he finished his daily prayer. While the holy man was waiting patiently, the emperor prayed to God for this thing and that thing. Hearing such a prayer, the holy man got up and was about to leave when Akbar finished his prayer and inquired why he was leaving without receiving his gift. The holy man replied, "I do not accept gifts from a beggar." The noble emperor realized his limitation and learned a great lesson from this incident. Most of the people in the world who are associated with religion are of this type. They seek things from God.

So it is necessary to have a prescription or a system of habits, ways, and actions for the cultivation of higher forms of love. Spiritual practices are the means of the cultivation of divine love. They are not mysterious as some critics seem to think. They are not incantations or processes of propitiation of certain deities. They are not allurement of God so that He will shower us with His blessings. Neither are they processes of self-hypnosis. They are mainly a method of cultivation of the thought of God, a method of manifestation of divine love. As we discussed in Chapter III, Jesus Himself practiced the path of love and repeatedly told His disciples to do the same through systematic methods of manifestation of love. Consider His parable of the ten virgins and their lamps. "And five of them were wise, and five were foolish. . . . the bridegroom came; and they that were ready went in with him to the marriage: and the door was shut."[138] By this Jesus made it apparent that people who are watchful and vigilant in their spiritual attitudes and practices can realize God. On the other hand, those who are lazy and careless in their spiritual life miss the mark and do not become aware of God. "Watch therefore, for ye know neither the day nor the hour wherein the Son of man cometh."[139] Again, when Jesus went to the house of Mary and Martha, Mary sat at His feet and listened to His words. He said: "Martha, Martha, thou art troubled about many things: But one thing is needful: and Mary hath chosen that good part, which shall not be taken away from her."[140] These incidents clearly indicate that spiritual practices and cultivation of love for God are prerequisites of the second commandment of Jesus.

Now some of the critics will again say that we do not need spiritual practices and that it is better to do the will of God. But how are we going to know what is the will of God? There are certain groups in Western countries who seem to think that they can get the guidance of God or know the will of God by just sitting quietly. Would to God we all had that power of knowing the will of God just by sitting quietly and remaining passive! However, this creates difficulties. In the first place, if we merely remain quiet, we generally become negative or we become restless. None of us can sit still without thinking of different things we have experienced previously. Our conscious or subconscious impressions come to the surface at that time, eliminating any continuous thought. Again we may enter into a negative state when the subsconscious bubbles arise to the conscious plane, and the thoughts or associations that we like are inclined to appear. Then we are likely to conclude that those ideas are the guidance or "voice" of God. We may make fanatical decisions. So again there is serious difficulty.

It is a problem to know what is the will of God and what is not. Some will say that they know the will of God and if people do not follow them, they are irreligious and have no right to live in this world. Others are a little more generous; they not only say that people who do not follow them are irreligious but also that they will not have any spiritual blessings nor attain heaven; they will suffer forever. The so-called non-believers may not lose their lives; their presence and existence will be tolerated with pity and contempt. The best thing they can do is to redeem themselves and follow the suggested method.

Acts performed in many religions in the name of God have flooded the world with human blood, from the Crusades to contemporary developments. The so-called expressions of the will of God darken the pages of history with the perpetration of inhuman and brutal acts performed by men and women in the name of God and for the expression of the will of God. They have destroyed many noble souls and institutions as well as the possibilities of their own spiritual evolution.

Objective observers or rationalists will find it impossible to subscribe to these interpretations of the will of God. When they consider basic ethical principles, they will refuse to accept such viewpoints. Their idea of ethics is that we must not hate anyone and we must not express base qualities. This is also the viewpoint of many Christians and other real religious leaders. The moment a religion based on the will of God expresses hatred in the name of God, they will run away from the threshhold of that religion. They try to find a reason, a background, an ethical explanation for religious activities. If these go against the established ethical principles of harmonious living and peace in human society, they cannot accept them. So they find it most difficult to follow this kind of religious attitude or expression of the will of God. It is true that Jesus says that we are to do everything according to the will of God, but very few persons ever demonstrate that they have an understanding of it. Often their imagination or subconscious urges are interpreted as such.

Now what should a man do? Real spiritual persons tell us that in order to know God's will we must cleanse our minds. Jesus says: "Blessed are the pure in heart: for they shall see God."[141] Unless the mind is cleansed, ambitions, preconceived notions, and subconscious urges will come between us and the will of God which is often interpreted in terms of these impressions. It has been done time and again by every one of us. That is the reason that the mind should be purified and cleansed. This is the prerequisite of the understanding of the will of God. As St. Paul says: ". . . Be ye transformed by the renewing of your mind, that ye may prove what is that good, and acceptable, and perfect, will of God."[142]

Some of the devout orthodox persons will say that we do not have to go through spiritual practices and exercises to cleanse our minds; if we do good to others, our minds are already pure. But, in fact, our minds are not pure. We may not harm anyone or steal or give slap for slap, yet our minds can remain contaminated by many subtle urges. Take for instance, ambition or self-expression as emphasized by certain schools of modern psychology. These urges possess us and appear in such a subtle way that we hardly suspect them as being anything ignoble. They can even be construed as the will of God. Until the empirical ego is disciplined and controlled, we can hardly differentiate between the will of God and our ambitions and desire for self-expression. We interpret those urges as the will of God. It is a psychological fact that many of us unwittingly fool ourselves.

Time and again we read in religious history how persons with well-meaning attitudes started a social gospel of service to man. Yet, in the course of a few days, all their ambitions and urges of self-expression stepped in and destroyed the possibilities for real service and real spiritual evolution for them and their followers. We know many such cases where people had serious setbacks so far as spiritual progress was concerned, even though their work objectively grew. Their external activities in the form of love of neighbor were also gradually affected by their inordinate ambitious tendencies. That is the very reason we must be careful about following the will of God and carrying out His purpose. We must purify our ego and cleanse the whole inner attitude; then and then alone can we understand what is really His purpose and His will. The intense spiritual practices of Jesus for forty days definitely indicate that such practices are absolutely necessary for mental purification and awareness of the will of God.

The mind has five distinct states. (1) It is extremely restless. In this state we can hardly expect to have one-pointed thought of God. The mind cannot even think of God; in fact, it cannot think of anything systematically and consistently. So it goes without saying that we must control extreme restlessness. (2) In another state the mind becomes a little quiet. For instance, when a person goes to a concert and hears a beautiful piece of music, it enchants him and he concentrates on it. Again, when a person sees a beautiful piece of art or looks at a lovely scene, his mind is attracted by that and it becomes quiet. It is possible to think of God for a little while in this quiet state. Unfortunately, the mind is not yet controlled. External conditions may calm it; but the moment they are withdrawn, the old tendencies and expressions of restlessness return. (3) There is yet another state in which the mind is dull and inert and does not like to exert itself or to think of anything. (4) The mind is one-pointed in a higher state; it is neither inert nor extremely restless. Through discipline and training, the mind can be kept in this state of attention for a fairly long time. (5) In the last state, the mind is completely concentrated. Very few of us experience the fifth state of mind; generally we are in the first three.

Religion teaches us how to apply the whole mind to

God so that it can think consciously and deliberately of God for long periods of time, if not constantly. As we develop this thought form, we develop love. This brings a gradual emotional satisfaction and joy and consequent awareness of God. Herein lies the utility of spiritual practices which train our minds so that we can ultimately think of God. We do not believe that any great mystic—whether he is a Hindu, Christian, Buddhist, Mohammedan, Jew, or Taoist—will gainsay that in the path of divine love or in the following of the will of God or in the imitation of Christ, we must deliberately, consciously, and continually think of God.

The question arises: How should we do it? As we mentioned, we seldom find a person who can deliberately think of God for more than a few seconds. The use of symbols of God in spiritual practices is a means of focusing the mind on Him. One method is to adopt an outside, objective aspect of God in the form of a symbol, picture, statue, or some other substitute of God to signify His universal qualities. Then we direct our attention to that particular form as they do in some of the orthodox churches through the use of the cross or crucifix, the statues of Christ or the Madonna. In the Hindu temples, statues, substitutes, and symbols are used to remind the devotees of God and His universal and glorious qualities. Swami Vivekananda gave a beautiful example of the utility of symbols in connection with an ordinary picture. It so happened that a man of high position in India asked the Swami why people practice idolatry. This man happened to be the prime minister of one of the native Indian rulers, and in his room he had a picture of the maharaja. Swami Vivekananda requested this man to bring the picture to him, and when he did so the Swami asked him to spit on it. The man was startled at the thought of spitting on the picture of his ruler. "Why?" asked Swami Vivekananda, "What stopped you from doing it? This is not the maharaja but only a picture of him." Nevertheless, the prime minister could not bring himself to do it because the picture reminded him of the maharaja. So the Swami explained to him that symbols signify whatever is represented in them. In the same way, symbols of God are not God; yet they remind us of Him. As such, symbolism has a definite place in the spiritual culture of a man. It is a mistake to think that symbolism can be equated to idolatry. Sri Ramakrishna explains it:

> As a toy fruit or a toy elephant reminds one of the real fruit and the living animal, so do the images that are worshipped, remind one of God who is formless and eternal.
>
> . . . .
>
> A marksman learns to shoot by first having big objects to shoot at; and as he acquires more and more facility in shooting, he aims more and more easily at the smaller marks on the target; so when the mind has been trained to become fixed on images having form, it is easy for it then to become fixed upon things that have no form.[143]

It is a mistake to criticize the use of symbols, rituals, and ceremonies, as some of the liberal groups often do. The result is disastrous. They neglect an important instrument of worship so far as the primary objective of religion is concerned. They confuse the use of symbols with idolatry, but there is a world of difference between idolatry and symbology.

The first part of the commandment of Jesus emphasizes that one must love God wholly. That implies knowledge or awareness of God. Without awarenes of God and immediate knowledge of Him, one cannot have the type of love for Him, which we described in the first part of this chapter. The primary objective of religion is naturally immediate knowledge of God and the consequent complete manifestation of divine love. These two are interdependent in spiritual development. A devotee does not have love without awareness of God nor can he be aware of him without simultaneous love. A study of highly developed persons will reveal that every one of them expresses awareness and love of God simultaneously. As they increase their love of God and consequent thought of Him, so they have immediate knowledge of Him, and vice versa. The lives of St. Francis, Swami Vivekananda, and others show that these are two phases of the same spiritual growth. We also observe a natural corollary of awareness of God in the form of love of neighbor and consequent service of Him. Very few people can boldly say: "Yes, I have seen God." Their lives will prove whether they have or not. The experience and consequent love of God changes a man's personality. As Jesus says: "Wherefore by their fruits ye shall know them."[144] So we feel that the use of external symbols is absolutely necessary for certain types of persons to enable them to develop their spiritual qualities and to manifest the will of God.

There are others who use mental symbols rather than external symbols to signify the universal qualities of the Infinite. There are various types of spiritual practices, devotional exercises, and worship. The repetition of the name of God is also used as well as the practice of concentration and meditation. There are many varieties in the methods of worship, concentration, and meditation.

A serious question will arise here: Did Jesus want His followers to go through practices? It is often argued by many liberals of the Christian groups that He did not intend that His followers should use rituals as He condemned some of the existing forms practiced by the Jewish leaders. We are told that many of the orthodox Christian practices were taken from old European, African, and Asiatic pagan methods. Suppose that we accept that they are pagan methods practiced by the pagans. Should they be regarded as wrong because they were practiced by non-Christians? Should not we study them to see if they have any real spiritual significance? Why should we discard anything that is done by another man because we do not know him and the significance of his practices? A thing is wrong because it is intrinsically wrong and not because it was done by someone else. A reasonable man does not discard anything because it was done by another person or religious group, whether pagan, Hindu, Mohammedan, Christian, or otherwise. After evaluating the significance of the spiritual practices in the manifestation of the love of God and awareness of Him, we should use them accordingly. No scientific or rationalistic thinker discards anything if it is useful for scientific investigation, even if it comes from an alien source. Similarly, a religious person should not have any prejudice against a practice which is helpful, even though it originates in another religion. Moreover, there is no reason to believe that Jesus Himself did not advocate spiritual practices and exercises for the development of the love of God. He prayed in the wilderness and communed with God and He taught His disciples to follow in His footsteps. From the few facts about His life, we can safely conclude that He Himself found it necessary to go through these practices, otherwise He would not have done so. He gave the Lord's prayer to His disciples. After the Last Supper He remained in prayer and communion with God in the garden of Gethsemane. The incident of Gethsemane is an evidence that Jesus observed spiritual practices and wanted His followers to do the same. When they slept, He reprimanded them, saying: "Watch and pray, that ye enter not into temptation: the spirit indeed is willing, but the flesh is weak."[145] This shows that unless a person goes through systematic spiritual practices, he easily falls prey to human weaknesses, such as falling asleep and becoming indifferent to higher values of life. This very incident indicates that a person must be extremely careful regarding spiritual practices. Slipshod or mechanical methods will not change the human personality. That is the reason Christian mystics who followed in the footsteps of Jesus were so emphatic about spiritual practices. It is historically evident that when this emphasis is minimized man and society fall prey to human passions. Jesus as a

Master and teacher knew these human frailties and so admonished His disciples and made it clear that spiritual practices are absolutely necessary for right action. We can take it for granted that an incarnation of God does not do anything that is not meaningful. He comes to set an example and finds it necessary to go through these practices, otherwise He would not have done so. His actions are purposeful and are demonstrations of real spiritual life so that others may follow His footsteps.

In India, we have a habit of evaluating a philosophy or religious system from its practical value. We do not take either a philosophy or a religion to be worthwhile if it does not change the life of a man. A founder of a religion must demonstrate in his life that it is practical and useful through integration of his own personality and awareness of God. This should, thereby, lead one to the primary objective of life. It must be demonstrated also in his followers and disciples; otherwise, the statements and ideas will not be accepted by the Hindus.

Jesus demonstrated His religion through practice, prayer and communion with God. He showed through successive generations that these practices were useful and practical. We have no reason or justification to say that these practices were just propitiation or incantations or means of alluring God. They are methods of training the mind so that we can understand and follow the will of God. Otherwise, our ego or our subconscious urges will run riot, which has happened in the lives of many persons. In the methods of Jesus, we find that He was a thoroughgoing teacher. He remained absorbed in God and taught His disciples to do the same through spiritual practices. It did not end there; the disciples and followers successfully introduced the same practices into the whole Christian Church. We have no reason to believe that they did this just for the sake of following habits and ways which they gathered from pagan sources from time to time.

It is true that the followers of Christ were considerably influenced by the existing thoughts and ways of the Jews, Buddhists, and Hindus, in the early days of Christianity. Contacts were made through trade as well as cultural, philosophical, and religious communication, and the early Christians became acquainted with the ways of living and the spiritual practices of the Buddhists and Hindus. There are many historical evidences to show that Alexandria was the seat of mutual exchange in cultural activities as well as worldly commodities. Plotinus, the teacher of Origen, was said to be the student of a Hindu teacher. Neo-Platonic ways of thought and action have been introduced a great deal into Christian thought and culture since the time of Plotinus.[146] From this we can conclude that there was considerable influence from Buddhist and Hindu sources in the early days of the Christian Church. This influence was even found in Greek thinkers such as Plato and others.[147]

Do we not find that the great Christian mystics, who systematically went through spiritual practices, reached the goal of life? Suppose that we accept that they themselves discovered those practices without being influenced by anyone. Even then we find that these exercises trained their minds so that they could comprehend the truth. They understood the utility of these practices; otherwise, they would not have advocated them for others or undergone such strenuous discipline themselves.[148] A modern Indian Christian says:

> Prayer forms or provides the binding factor between God and man. It is the medium by which man establishes union with God. Therefore, one who wishes to do the will of the Father has always to pray. Indeed, such a person's life itself should be one continuous prayer. . . Through prayer it is that man remains in communion with God and derives his strength.[149]

That is the very reason St. Teresa of Avila gives us a systematic method of contemplation and meditation in her *Way of Perfection.* St. Ignatius also prescribes a system of *Spiritual Exercises* for arousing the thought of God. George Fox, the founder of the Quaker group, emphasizes "quietism." John Wesley advocates meditation and communion with God. Some of the Christian leaders describe all this as "heart warming" or as finding the "inner light," but they certainly mean the cultivation of the continual thought of God. This is what we mean by the necessity of spiritual practices or mystic exercises. Professor Eddy Asirvatham, a Protestant Indian Christian leader, sees the necessity for such practices. He suggests that religious retreats be incorporated into the church organization in India.

> While the Christian ashram should not be an exact replica of a Hindu ashram, it would provide ample opportunity for prayer, meditation, and unhurried thought and study followed by Christian action. Its emphasis would be on simplicity of life, corporate

> living, and the sharing of material goods to the utmost practicable limit. Organization and doctrine would play a relatively minor part.[150]

Spiritual practices must be followed if we really want to integrate our emotions. We know that misdirected emotions, conscious or unconscious, create stumbling blocks in our expressions of love. If we admit with the followers of the social gospel that they are doing the will of God, which is the highest expression of religion, we still find historical evidence that, in spite of the lofty teachings of Jesus in the Sermon on the Mount, many followers are not equipped to carry out what they think is the highest goal of life, the service of man. On the contrary, they destroy and advocate the destruction of man. Is it that they lack the teachings of Jesus? Not at all. It is because they cannot integrate their emotions. A foolish man "built his house upon the sand. . . and the winds blew, and beat upon that house; and it fell: and great was the fall of it."[151] In the same way, the houses of spiritual culture of these people are destroyed. It is all right when the wind does not blow, when there is no storm; then they can talk nicely. But when the test comes, they have no strength to follow the will of God, as their emotions are not integrated. They react in an ignoble, irreligious way against the will of God, although they often try to explain that their actions are according to His will. Take, for instance, the Crusades and the Spanish Inquisition. Even if we stretch our imagination, we still cannot find justification for their support of such destructive activities. They are not consistent with the Sermon on the Mount.

Some people may argue that the Christian Church lost its fervor of spiritual regeneration during the Dark Ages, but since the period of the Reformation it has regained its religious force. We admit that there have been men and women who were integrated personalities in the post-Reformation period. We must also equally admit that there were great personalities, like St. Francis, St. Anthony, and others, who lived during the pre-Reformation period. It is not that the people of earlier periods had no power of integration while those of later generations had strong religious dynamics to mold their lives. If we just casually observe the writings and utterances of many of the religious leaders during the last two world wars, we are convinced that the people failed to translate the religious ideals of Jesus into action in spite of their philosophical and theological flights. Many of the religious leaders of Europe and America not only diluted the gospel of love during the period of emergency but they also condemned those who struggled to live according to that ideal during the days of world-wide destruction. Some of these theologians did not hesitate to condemn the peace-loving people who believed in the absolute efficacy of the gospel of love and consequent soul force for the adjustment of individual and collective disputes and conflicts. They were called heretics, as Professor Niebuhr says:

> . . . Yet most modern forms of Christian pacifism are heretical. Presumably inspired by the Christian gospel, they have really absorbed the Renaissance faith in the goodness of man, have rejected the Christian doctrine of original sin as an outmoded bit of pessi-

> mism, have reinterpreted the Cross so that it is made for the absurd idea that perfect love is guaranteed a simple victory over the world, and have rejected all other profound elements of the Christian gospel as "Pauline" accretions which must be stripped from the "simple gospel of Jesus." This form of pacifism is not only heretical when judged by the standards of the total gospel. It is equally heretical when judged by the facts of human existence. There are no historical realities which remotely conform to it. It is important to recognize this lack of conformity to the facts of experience as a criterion of heresy.[152]

Such a philosophy of defeatism and glorification of the lower propensities of man is not amazing. The people who do not or cannot integrate their emotions and harmonize their ideal with actual living will either rationalize their upset emotional conditions or dilute the ideal by stretching the spirit of the ideal of the gospel of love. It is but a common human failing to feel satisfied in one's own weakness and to be defensive about self-condemnation of the higher ideal that one gathers from religious study.

In our spiritual practices, we establish an emotional relationship with God. Some persons look upon God as father or mother or friend. To others He is the Master or the beloved. Through these relationships, they emphasize and manifest their love for God and direct their emotional inclinations to Him. It is a mistake to think that spiritual exercises can be performed without cultivation of love toward God. This is impossible. Spiritual exercises are meant for the culture of inner urges and emotions. That is the very reason that Jesus says in the Fourth

Gospel: "Henceforth I call you not servants; for the servant knoweth not what his lord doeth: but I have called you friends; for all things that I have heard of my Father I have made known unto you."[153] His disciples started their spiritual life as servants of God; their relation with Jesus was as servant to master or as disciple to teacher. Gradually, as they evolved, the disciples transcended their limitations and became friends of God — a very sweet relationship indeed. The tendencies that create separation between the lover and beloved vanish. The sweetness of friendship and love has no fear, wonder, embarassment, or other such separating tendencies. So Sri Ramakrishna says: "One cannot succeed in religious life if one has shame, hatred, or fear. These are fetters."[154] When these tendencies of mind vanish, then alone the relationship of servant and master culminates in friendship. It is a very intimate contact between the devotee and God and it cannot be experienced unless one's inner nature evolves and grows into it. There are, however, outstanding Christians who attained this intimacy through purification of their inner nature. St. Anthony looked upon Christ as a baby and established an intimate relationship with Him. St. Teresa of Avila took Him as the supreme objective of her life. St. Thérèse, the Little Flower, thought of Him as her dearly beloved; Brother Lawrence practiced what he called the "presence of God"; George Fox considered Him as the Inner Light; and Jacob Boehme also developed his own relationship with God. We find that a number of Christian mystics have adopted various relationships and have reached the highest state of God-consciousness through culture of the emotions. It is also noted that some devotees, in the early days of spiritual culture, try to cultivate that state of friendship with God by imitating the great mystics and saints and recapitulating their relationships with God. In this way, these devotees establish themselves in the love of God and friendship with Him.[155]

When we establish a relationship with God, we do certain things for Him, our beloved. Those are the spiritual exercises. Some of us decorate the beloved with flowers and burn incense. Some cook food for Him. Mirabai, a saint of medieval India, used to treat Krishna as her little boy, the veritable embodiment of love and her object of supreme love, and she used to cook for him as a mother would cook for her child. Through this relationship she reached the highest spiritual consciousness. Similar practices have been followed by Christian devotees; they followed wholly the teachings and footsteps of Jesus and derived their inspiration from Him.

Those who cannot understand the wind and storm of their emotions are not the ones to develop their will power. Consequently, they cannot carry the ideal into actual life, as the will cannot be developed unless the emotions are unified. Even if anyone wants to follow the social gospel and love of neighbor, he must basically develop his emotions and will power; otherwise, he finds it very difficult to carry on against certain obstacles and disturbances in the reality of his activities. He expresses base emotions of hatred and anger and often gives up his higher ideals. He does not follow the teachings of Christ and frequently dilutes His teachings to suit his own emotional urges. So if any of us want to reach the goal of life, we must take up some form of spiritual exercise. Then and then alone can we unify and purify our minds. So in the words of Jesus: "Take ye heed, watch and pray: for ye know not when the time is."[156]

There may be a narrow interpretation regarding spiritual exercises, as we have mentioned already in connection with the will of God. Often some of the devout thinkers and narrow thinkers conclude that a particular method must be followed in order to have spiritual realization. If a particular ritual is not followed or performed in a particular manner, then a person cannot grow. We cannot accept that viewpoint. From an Oriental point of view, we find that in Christianity there have been various methods and exercises practiced by the followers of Christ. The methods of St. Bernard were different from those of St. Teresa. They were again different from certain practices of St. Ignatius. These were not the same as the Franciscan methods. Jacob Boehme, John Wesley, George Fox, and such others also prescribed methods of their own. Nevertheless, the different groups of Christians reached the highest state of God-consciousness by following their own individual methods.

When we take the world viewpoint, as we are living today in one world, we find that there are many types of mentalities. Therefore, every one has to follow his own particular method of practice in order to attain the goal and carry religious principles into the various activities of his life. Spiritual exercises and consequent religious experiences or direct and immediate knowledge of God have a definite influence on the everyday life of man. As such, religious realizations cannot be divorced from life in the world.

---

129. Matt. 7:21.
130. Luke 21:36.
131. Matt. 6:6.
132. **Srimad-Bhagavad-Gita** IX:25.
133. "Narada Bhakti Sutras," (A free translation dictated by Swami Vivekananda), **Works,** VI, 116-117.
134. **Works,** III, 85-86.
135. **Sayings of Sri Ramakrishna** XV:528.
136. The nature of divine love is explained more fully in Chapter III.
137. **Works,** III, 86-88.
138. Matt. 25:2, 10.
139. Ibid., 25:13.
140. Luke 10:40-42.
141. Matt. 5:8.
142. Rom. 12:2.
143. **Sayings of Sri Ramakrishna** XVI:336, 340.
144. Matt. 7:20.
145. Ibid., 26:41; Mark 14:38.
146. **Encyclopedia of Religion and Ethics,** ed. James Hastings, (New York: Charles Scribner's Sons, 1917), IX, pp. 318-319.
147. Edward J. Urwick, **The Message of Plato** (London: Methuen Co., Ltd., 1920).
148. The **Spiritual Exercises** of St. Ignatius; St. Teresa's **Way of Perfection** (London: Thomas Baker, 1935); and the teachings of St. John of the Cross should be especially studied for further details, as also the rules of monastic orders of St. Basil, Pachomius, St. Anthony, St. Benedict, etc.
149. J. C. Kumarappa, **Practice and Precepts of Jesus** (Ahmedabad: Navajivan Publishing House, 1945), p. 37.
150. Eddy Asirvatham, "Problems of the Christian Church in India," **Christian World Mission,** ed. William K. Anderson, (Nashville: Commission on Ministerial Training, The Methodist Church, 1946), p. 110.
151. Matt. 7:26-27.
152. Reinhold Niebuhr, **Christianity and Power Politics** (New York: Charles Scribner's Sons, 1940), pp. 5-6.
153. John 15:15.
154. **The Gospel of Sri Ramakrishna,** trans. Swami Nikhilananda, p. 689. See also pp. 243-244, 438. There are eight fetters: shame, hatred, fear, castle lineage, good conduct, grief, and secretiveness.
155. For reference, the teachings of Sri Ramakrishna and the Vaishnava literature of India are suggested for clarification of the loving relationship between devotees and God, which Jesus glorifies in the Fourth Gospel.
156. Mark 13:33.

CHAPTER V

CHRIST AND EVERYDAY PROBLEMS

> Enter ye in at the straight gate: for wide is the gate, and broad is the way, that leadeth to destruction. . .
>
> . . . .
>
> Ye shall know them by their fruits.
>
> Even so every good tree bringeth forth good fruit; but a corrupt tree bringeth forth evil fruit.
>
> A good tree cannot bring forth evil fruit, neither can a corrupt tree bring forth good fruit.[157]

There is considerable misunderstanding of the true meaning of religion. Consequently, many persons do not clearly comprehend its place in everyday life. Some think that it implies accepting certain creeds and dogmas, believing in certain personalities, or merely saying "Lord, Lord." As a result of this misconception, there is a great deal of criticism of religion. Many Western thinkers have revolted against it, saying that it is nothing but an opiate which stupefies the people and makes them victims of designing and unscrupulous schemes. The pages of European history reveal how the innocent and illiterate have been exploited by unethical and selfish persons associated with religion. We cannot, therefore, wholly blame the critics for having rebelled against such interpretation and understanding. They found that religion was not only associated with the exploiters of the common man but it also gave support to the exploitation. Moreover, the common people were given to understand, directly or indirectly, that if they gave no opposition and tried no other methods, they would enjoy peace in the life after death. They were led to believe that what happened to them here did not matter, they would be rewarded in heaven. Directly or indirectly, the people were, in a way, hypnotized and they submitted to the instructions of the religious groups. Consequently, they were left powerless to assert themselves.

In other parts of the world there have been many abuses in the name of religion. Exclusive rights and privileges were claimed by some who preyed on the ignorant and underprivileged masses. A large number of people were kept in a state of misery — physically, mentally, and spiritually.

Although the revolt of European thinkers was prompted specifically by abuses in the Judaeo-Christian religion, their criticism has actually been levelled against religion as a whole, including Oriental religions — Hinduism and Buddhism. However, relatively few thinkers in either Europe or America have studied Oriental religions or have any deep understanding or knowledge of them.

From a rational point of view this attitude is extremely uncritical and dogmatic. One cannot condemn religion itself on the basis of certain habits and ways of persons who are associated with particular religious groups. Affiliation with a religious group does not necessarily make a man religious, any more than association with a university makes him a scholar. If this were so, every janitor of every university would have been scholarly. We cannot conclude that the universities are to be blamed when those associated with them are not intellectual. Therefore, it is irrational to condemn religion because some of the followers fail to live a religious life.

It is unfortunate that Orientals who have been nurtured by certain European traditions and influenced by European scholars have accepted unconditionally the criticism against religion itself. This uncritical attitude on the part of Oriental countries, like India and China, has created a great deal of confusion in the minds of many thoughtful young people of those countries. They have come to believe that religion is the cause of their degradation, subjection, and misery on the physical plane. The Orientals are justified in suspecting the motives of some of the Occidentals who have been patronizing in their attitude. "You have your religion; you take care of that and we will take care of your political and economic welfare." Such are the sentiments of the Earl of Ronaldshay, Marquis of Zetland, who made a similar statement as a member of the British Cabinet a number of years ago.

Young people in those countries are also influenced by the criticisms against religion itself. They are attracted by the glamour of the modern, scientific achievements and its consequent application in the economic system of the West, so that when Western critics condemn religion they assume that there must be some truth in it. Without question they accept the criticisms as valid, not because they understand the religions of the East and the West but because certain European or American intellectuals have spoken. Lord Ronaldshay writes of India:

> By the middle of the nineteenth century a period of intellectual anarchy had set in, which swept the rising generation before it like a craft which has snapped its moorings. Westernism became the fashion of the day — and Westernism demanded of its votaries that they should cry down the civilization of their own country . . . . ancient religion was decried as an outworn superstition. The ancient foundations upon which the complex structure of Hindu society had been built up were undermined. . . .
>
> . . . .
>
> And following hard upon this new spirit of contempt for their own past, came religious scepticism, which ate its way into the moral fibre of young Bengal with all the virulence of a corroding acid.[158]

The criticism against Christianity should first be evaluated, and then we should also consider whether or not Christianity and other religions can make any contribution to our everyday life. The abuses that are criticized by the humanistic thinkers and Marxists are either the inherent qualities of Christianity or they are the result of erroneous practices. If they are inherent in the teachings of Christ, we can safely say that Christianity is incompatible with civilization. On the other hand, if they are not, the critics have no justification for condemning religion in general and Christianity in particular. However, no trace of abuses nor justification for them can be found in the teachings of Christ. The Sermon on the Mount gives no basis for the exploitation of others by selfish and designing persons. Jesus said: "Blessed are the meek: for they shall inherit the earth." "Blessed are the pure in heart: for they shall see God."[159] And He further stated: "And thou shalt love thy neighbor as thyself."[160] Jesus never mentioned that only a selected few — Gentiles or Jews, Europeans or Asiatics — would attain the Kingdom of God. There is no trace of any such differentiation in His teachings; they had universal implications. Christ Himself was universal. He meant His teachings to include all persons without distinction of creed, class, color or race. So when He said to "love thy neighbor as thyself," He meant us to love all persons as veritable manifestations of God, the divine Self, with no distinction as to this or that type of person or this or that family. This is clearly indicated in His parable of the good Samaritan, which He told in answer to the lawyer's question: "Who is my neighbor?" He instructed the man: "Go, and do thou likewise."[161]

In His own life, Jesus demonstrated that the principle of love is applicable in everyday life. His teachings were powerful because they were supported by His activities. Every one of the passages in the Sermon on the Mount was fulfilled in His life. As an incarnation of God, He did not utter a word that He did not demonstrate. His methods were not aggressive nor destructive, which is often the case with people who take His name. But Jesus cannot be held responsible for any abuses of which His followers are guilty. He did not behave in any such manner nor did He teach others to do so; on the contrary, He condemned such behavior and stopped expression of any but the purely religious method. He did not want St. Peter to be violent in spite of provocation by the mob which had come to get Jesus in Gethsemane. When Peter cut off the ear of the servant of the high priest with a sword, Jesus immediately reprimanded him and said: "Put up again thy sword into his place: for all they that take the sword shall perish with the sword."[162] We know how He treated even Judas who betrayed Him and was the cause of His Crucifixion. Jesus was fully aware that Judas would submit to temptation and express low tendencies. Yet He showered His love and blessings on Judas and did not exclude him from the Last Supper with the other beloved and staunch disciples.

Every one of the utterances of Jesus was justified by His action. "Blessed are the pure in heart . . ."[163] Can any trace of impurity be found in Him, any envy, jealousy, hatred, selfishness, lust, or greed? They were non-existent in the mind and life of Jesus. He trained His disciples accordingly and thoroughly established them in purity. He could never make any compromise or dilute the spirit of purity with inordinate tendencies of any type.

It should also be remembered that when impure persons went to Jesus, He took them into His fold with all His love and blessings. He did not make any distinction between saint and sinner. It is said in the teachings of the *Bhagavad-Gita* that a wise man never makes such distinctions. "He attains excellence who looks with equal regard upon well-wishers, friends, foes, neutrals, arbiters, the hateful, the relatives, and upon the righteous and the unrighteous alike."[164] Jesus gave shelter even to a Mary

Magdalene. He blessed and transformed everyone who went to Him. Did He condemn or curse them? Never. You will never find that a curse came from the lips of Jesus, although He did speak harshly of hypocrites.

In the light of the incidents in His life, let us consider how He handled life's problems. When two or more persons live together, there are conflicts and disturbances among the personalities. No two persons have the same mentality or likes and dislikes; nor do they face the same conditions and problems with the same sense of responsibility. Consequently, there are difficulties arising from contacts with other human beings. How did Jesus solve social or family problems that arise from relationship with others? He emphasized the spiritual approach with no compromise whatsoever to them, as He was the embodiment of spiritual light. Again, consider His treatment of Judas and Mary Magdalene; think how He dealt with Nicodemus.

Is there any justification in the teachings of Christ for the abuses in religion? Certainly not. Unfortunately, however, as time rolled on after Christ came to the world, many persons could not remain at the highest peak of spirituality nor could they apply His religious ideals in their everyday life. They eventually began to justify the iniquities and weaknesses of themselves and others by stretching the text of the teachings of Christ. They promised heaven hereafter if the people believed in Him and in certain creeds and dogmas and practiced certain rituals and ceremonies. The Dark Ages give many sad pictures of European society until the advent of great personalities like St. Francis of Assisi, St. Anthony, and other Christian saints. Unfortunately, many Christians of that era lost sight of the ideals of Jesus. However, as previously mentioned, Christ or Christianity or religion itself was not responsible for such abuses; they occur in every society. The history of India shows also the periods of decadence of religion and rise of selfishness and irreligion. When a great religious leader or an incarnation is born, human minds are lifted to a higher plane. Many people follow in the wake of such an advent, and religious ideals are practiced for centuries. However, in the course of time men forget them and act deplorably. They abuse the ideals so much that they defeat the purpose of the personality they profess to follow. People ask: "How do you justify the Spanish Inquisition?" It cannot be justified according to the teachings of Christ.[165] It is very important to note what R. H. Tawney has to say in his book, *Religion and the Rise of Capitalism.* "It was partly that political changes had gone far to identify the Church with the ruling aristocracy, so that, . . . in England it was rarely that the officers of the Church did not echo the views of society which commended themselves to the rulers of the State."[166] In fact, the abuses that have been practiced in different parts of Europe and other places are unjustifiable in any religion. Neither can exploitation of the weak by the strong be justified, as some thinkers and religious leaders advocate. Such exploitation positively contradicts the basic ideals of Christ.

There is a point for argument here. We accept the premise that the teachings of Christ do not support the abuses of religious ideals. Yet we find that man in the name of religion has caused much bloodshed and destruction. Critics ask why one should cling to religion when it deteriorates. Why not give up religion itself as it has the possibility of demoralization? Of course, they advocate a moral life and harmonious society, as there cannot be a harmonious society without sound moral principles. They want to establish brotherhood and so they accept certain codes of behavior. But religion, as they understand it, brings narrowness and bigotry; therefore, it removes the possibility of universal brotherhood in society, so it should be left out. Their contention is that brotherhood and a harmonious society, along with everyday activities, can be based on sound ethical codes of behavior alone.

These critics forget that religion is the basis of equality, brotherhood, and a stable society. It furnishes the basis for stability in human relationships as it induces the votaries to become unselfish, patient, and enduring. Above all, its teachings are of love and sympathy, without which no stable society can be established. In the history of India, Hindu groups, being inspired at different periods by the lives and teachings of great personalities, established true brotherly love and a harmonious society. Buddhists, Taoists, and Confucianists also laid the foundations for harmonious social behavior at different periods in the history of the East. In fact, the followers of Buddha, Laotze, Confucius, and other great personalities established what the critics of religion aspire to — namely brotherhood and equality. The early Christians, who were inspired by the life and teachings of Jesus, started what is known today as the Christian civilization by stimulating the noble tendencies in man. "Love thy neighbor as thyself" was a guiding force in their harmonious living. The early Christian civilization was based purely on love of God and neighbor, and there have been many revivals of this spirit in various groups in Christian society at different times. Any casual observer can see the effectiveness of the teachings of Christ in the lives of the people. They not only established brotherhood amongst their own groups but they also expressed, and are expressing, brotherly love to non-Christians and even to their so-called enemies. The activities of some of the Christian churches, especially the Society of Friends, and such other organizations, merit special mention. The statements and actions of the present Pope and some other groups in Christianity refute the uncritical comments of the critics of religion. It does not require a stretch of the imagination to understand that brotherly love and harmonious society were established only by religious people, Christians and others, who were thoroughly inspired by the love of God and consequently by love of neighbor. Noble sentiments in human society can be directly traced to great spiritual personalities like Christ, Buddha, and Sri Ramakrishna. Karl Marx and other allied thinkers inherited the contributions of Christianity in Europe. It is the teachings of Jesus which really inspired many persons to try and remove the spirit of exploitation from society and establish justice, brotherhood, and equality. Unfortunately, they do not seem to realize the importance of the contribution of Jesus to the building of Western civilization.

It is important to understand the significance of the practice of religious ideals in our everyday life. Such religious methods are not abusive, do not encourage bloodshed, nor do they inculcate the spirit of competition and coercion. On the contrary, they remove these abusive expressions of human beings from society. So our advice to the Occidental and Oriental critics of religion is: Do not condemn anything without knowing it thoroughly. Very little religion can be understood without the practice of religious ideals. The values of scientific discoveries cannot be understood without laboratory experiments and appropriate technical training. You can have some idea of the contribution of science in the form of light, heat, and motion; but in order to know how they function, laboratory work is necessary. Similarly, religion cannot be properly evaluated until its principles are applied in life. So let the critics make experiments.

Another argument put forth by critics is that religion may have been applicable in other periods of history but today it is rather obsolete and not applicable in this industrial civilization, as Ingersoll stated. Many modern thinkers have this point of view, that religion is for medieval monasteries or perfectionists, but not for the people of today. This is expressed by Niebuhr:

> His [Hitler's] victories thus far are partly due to the fact that the culture of the democracies was vapid. Its political instincts had become vitiated by an idealism which sought to extricate morals from politics to the degree of forgetting that all life remains a contest of power. If Hitler is defeated in the end it will be because the crisis has . . . given us the knowledge that ambiguous methods are required for the ambiguities of history. Let those who are revolted by such ambiguities have the decency and

consistency to retire to the monastery, where medieval perfectionists found their asylum. [167]

However, our answer to that is that religion in general is not obsolete; as such Christianity in its pure form is not out of date. When we consider the teachings of Jesus, as already mentioned, they are applicable in our everyday life. We go still further to say that when they are not applied, life is not worth living. The disturbances in Christendom which have been prevalent for the past two or three centuries, and which threaten Christian and consequently non-Christian societies with destruction today, exist because of negligence and utter ignorance of Christian principles, which are mentioned in Chapter VII. It is not that the teachings of Christ are obsolete or inconsistent with modern mechanical civilization, but rather that man becomes selfish and arrogant because he does not follow His teachings and emphasizes the hedonistic view of life. So life is not peaceful and harmonious in the Christian community; moreover, the people have become extremely destructive and miserable. We make bold to say that these destructive activities are conducted and supported by the Christian nations because they have forgotten the spirit of Christ in the Sermon on the Mount. It is not the fault of His teachings that the Christians are behaving in this way, but it is their inability to follow Him in their practical life.

In everyday life we find problems arising from contacts with different human beings, changing climatic conditions, undesirable surroundings, economic conditions, and any number of other conditions which affect us. When the problems are there facing us, how can we apply the basic principles of religion to meet them?

Let us now consider how we can apply religious principles in our interpersonal relationships. When we know that we are abiding in God and that the members of our family — parents, children, husband, wife, father, son, brothers, and sisters — are also part of the same All-Loving Being, as the rays are of the sun, then we realize that we are all inseparably connected with one another and our interests will not clash. We may be different from each other on the relative plane but we realize that there is the same spirit in all of us; consequently, we cannot express the egocentric, selfish attitude of life. We cannot be greedy or think that we must take care of "Number 1" — ourselves. We are often amused when we hear married persons say that they are very unselfish because they have money in joint bank accounts, in the name of both husband and wife. To a religious person it seems stupid that these people even have to talk about it! Of course they will have to keep separate accounts so long as they are conscious of their difference, so long as they think that they are not united, so long as they consider marriage a contract which can be broken at any time, and so long as they do not understand the real implication of love. On the other hand, when people realize that union in marriage is for a greater unfoldment — that the two parties are united for mutual good, mutual happiness, and mutual spiritual evolution — when they understand that man and wife are united to help each other toward a knowledge of the Reality, then they will generate real and unselfish love. As a result, the children of such unions will be extremely sympathetic, affectionate, and loving toward one another. The spirit of the parents is spontaneously inculcated in the minds of the children. We have seen time and again that when parents are unselfish and devoted to one another and society, the children unconsciously imbibe those qualities. The surest way to have good children is to live a good life. If parents want them to be unselfish, considerate, and thoughtful, they must show thoughtfulness and consideration to each other. So it is that this spirit of oneness of existence, this spirit of abiding in the Father will reflect in our family life. A person who cultivates that spirit can never remain selfish and egocentric or boast that he has a joint bank account. He is not doing anything unusual. If a husband and wife cannot have a joint account, then who will have one? So a society where such selfishness is prevalent can only encourage a man to be proud when he has a joint bank account. But what really matters is not the kind of bank account, but the spirit expressed through it.

This very egocentric and individualistic attitude of life creates a consciousness of separateness in every sphere of activity. The over-emphasis on what people term "rugged individualism" has created all sorts of social problems. The desire for more and more personal satisfaction and gratification on the sense plane creates the spirit of competition and coercion in the family, society, and the world. Professor Sorokin, a distinguished contemporary sociologist, gives the conclusions of his lifetime of research in his recent masterful book. He writes:

> Thus sensate society, with its sensate ethics, has prepared its own surrender to the rudest coercion.

> Liberating itself from God, from all absolutes and categoric moral imperatives, it has become the victim of undisguised physical coercion and fraud. Society has reached the nadir of moral degradation and is now paying the tragic price of its own folly. . . . Without any compunction, remorse, regret, or compassion, millions of guiltless people are uprooted, deprived of all possessions, of all rights, of all values, subjected to all kinds of privations, banished, or killed by bombs or bullets, simply because their mere existence is an unintentional obstacle to the realization of a lust for power, for wealth, for comfort, for some sensate value. Rarely, if ever, have even cattle been treated with such cynicism![168]

And he warns his readers that:

> As long as society attempts to function in a disintegrating sensate framework there is no hope of arresting this process of dehumanization, demoralization, and brutalization, this progressive substitution of physical force for all moral, religious, and social values. [169]

Of human relationships in the sensate culture he says:

> Relationships of employers and employees, bankers and labor unions, of social classes to one another, of rich and poor, of educated and noneducated, of privileged and underprivileged, of political parties, occupational groups, and finally, of nations, are at the present time in an incessant war, controlled mainly by the rude force and trickery which a given group has. He who has greater force triumphs, while the weaker party is pitilessly trampled on and crushed.[170]

R. H. Tawney writes in his book, *Religion and the Rise of Capitalism*:

> Religion has been converted from the keystone which holds together the social edifice into one department within it, and the idea of a rule of right is replaced by economic expediency as the arbiter of policy and the criterion of conduct. From a spiritual being, who, in order to survive, must devote a reasonable attention to economic interest, man seems sometimes to have become an economic animal, who will be prudent, nevertheless, if he takes due precautions to assure his spiritual well-being.[171]

The problems arising from relations between capital and labor, between landlord and tenants, and between other groups, will continue as long as the relationships are based on the Darwinian theory of struggle for existence and survival of the fittest, however politely couched the modern interpretations may be. We may cover an ugly sore with beautiful clothing, yet the sore remains within the covering. We may express socialistic and humanistic ideas, in spite of our philosophy of material and sense enjoyment. We may also try to introduce economic adjustment and all sorts of welfare activities which are good, yet the problem of real social security will not be touched as long as man still remains on the selfish plane. So co-operation and co-ordination in society will still remain limited to philosophical discourses and the science of sociology, and they will not be actualities so long as man basically emphasizes the greatest amount of individualistic pleasure. It is true, however, that social scientists are trying to establish better social relationships. Although they are making noble attempts, they are bound to fail when they ignore the basis of co-operation and co-ordination, namely divine love and divine realization, as expounded by Jesus and other great world teachers like Buddha, Krishna, and Ramakrishna.

In the first place, the objective of religion is awareness of God in everyday life. We beg to differ from those who seem to think that this awareness will be experienced in the life after death. Some groups revert back a few centuries and console human beings with the idea that they can call on the Lord and get peace in the other world. Christ definitely refutes such an interpretation of religion: "Not everyone that saith unto me, Lord, Lord, shall enter into the Kingdom of heaven; but he that doeth the will of my Father which is in heaven."[172] We may say, "Lord, Lord"; yet if we do not act according to the will of God, according to the principles of religion, we cannot have the Kingdom of God here or hereafter. This very statement of Jesus implies that our life must be saturated with religious ideas and ideals. The implication of religious ideals is awareness of the presence of God. We must practice the presence of God, as Brother Lawrence describes it:

> I cannot imagine how religious persons can live satisfied without the practice of *the presence of* God. For my part, I keep myself retired with Him in the fund or center of my soul as much as I can; and while I am so with Him I fear nothing, but the least turning from Him is insupportable.[173]

Sri Ramakrishna tells us that we must live in this world with constant thought of God. To quote His own words:

> As a boy holding to a post or pillar whirls about it with headlong speed without fear of falling, so perform thy worldly duties fixing thy hold firmly upon God, and thou shalt be free from danger.[174]

Man is constantly seeking security in life. The secret of a secure life is not social security, old age assistance, and such measures; it is a way of life based on higher philosophy. That is not to say they are not good; what we mean is that even their social service activities do not and cannot give a sense of security unless a person has an awareness of the presence of God in his everyday life. When a person is aware of God he focuses the mind on Him or takes Him as the primary objective and subordinates all other activities to that ideal. Then his life becomes secure and happy. So Sri Ramakrishna tells us first to get hold of the pillar, or God, and then move around the world with various activities and objectives, holding fast to Him. He means that the attitude toward work itself is far more important than the nature of the work. With the knowledge of God within, every action is converted into worship. Not every man or woman is capable of or in a position to enter a monastery or convent; nor is it necessary that everyone become a monk or a nun, whether they are Christian, Hindu, or Buddhist. It is of far more consequence to practice awareness of God in life. As Jesus says: "But seek ye first the kingdom of God and his righteousness; . . . " Unless one first seeks God, his life is full of conflicts and confusion, as we observe in modern society. Jesus, as a living divine incarnation, expressed the same attitude toward everyday life as other masters like Sri Krishna, Buddha, and

Sri Ramakrishna. All these great teachers were explicit in their assertions that it can be made successful and happy if God is the center.

The question will arise: Can we remain aware of God during our daily activities? We have so many things to do. In American life for example, people have to struggle for an existence; opportunities are available to everybody. But think how much of his time a man has to give for the bare maintenance of his body. Business women and girls in this country have to work many hours a day and then they have to spend considerable time to keep themselves fit for their work. What is left for their intellectual pursuits, their cultural activities, and above all for their religious development? Practically nothing. They either do not think of the necessity of spending time for spiritual practices or they give them up. In this age they have reason to say that they cannot be too deeply religious because they do not have the time.

What can we suggest to working people in America who are under the pressure of work for their existence? Can the teachings of Christ offer any solution? Is religion meant only for a few persons who can go to a convent or a monastery? Our answer is that whether it be Christianity, Hinduism, or Buddhism, Judaism or Mohammedanism, religion is meant for all persons regardless of position, culture, or race. It should not be divorced from everyday living; otherwise it will have no meaning in life.

> Therefore, if thou bring thy gift to the altar, and there rememberest that thy brother hath ought against thee,

> Leave there thy gift before the altar, and go thy way; first be reconciled to thy brother, and then come and offer thy gift.[175]

Every man can find a way to apply religious principles in his life. So let us consider those who are working in the business world. They will have to cultivate a new outlook on life and apply religious ideals in their own activities—industrial, office, executive, or any other type of work. In fact, religion must be shown to have a place in every sphere of life in order to prove its utility in human society. Religion is a way of life and not one of its pursuits. That is the very reason Jesus said that those who enter the Kingdom of God are not the ones who cry "Lord, Lord," but rather those who do His will. Jesus teaches us that religion is an attitude that can be applied to ordinary activities of all types. Whether a man is in industry, commerce, education, or any other work, he must try to remain aware of the presence of God in and through his activities.

We should remember that we are here to serve the All-Loving Being. As Jesus says: "Thou shalt love the Lord thy God with all thy heart, and with all thy mind." And "Thou shalt love thy neighbor as thyself."[176] It is not so difficult to bring these principles into our daily lives, to remember God as a reality in the midst of activities, as we might think. But we have to struggle to be aware that it is He who is receiving our worship in the form of employers or employees, through dedication of our work in the industrial plant or commercial institution. We must constantly think that we are serving Him whether our work is in the kitchen, department store, law office, hospital, or school. All the different members of society are veritable manifestations of God; we have to translate the knowledge of this fact into action.

A question is raised by many persons who are devoted to their families. They say that when they take care of their families, they are doing their duty and they cannot be too religious. They do not have any time for special exercises like meditation and prayer and it is perfectly all right if they attend church once a week. This argument is implicitly or explicitly put forth by many people in modern Christendom. Our answer to such an argument is that it is not all right for them to be satisfied if they only remain religious on a specific day in the week. This habit does not fulfill their religious obligations. The meaning of religious obligations is the awareness of God in everyday life, not just once a week. Let us suppose that we accept the fact that when a person is in church he is constantly thinking of God. Even so the rest of the week is spent in secular thought and activity. So long as a man makes that distinction, he cannot be a religious person. Life cannot be divided into secular and spiritual compartments; it must be one or the other. We do not minimize the importance of observing a special day for religious purposes, as it has its value, but it does not enrich the entire life with religious strength and understanding. Experience convinces us that remembrance on one day is not sufficiently powerful to create awareness of God throughout man's everyday existence. That is the very reason special religious exercises were adopted by the devotees of Christ for each day in the week. What a man makes of his life entirely depends on his attitude. He becomes religious when his attitude is one of awareness of God; and he becomes secular if he does not cultivate that awareness, even though he may be associated with a church or synagogue. We find many persons in different communities of this country who hold important positions in church organizations, yet they are the most irreligious persons imaginable, insofar as awareness of God is concerned.

Recently, in a discussion with some friends on the problem of capital and labor and the conflict between capitalism and communism, a gentleman enumerated a few prominent persons who accumulated an enormous amount of money by questionable means and then gave considerable to charity. They contributed large sums to church organizations, particularly for the rescue of the souls of the poor heathens through missionary activities abroad. The question arose as to whether or not such persons were religious just because they were contributing to their church. Our answer is that this kind of contribution, although generous, is only consoling to the person who gives it but it does not make him religious or a follower of Christ. He may be respected in the church organization as a great contributor, but he will not be respected in the eyes of God, because he has not observed the commandments to love God and neighbor. His contribution is not motivated by the love of God and man but by the thought of name and fame. We do not minimize the value of the gift to the community or the beneficiaries, yet it does not purify the heart of the donor. It may ease his mind in view of his vicious exploitation of the poor, yet it does not make his inner nature spiritual. On the other hand, a person may not have any money but he will possess the treasure of awareness of God and love of man. With that, if he gives only a few grains of rice to others, the very act becomes deeply spiritual. Even if he has nothing to give but has kind thoughts of others and expresses love and prayers for their welfare, this in itself will be a religious act and his contribution will be a blessing to the world. We have known many cases in religious history when a gift of a few grains of food was regarded as a deeply spiritual act. On the other hand, if a person exploits others, robs them, and then gives several million dollars to charitable or religious organizations, his contribution cannot be regarded as spiritual action. So we must remember that it is not the amount of the contribution that is spiritual but it is the attitude itself, the way of life. Again, if someone lives a questionable life and at the same time says a few beautiful words, he will not be regarded as a spiritual man. On the contrary, if a man is not given to beautiful expressions, or what are known as "soul talks," but he has deep love and sympathy in his heart and leads a life of God-consciousness in and through his activities, he will be an inspiration to his neighbors and community.

---

157. Matt. 7:13, 16-18.
158. Earl of Ronaldshay, The Heart of Aryavarta (London: Constable & Co., Ltd., 1925), pp. 45-46.
159. Matt. 5:5 and 8.
160. Ibid., 22:39; and Mark 12:31; Luke 10:27.
161. Luke 10:29-37.
162. Matt. 26:52.
163. Ibid., 5:8.
164. Srimad-Bhagavad-Gita VI:9.
165. Fedor Dostoevski, The Brothers Karamazov, trans. Constance Garnett (New York: Random House, 1933), Part Two, Book

V, chap. V.
166. R. H. Tawney, Religion and the Rise of Capitalism (New York: Harcourt, Brace & Co., Inc., 1947), p. 248.
167. Niebuhr, Christianity and Power Politics, pp. 174-175
168. Sorokin, The Crisis of Our Age, pp. 163-164.
169. Ibid., p. 231.
170. Ibid., pp. 314-315.
171. Tawney, "Religion and the Rise of Capitalism," p. 246.
172. Matt. 7:21.
173. Brother Lawrence, The Practice of the Presence of God (New York: Fleming H. Ravell Co., 1895), p. 32.
174. Sayings of Sri Ramakrishna XXXIV:631.
175. Matt. 5:23-24.
176. Matt. 22:37 and 39; Mark 12:30 and 31; Luke 10:27.

CHAPTER VI

CHRIST AND POWER

> Blessed are the poor in spirit: for their's is the kingdom of heaven.
>
> Blessed are they that mourn: for they shall be comforted.
>
> Blessed are the meek: for they shall inherit the erath.[177]
>
> . . . .
>
> Ye are the salt of the earth: but if the salt have lost his savour, wherewith shall it be salted?[178]

It is but natural that Christians and non-Christians should question whether or not the ideas described by Jesus in his glorious Sermon on the Mount are practical and useful today. We are going through a serious intellectual, political, and spiritual crisis—a cultural crisis. There is conflict between the materialistic, hedonistic outlook on life and the religious outlook. It is not confined to one part of the world alone; all groups, all races, all nations are seriously affected. Men and women everywhere are asking whether there is utility in the higher values, the religious values of life. They want to know if religion has any solution for the complex problems of the modern world; and they wonder if religious teachings are not making the problems more complicated by injecting doctrinal and ritualistic differences and by exaggerating religious and racial differences among individuals and groups.

We are discussing this problem because the people who are in power today are those born in the Christian tradition. Whether their power is used according to the principles and teachings of Christ or imposed externally is the question. We are concerned with the teachings of Christ and their application in the Western world because the people of the West claim to be Christians. They want to establish what they call the "Kingdom of God" in the world, to quote the late Archbishop of Canterbury.

What is this power? What do we understand by it? Ordinarily, man understands its external expressions. The ordinary man does not understand the real value of intellectual and spiritual power. No doubt he has a little understanding of intellectual power as it is used today; but according to its use in scientific achievement, it is utilized for domination and exploitation and, thereby, the establishment of smaller and larger empires.

When we came to this country more than twenty years ago and when work was started in Providence, Rhode Island, it so happened that some good Christian ministers became very friendly to us. They appreciated the message of India very much. When their appreciation was expressed through the pages of the newspapers, and when our views were frequently presented in the same papers, the Providence Journal and Evening Bulletin, there were a few controversial comments given by persons who were not actuated by what they call the Christian life, but rather by something ignoble—jealousy. They expressed the idea that if India has such a glorious message, why should she remain under the domination of a foreign government? If the Indian religion is so powerful, the Indian people should be free and have the conveniences and commodities as we have in Christian countries. This expression was given not by one person alone, but by many outstanding religious leaders, including some high officials of certain religious denominations. These very sentiments are often expressed in different communities, even today. It is evident that these people felt that Christianity is superior because of external expressions of power in the West and because many of the followers of Christ have had material achievement and success. The standard for the success of Christianity was that it helped people to express their power all over the world. They also said that Christianity enabled scientists to discover the airplane, telephone, and radio. Fortunately, the atomic bomb and the use of atomic energy had not been discovered at that time, so these were not included in the statements concerning Christian power.

The other premise was that Christianity can be equated with the airplane, telephone, radio, or other modern inventions. So far as we understand the teachings of Christ, they have nothing much to do with these discoveries. Such contributions were not made by the Christian spiritual leaders nor inspired by Christian ideals. They were done because of man's interest in the study and control of the laws of nature and love of nature. Their primary interest was not in God but in the discovery of scientific truths through controlled observation of objective nature. They were discovered and used by people who had very little interest in the teachings of Christ.

Perhaps the eighteenth and nineteenth century politicians were responsible for the establishment of the smaller and larger empires. This, too, had very little to do with Christian principles, although it must be admitted that when these Europeans went out for conquest they often paid money to churches and synagogues and justified their exploits in the name of God. When we analyze the activities of those persons, whether they were political or scientific leaders, we find very little influence of the teachings of Christ in their lives. So we can dismiss the claim that Christianity can be equated with the discovery of the airplane, radio, telephone, and other modern inventions.

The second point in question is: Is the power of Christ allied with material achievements or antagonistic to them? Our study of Christianity, if we understand the teachings of Christ aright, reveals that material power is not the goal of His teachings. In fact, nations that claim to be Christian powers do not seem to understand the teachings of Christ. He tells us: "Blessed are the meek: for they shall inherit the earth," and "Blessed are the pure in heart: for they shall see God."[179] There can be only one interpretation of these sentences: the meek, the noble will inherit the earth; and those who are pure will gain the Kingdom of God.

What do we mean by "those who are pure"? The people who are selfish and greedy and yet use words of metaphysics or theology? Certainly not. As we find in the teachings of Christ time and again, purity is equivalent to unselfishness. Once a man becomes supremely unselfish, he does not seek power or position, he becomes a pure man. If we follow the teachings of Christ to a logical conclusion, then domination over the world can no longer be practiced, and unselfishness and sympathy must be extended to all races and countries, as we find in many true devotees of Christ throughout the ages.

There are persons who seem to obscure the teachings of Christ and thereby establish a connection between them and the modern spirit—the seventeenth, eighteenth, nineteenth, and twentieth century Christianity. Let us examine some of the ideas expressed by a man who was one of the most outstanding Christians known in the modern Western world, the late Archbishop of Canterbury. In one of his very interesting books, *Mens Creatrix*, the great theologian argues that the British Empire was not built on the same principles as the Roman, Macedonian, Babylonian, or the Assyrian Empires. In this sense he holds it was a pure fact that previous empires were built on the spirit of conquest, while the British Empire was built on the spirit of co-operation, and co-ordination among free nations with their free will. The Archbishop says:

> But there is in the world a political institution which, just because it is a natural growth and not an artificial construction, seems to supply the clue to one part of the problem. The so-called British Empire was never planned by any persons or group of persons; it is the spontaneous product of the energy of the British people . . . Here already we see

> in the Imperial Government the germ of a World Government deriving its authority from a moral need. This Empire does not stand in the line of succession with Assyria, Babylon, Macedon and Rome; it is a new kind of fact . . . In this fact of the British Empire, then we have "the noblest project of freedom that the world has seen."— Curtis, *The Commonwealth of Nations*, p. 705. It has grown, but in its growth has been true upon the whole to the principle of freedom, and in that principle has found its bond of unity. That is the new fact; other empires were united by a force imposed upon them from above; the Commonwealth of the British Empire is united by the free loyalty of its constituent parts.[180]

We do not know whether any historian will support the statements of the Archbishop, but this information is contrary to much historical evidence. We do not understand how he could draw this conclusion. We wonder what he would have said about the conquest of India, part by part. Were these wars of conquest, at different periods in India, Christian methods of expressing love? Were the conquests of Burma, Singapore, and some parts of the Near East and Africa expressions of brotherly sentiment? Were all these conquests and "annexations" equivalent to free will and co-operation of free nations? It requires a tremendous stretch of the imagination to find the spirit of Christianity in such activities.

To be fair to the Archbishop, he devotes one paragraph to the question of India. The people of India, he says, want freedom and they will gradually have a larger share of the administration of their country when they are educated. Did he remember the spirit with which Lord Macaulay introduced the English educational system in India[181] and how the idea was carried out by the British Government? However, according to the Archbishop, the sooner other nations join the British Commonwealth, the better it will be for the world. Of course, he admits that some of the elements of the Commonwealth will have to be changed, and some might want to change even the name of the British Empire. Nevertheless, the British model is the one that should be followed in the world, one that he describes as being pretty nearly equivalent to the Kingdom of God. To quote the Archbishop:

> We must arrive at a real Federation of the Empire if we are to be true to its own root principle; but so soon as that is done there seems no reason why other nations should not seek incorporation in this Commonwealth, thereby of course gaining the right to a voice in its control, so that on the basis of freedom and equality all nations might be linked to one another. In that case of course the title "British Empire" would have to go for it would no longer be specifically British. The final stage in such incorporation would be a definite Act of Union, . . . The nations themselves need some society that may include themselves, whose basis shall be a common purpose, . . . arising out of loyalty to an all-inclusive Kingdom and a common Master, and expressing itself in common action in service of that Master and Kingdom.[182]

The question is: Spiritually or intellectually can we justify such claims of an advocate of the Kingdom of Heaven on earth by appeal to the teachings of Jesus in the Sermon on the Mount? Intellectually speaking we cannot justify such claims, not to speak of spiritual justification. In the first place, the British Empire, which has been so much appreciated by the late Archbishop, does not indicate that the teachings of Christ in the Sermon on the Mount were followed. We admit that some groups in the British Empire have a certain amount of freedom; but the basis of the Empire was not in Canada, New Zealand, or Australia; it lay in India and other conquered countries. Now that India is free, the Empire has changed.

No practicing religious man can find spiritual qualities in the building of empires based on selfishness and love of power, both of which are hostile to religious culture. Apart from that, imperialism demoralizes the builders themselves as well as those who are exploited. History reveals that empire builders become more and more selfish, greedy, and ruthless in the very process of preserving and protecting the empire; and the administrators demoralize themselves in the very process of administration. To be frank, they sell their souls for "thirty pieces of silver." All the non-spiritual qualities are manifested in their lives and activities. Moreover, the subject nations also become demoralized and they develop slavish mentalities of various types. Any nation that remains under the subjugation of an imperialistic system becomes selfish, sneaky, and fearful. Its people sell themselves as spies and indulge in other such deplorable activities.

So both the rulers and the ruled are deprived of the opportunity to develop spiritual culture. Can anyone find the power of Christ in these imperialistic practices?

The learned Archbishop Temple supported his viewpoint when he came to visit this country as Archbishop of York in 1935. During an interview with the religious editor of the Evening Bulletin in Providence he said: "I think it should be accepted as a principle, however, that advanced nations in the future should have a definite say as to backward nations: otherwise equity is impossible."[183] This raises the question: Who is to judge the forwardness or backwardness of nations? What is the standard of forwardness or backwardness? Are the men who invented the atomic bomb, which destroyed tens of thousands of persons in a few minutes, to be considered as men of advancement? Is it the expression of material power or manifestation of spiritual qualities? We have not found any evidence that he changed his ideas later, so far as the application of the teachings of Christ to political and economic activities was concerned.

It is true that the late Archbishop expressed more liberal views in recent years so far as laborers and other underprivileged persons in England are concerned. However, did we hear him uttering a word of liberalism in connection with the Christian principle of brotherly love toward the people of the British colonies? In a mysterious way he felt that the subject nations of the British Empire were willing to be under British rule! When about three million people died of starvation in Bengal, India, in 1943, we did not get any report that the Archbishop expressed or did anything for those starving people, even though the famine could have been avoided by the British rulers and their underlings in India. It is made clear to the world that abject indifference may be the deliberate policy of the ruling powers who created such a situation. There is no record that the leader of the Church of England did anything to undo the un-Christian acts of his government. Nor do we find any protest against the utterances of Churchill, the then prime minister of England, when he expressed his old die-hard imperialism. We did not hear any protest by the Archbishop against the ruthless persecution of Indian men and women, when they were clamoring for the legitimate independence of their country. We have to admit frankly that none of the ecclesiastical lords of England protested against the imperial policy of their government. However, we are very grateful to the Quakers and others who tried their best to do something for the starving people of India. They expressed true Christian spirit.

It is refreshing to note that there are Christians like Professor Paul E. Johnson who have lived in the mission field in Asia as well as America. Professor Johnson has had wide experience in both the domestic and foreign fields. Being a Christian leader, he has authority to speak on the teachings of Christ. Of imperialism he writes:

> Christian imperialism is a contradiction of mutually repellent forces. The essential nature of Christianity is inherently opposed to the essence of imperialism. Christianity is anti-imperialistic as imperialism is anti-Christian. Those who renounce imperialism are thereby allied with the religion of Jesus. The entanglement of Christian movements

> with imperialistic enterprise is an unholy alliance, betraying both parties in a false union that is mutually antagonistic.[184]

Dr. E. Stanley Jones, who is a very great Christian leader in the missionary field and also in America, very strongly expresses his feelings against the domination of the West over Asia. His sympathy for the freedom of India is well known. Of late many Christian leaders in America have been unequivocally expressing their Christian idealism against any form of imperialism or power politics.

There is another opinion found in the utterances of some groups, which is even more confusing and misleading than the statements of the late Archbishop of Canterbury. Professor Reinhold Niebuhr, an outstanding theologian of this country and a leader of the neo-orthodox school of thought, published the book, *Christianity and Power Politics*, on the eve of World War II. The first chapter creates a feeling of mixed Christian spirit and non-religious sentiment. It is extremely confusing, to say the least. It is a philosophy of defeatists who feel utterly incompetent to follow the teachings of Christ yet who want to justify their non-religious tendencies in terms of Christian ideology.[185] It seems that the learned theologian cannot wholly destroy his intellectual power and higher appreciation but, at the same time, he is determined to justify certain of his urges or feelings that are prevalent among people in modern materialistic society. He takes the stand that the lofty ideals of Christ such as: "Love thy neighbor," "Be ye perfect," "Blessed are the meek," and "Blessed are the pure" are not absolutely false doctrines, but they are not workable in this age. According to his point of view, the medieval ascetics, the secular perfectionists, and, he implies, the Wesleyans, Quakers, and Mennonites are, in a way, heretical because they emphasize the absolute ethics of the teachings of Jesus.

He admits that lofty ideals are doubtless in accord with the teachings of Christ. That cannot be denied. But he says that in this world of sin, you cannot use the absolute ethics of Christ. He writes that the ethics of Jesus is "finally and ultimately normative" but "not immediately applicable to the task of securing justice in a sinful world."[186]

In order to handle political problems, relative ethics is necessary. This means using force against force, force for the sake of justice. "It may also be necessary to resist a ruling class, nation or race, if it violates the standards of relative justice which have been set up for it."[187] Use any kind of action that is required, because after all this is a sinful world. Man is sinful from the beginning to the end of his life; consequently, so long as he has his sin to conquer, he cannot follow the absolute ethics of Christ. "It is because men are sinners that justice can be achieved only by a certain degree of coercion on the one hand, and by a resistance to coercion and tyranny on the other hand."[188]

What does Professor Niebuhr promise to "sinful" man? Is there any philosophy of life for us, according to him? We wonder if the learned theologian wants us to wait until we die to attain the Kingdom of Heaven and follow the absolute ethics of Christ. We do not find any sound basis for the philosophy of a sinful world that should follow relative ethics. This leads to no end of compromise. Already compromises are being made by politicians to such an extent that they do not show any trace of the teachings of Christ.

Once the theologians begin to dilute spiritual principles, human nature hastens the dilution until there are no longer any principles. That is what is happening in the affairs of the world today. We do not find the influence of the words of Jesus: "Blessed are the meek," or "Blessed are the peace-makers."[189] These exalted ideas are not in evidence because the religious leaders have been compromising the principles of Jesus. For example, Karl Barth, one of the great theologians of the present century seems to feel that World War II was a "Christian cause." He writes:

> The Churches ought today to pray in all penitence and sobriety to bear witness to all the world that it is necessary and worth while to fight and to suffer for this *just peace*.[190]
>
> . . . .
>
> It is precisely Christian thought which insists that resistance should be offered, and it is the Christians themselves who must not withhold their support. . . . The cause which is at stake in this war is our own cause. . . . The Christians who do not realize that they must take part unreservedly in this war must have slept over their Bibles as well as over their newspapers.[191]

A Hindu cannot help but wonder about this. We make bold to say that many Christian leaders like Professor

Rufus M. Jones, Professor Henry Cadbury, Professor Edgar S. Brightman, Professor William E. Hocking, and Bishop W. Appleton Lawrence (of Massachusetts) would also wonder how a religious person, especially a follower of Christ, could disregard the teaching and practice of Jesus in settling interpersonal and international problems. It seems to us that Barth, Niebuhr, and such other leaders disregard wholly the advice that Jesus gave to Peter in the garden of Gethsemane when He said: "Put up again thy sword into his place: for all they that take the sword shall perish with the sword."[192] We are told that during the Christian era more than five hundred wars have been fought on the European continent. Many of them were given a religious coloring as Barth, Niebuhr, and others, would give to the last war. They were a kind of religious crusade. A Hindu cannot help wondering how such brilliant minds could ignore the words of Jesus. This is the very reason Hindus in general like to study the teachings of Christ rather than the interpretations of the Christian leaders. Professor J. C. Kumarappa, a third generation Indian Christian, gives us his impressions of the interpretations of modern theologians:

> Again, as a student in England during the World War I, when I attended war services at St. Paul's Cathedral or at Westminster Abbey, however imposing the service may have been, I failed to reconcile the worship of an Universal Father and the Prince of Peace with tribal appeals to destroy the enemy. Nor could I understand the use of the pulpit by Bishops and other clergy for recruiting. The blood bespattered banners of many a battle and the tombs

> of noted generals in these places of worship seemed a desecration. These and such other contradictions between Jesus and the churches shook my faith in the "Christianity of the Churches."[193]

Then he asks:

> What are the Churches doing to undo the mischief brought about by their failure? They are holding up their holy hands on either side of the fighting lines praying to the Father of mankind to help them to devise more and more deadly ways and means of destroying His children on the opposite side.[194]

A religious man should always keep the highest principles in view and live the life accordingly. But what about those who are not deeply spiritual and cannot follow absolute ethics because of their inordinate tendencies? Are we to create great tension and conflict in them by advocating absolute ethics? Are we to create a superego of the Freudians in the form of strong censorship and thereby disturb them throughout their lives? Our answer is that a religious leader should always live a life of intense spirituality and keep the ideal bright through demonstration in everyday living. He should teach and lift to a higher plane those people who are not capable of following absolute ethics intead of urging them to compromise, as Professor Niebuhr does. It is pertinent to note what R. H. Tawney says in his *Religion and the Rise of Capitalism* in connection with compromising the religious ideal with power politics and capitalism. "Compromise is as impossible between the Church of Christ and the idolatry of wealth, which is the practical religion of capitalist societies, as it was between the Church and the

State idolatry of the Roman Empire."[195] It is wrong for a religious leader to compromise the ideal, if our understanding of the teachings of Christ is correct. A teacher should always be sympathetic toward his weaker sisters and brothers and gradually lead them to higher ways of life through application of religious principles. An efficient and strong spiritual personality can change a weaker person without creating any conflict in his ways of life. He can lead an individual gradually from lesser to higher truth and then to the highest, convincing him that the ultimate goal is, in the words of Jesus: "Blessed are the meek: for they shall inherit the earth," and "Blessed are the peacemakers: for they shall be called the children of God."[196] If the religious leaders lose their spiritual ideal, there will not be anyone left to inspire and elevate the followers. If a flame is not kept burning but is allowed to go out, it is not possible to build another fire even though the fuel and straw may be around. Similarly, if the ideal of Christ is extinguished in Christian society, it will no longer be possible to light the flame of Jesus in the people. To quote once more the words of St. John: "And the light shineth in darkness; and the darkness comprehended it not."[197] If religious leadership also remains in darkness, the light of Jesus will not shine through His followers.

Let us further evaluate the ideas of some of the modern neo-orthodox schools of theology. In their interpretation of religion, they make it seem hopeless and helpless. Aside from the fact that there is practically no hope for man because he is sinful from beginning to end, they tell us that the only possible hope for him is in the life after death. Are we to trust the words of these people, that God will save us after our death but we have to remain in sin here? Not at all. Jesus says: "Be ye therefore perfect, as your Father in Heaven is perfect."[198] This statement presupposes that man has the possibility of becoming perfect, at least in the love of enemies. It has also been proven by many ancient and modern Christians that it was possible for them to lead a life of perfection in the world, and it has been demonstrated successfully by many great Christian leaders, secular and ecclesiastical. The teachings of Christ concerning perfection can be lived in this world. We do not have to live a sinful or selfish life or a life of greed and power politics, that is, not unless we want to.

We suspect that the arguments of these theologians are based on the failures of some individuals to reform their lives. It is true that all persons in a given society do not live a highly spiritual life. It is not that religion is incapable of giving perfection and redemption to sinful persons; it is rather that the persons concerned do not care to mend their ways and manifest love of God and neighbor. These failures do not warrant a theory that man is basically sinful and will remain so in "Immoral Society." He has the possibility of transforming himself and influencing others to do so.

We do not have to go to India or China to understand that man is divine and not sinful. In the teachings of St. Paul we read that we are joint heirs with Christ. How do some of these theologians interpret this statement: "We are the children of God . . . and joint heirs with Christ."[199] As such, we have the possibility of attaining perfection and pure Christianity in a positive sense through the manifestation of divine love and conquest of the lower self. These theologians may like to compromise Christian ideals, but we are not prepared to understand that the power of the teachings of Christ lies only in the establishment of the Kingdom of God after death. On the contrary, it is in the rebuilding of our lives here and now. When Jesus says: "Blessed are the pure in heart: for they shall see God."[200] He implies that whenever one becomes pure, one can see God. That is to say, he can attain perfection.

To Hindu thinkers who study the life and teachings of Jesus, the interpretation of the neo-orthodox theologians, Niebuhrian and Barthian, does not conform to true Christian principles. We do not find any trace of compromise in the teachings of Christ nor in the ethical principles of His life. Neither did He advise His followers to make a distinction between absolute and relative ethics. We are sure that if these theologians would accept the ethics of Christ and follow His teachings, perhaps the Mennonites and Quakers would be allowed to live in the world without persecution or condemnation, as heretics. We do not find any justification for an expression or interpretation of the teachings of Jesus, which necessitates that these people be placed in a camp, whether it is called a concentration camp or by any other name.

In spite of the confusing and misleading theological doctrines of some of the followers of Christ, there are noble souls who do not hesitate to express and live the ideals of Christ, as seen in the efforts of the great Christians we already mentioned. There are many devout German, British, and American and other Christians who did not compromise their ideals nor hesitate to express them, at the cost of being in a concentration camp or in prison. These conscientious objectors to totalitarianism or to war are to be found in many Christian lands. They do not even hesitate to become so-called guinea pigs and suffer other humiliating treatment, according to what we hear from earnest souls who are known as conscientious objectors. These outstanding thinkers and their young followers are true to their conscience and demonstrate the Christian spirit of equality and brotherly love, even to the erring human beings who are known as enemy nations. They do not withdraw the milk of human kindness from the distressed and suffering humanity all over the world. They are true to the words of Christ: ". . . Love your enemies, bless them that curse you, do good to them that hate you, and pray for them which despitefully use you, and persecute you."[201] This is very encouraging to a Hindu who looks at Christ and His followers with great respect, love, and adoration. True Christians indeed deserve all of that because of their uncompromising spirit of religion.

The editorial staff and management of the *Christian Century* also deserves not only appreciation but also respect for their uncompromising spirit of Christianity. Time and again they request the Christian world to kneel and confess their sins to the Almighty God and ask to be forgiven by Him. They do not hesitate to advise political and military leaders of the Western world to adopt the undiluted spirit of Christianity. Non-Christians feel extremely encouraged that the spirit of Christianity is being voiced unequivocally, at least by some in the Christian world.

It is just fitting to say here that the late Mahatma Gandhi of India, who represented a true ideal of religion as taught by the Hindus, showed an uncompromising spirit of religion in his political and social activities. Any Christian who is unwilling to dilute the teachings of Jesus will find kinship with him and such other personalities. That is the very reason that many devout and prominent Christians in India and the West — Professor Asirvatham, the Kumarappa brothers, Dr. John Haynes Holmes, Dr. Stanley Jones, and others already mentioned — find a manifestation of the Christian ideal in him. He and his colleagues have demonstrated explicitly that political and social reform can be attained by non-violent means. Farsighted leaders of the British Empire recognize the power of religious idealism in political activities. Every student of history understands the tremendous effect of the non-violence of Gandhi in the independence movement of India.

The highest religious ideal in political activities is followed by those who do not want to compromise or dilute the ideal of soul force. Mahatma Gandhi advocated the conquest of enemies by adoption of the non-violent, non-co-operative methods, by soul force and by the positive expression "love your enemies." We are often told by devout Christian leaders that he demonstrates the power of love as taught by Jesus. They also tell us that he is the modern example of the principles of Jesus which are being carried out in political and social activities. Whether we are Hindus or Christians, we must admit that the religious ideal in ordinary activities, such as political, social and economic reforms, ultimately comes out victorious. However, we must also admit that in order to practice that ideal in conflicting situations, one must have the glorious spiritual qualities of patience, endurance, and, above all, forgiveness. He must be an integrated personality.

Our understanding of the power of Christ is not in materialistic advancement, scientific discovery, or even in philosophical flights; it is in the spiritual unfoldment of our lives. Religion must be valued by its power to transform human life and not by physical or material achievement. Swami Vivekananda gave a wonderful illustration. A man asked him: "What can religion give me?" The great Swami replied: "A child would ask, 'will your God of religion give me gingerbread?' If the answer is negative, he will say that he does not want it." So, we do not go to religion for gingerbread; we do not go to religion for conquest of empires or the world.

Let us evaluate religion for its own intrinsic value. What is the real value of religion? The religious teachings of Christ or any other great personality should give us control of our lower selves and knowledge of our higher selves. If that is not given by religion, it is meaningless. To refer to the teachings of Christ, religion ought to give us a complete love of God and neighbor. When a person loves God wholly with all the strength of his mind, heart, and soul, he will have an understanding of his real self and God. "If any man will do his will, he shall know the doctrine, whether it be of God, or whether I speak of myself."[202] As a result, he will also have an intense love for his neighbor. He has become the conqueror of his lower self.

A very pertinent question is being asked by many non-Christians, such as Indians and Chinese. In fact, they are asking over and over again: "Well, if we are to follow the theory of 'blessed are the meek,' then we will always remain in subjugation. Other nations will rule us." About three years ago, we had occasion to meet a number of Chinese boys. When they realized that we were from India, they remained to talk. They had come to this country to study for their doctorate in various universities. In the course of the conversation, almost unanimously, these boys expressed the idea: "Your country and our country are in their present plight because we give too much emphasis to religion, because we are a religious people; so these white people exploit us and rule us. You must do something about it, and we must do something about it." After they had presented their arguments, we said: "My friends, are you sure that it is religion that is making you suffer, or lack of application of the spirit of religion that is causing you to be exploited and that causes us in India to be conquered or exploited by other nations? Do you think that people who are ruling the Asiatic countries are religious people?" Actually they are irreligious. They do not follow the teachings of Christ in their imperialistic activities. But there is a danger in this belief of the non-Christians that the people who are expressing such dynamic power in the field of politics and economics may have something which we do not have in spite of our understanding of the values of religion. They think that it may be worthwhile to imitate them.

Many leaders are using elegant phrases, professing to establish brotherhood and equality all over the world and promising freedom for all, while at the same time they are doing deplorable things, as has happened since the Atlantic Charter was framed. The real power of Christianity is not in what the pseudo-Christian leaders want us to believe. We expect from Christianity the power to lift a man from the grave of selfishness and materialism to divine consciousness. The nations who are truly meek, truly spiritual, in the spirit of the New Testament, will remain intact even though wave after wave of conquest comes over them.

Do we not find this illustrated in India? Although people have often contemptuously referred to the Indians as being meek, Indian culture is still surviving in spite of the onslaught of time and waves of conquest. There must be something in Indian culture which preserves its continuity. The power that sustains India's culture is her spiritual ideal. Professor Hocking, in his magnificent book, *Living Religions and a World Faith*, describes the contributions of other religions to Christianity and evaluates what it is in the Hindu religion which is sustaining the life and tradition of India intact:

> I would mention, too, the naturalness of the meditative element of religion [in India], so that school children know instinctively what is to be done in an hour of "meditation." The psychological principle is accepted that a price must be paid for insight: . . . time, preparation, and effort must be spent in order to see. . . There is . . . the willingness among all groups, and not alone among the devotees, to pay

> the price of spiritual gifts, the capacity to renounce the lesser for the greater. . . . The Orient is less a despiser of this world than repute has accused it of being, but it more instantly realises the insidious hold of physical enjoyment on the proportions of moral sanity; and more promptly renounces, with large and magnanimous thoroughness, what it discovers to be a personal peril to the soul.
>
> There remains a third point of excellence: the actually achieved serenity of spirit in many an Oriental saint. . . . with the actuality of renunciation there follows at once a freedom from petty fears, from angers, and from anxiety about many things.[203]

Some of our Indian friends may not like to admit this, as they are dazzled by Western achievements. Some of them are confused by the power politics of the West and think that they have to imitate these methods. (Unfortunately, this also seems to be true of many Chinese, according to the expressions of the young Chinese graduate students). We know that the principles of religion are being worked out in the lives of some of the Indian people. They may not succeed immediately in the objective sense, but a great experiment has been made in political, social, and economic life by Mahatma Gandhi through soul force. If the new India builds on it, it will be great.

So let not anyone think that those who are meek have no right to live in the world, no matter how sneering the expression may be. They may suffer because there is a lag in their scientific achievements and they have not wholly fulfilled their religious responsibilities. It may be that, to some extent, they were responsible for their own exploitation by physically stronger groups. Yet, in many of them, the spirit of religion has been functioning dynamically and fulfilling its primary objective, religious illumination. Religious development may not always go hand in hand with material achievement and objective improvement, but it sustains an individual and a nation for its own intrinsic value. For that matter, the spiritual ideal is much greater than worldly achievement. The achievement will be forgotten in time, despised, ignored, and often hated, as were the Roman and other materialistic cultures. But the example of Christ and His sacrifice for the sake of truth, love of God and humanity, is still there even after twenty centuries. This ideal is still operating in the heart of man. Herein lies the real power of Christianity.

So the power of Christianity can be understood in its effect on individual and collective life. Of course, collective life can be changed only when the individuals are thoroughly inspired by the ideals of love of God and love of neighbor and are transformed by that dynamic force. Great reformers like St. Francis and others introduced reformation in society and influenced the lives of the people by their own transformed personalities. The history of Christian tradition convinces us that the power of Christianity not only can change individuals but it can also change society.

The influence of spiritual power is felt in all phases of society if society keeps the spiritual ideal as the supreme objective of life, and all other ideals are subordinated to it. When we think of Christian culture or civilization, we mean that civilization in which the spirit of Jesus was dynamic and manifested in all the activities of that society. The highly spiritual man and woman were appreciated and admired rather than the symbols of material power in the form of political, economic and military personalities. Such people had subordinate status in Christianity, while the power of St. Francis and such other exalted personalities was considered supreme. They were admired because of their love of God and love of neighbor.

It is refreshing to note that a Christian leader of India, who was brought up and nurtured in the Christian tradition, states unequivocally that the real strength of religion lies in sainthood and not in institutional efficiency. The power of Christianity should be equated with the production of saintly characters. Professor Eddy Asirvatham of Madras, India, writes:

> In addition to doing all that has been said above, the Church in India will fail woefully if it does not produce saints and prophets even more than stewards and administrators. Saints and prophets can not be produced to order. But the Church can at least strive to provide the climate where sainthood and prophecy can have a fair chance of development and survival.[204]

---

177. Matt. 5:3-5.
178. Ibid., 5:13.
179. Ibid., 5:5, 8.
180. William Temple, **Mens Creatrix** (London: Macmillan & Co., Ltd., 1917), pp. 249-251.
181. See Evidence before Parliament, Com., 1853.
182. Temple, **Mens Creatrix**, p. 251-252.
183. **Evening Bulletin** (Providence), December 24, 1935, p. 10.
184. Paul E. Johnson, "Is Christianity Imperialistic?" **Aryan Path**, VIII, No. 5 (May, 1937), 206.
185. Niebuhr, **Christianity and Power Politics**, pp. 1-32.
186. Ibid., p. 9.
187. Ibid., p. 15.

188. Ibid., p. 14.
189. Matt. 5:5, 9.
190. Karl Barth, **This Christian Cause** (New York: The Macmillan Co., 1941), chap. I.
191. Ibid., chap. III.
192. Matt. 26:52.
193. Kumarappa, **Practice and Precepts of Jesus**, pp. vii-viii.
194. Ibid., p. 35.
195. Tawney, **"Religion and the Rise of Capitalism,"** p. 253.
196. Matt. 5:5, 9.
197. John 1:5.
198. Matt. 5:48.
199. Rom. 8:16, 17.
200. Matt. 5:8.
201. Ibid., 5:44.
202. John 7:17.
203. William Ernest Hocking, **Living Religions and a World Faith** (New York: The Macmillan Co., 1940), pp. 256-258.
204. Eddy Asirvatham, "India," **Christianity Today**, ed. Henry Smith Leiper (New York: Morehouse-Gorham Co., 1947), p. 178. Dr. Asirvatham has since become a professor in Boston University.

CHAPTER VII

CHRIST AND THE CROSS

> Awake to righteousness, and sin not; for some have not the knowledge of God.[205]
>
> . . . .
>
> Therefore doth my Father love me, because I lay down my life. . . No man taketh it from me, but I lay it down of myself.[206]

Jesus died on the Cross freely. He refused to resist evil or to use His miraculous powers to prevent it. This voluntary death has become a very important factor in Christianity. To a devout Christian, the Cross is a symbol of God's love and forgiveness.

Very few of us actually understand the significance of the Cross. It has profound meaning both in individual and collective life. When Christians take up religious life or join an order or religious organization, we feel that they have some understanding of the Cross because they are imitating Christ. It is true that they are following the example of Christ. There are many persons who recapitulate and think of the incidents of Calvary. Yet when we consider the life of Jesus as a whole, we see the importance of the message from the Cross. He willingly allowed Himself to be crucified; He did not run away from those who wanted to do this to Him but voluntarily submitted Himself to it, even though it was possible for Him to leave that section of the country. According to the Indian standpoint, an incarnation is a person who is thoroughly established in the All-Loving Being, who has no trace of cosmic ignorance, who is completely illumined (namely, who has direct knowledge of God and consequent understanding of the world process), and who understands the meaning and value of historical events. As we said in Chapter I, one of the most important factors which we understand from the life of an incarnation is that he does not do anything that is not deeply significant. You can write a book on one of the incidents of his life.

As we explained in Chapter V, the greater portion of our life is full of problems. We have our physical and mental problems, individual and collective problems, and our problems of human relationships. They are likely to exist as long as there remain differences in reactions to personalities as well as to situations. St. Paul said that the sun, moon, and stars are different from one another; there is even variety among the stars.[207] Variety is a natural condition. We know that no two persons are alike. Consequently, there are differences in our likes and dislikes which result in conflicts. If we demand satisfaction in our preferences regardless of the feelings and attitudes of others, we naturally create disturbances within ourselves and them. There are conflicts in the business world, social life, national and international affairs, and interpersonal relationships so long as these conflicts are not dissolved by higher understanding of life and its values.

When we study all the solutions that are offered to the world by those who are trying to remove the conflicts and tension, we can classify them into two groups: the physical, materialistic solution and the spiritual solution. The first method leads us to natural, physical, and animal reactions to conflicts and disturbances. We try to remove the obstacles. If an insect is troublesome, kill it. Do not let anything interfere with your life. If the forces of nature present difficulties, become invincible so that they cannot affect the system. Man has been trying to overcome the onslaughts of nature and has succeeded greatly in overcoming certain of its phases. But he has not yet conquered the final onslaught of death. We may try to forget it or ignore its existence, yet that cruel death appears and snatches us away from here. It is something that man will not be able to conquer because it is the very nature of physical life. Anything that is born goes through various changes and ultimately dies. However, this does not mean annihilation; it means only a change of condition. These changes will be in the world so long as we are living in the realm of time, space, and causal relationship. So man has been trying to overcome difficulties, limitations, pains, and agonies as best he could through the aggressive method, in which he asserts himself and overcomes nature.

The same principle is used in dealing with our problems of human relationships. If anyone is troubling us, aggressively overcome him; he has no right to trouble us, so give him a slap. If a group becomes troublesome, then go out with a gun and overcome them. Nowadays they are going out with atomic bombs to destroy each other in the name of self-preservation and national protection. In either individual or collective conflict, man follows the same urge. He has not changed for the better; rather his very nature is degraded.

Now this method of overcoming obstacles by force has been going on in human society for centuries and centuries; still man has not conquered the problem. He is making it more and more complicated. When we consider contemporary history, we find that the problems have become so acute that no one seems to know how to solve them. Some people seem to think that they are prophets because they prescribe this or that conference or this or that alliance, or perhaps they meet in certain parts of the globe and try to divide the world in certain ways. This solution is no solution. It has made the problems much worse than they ever were. Consider the meetings held in certain parts of America, Africa, and Europe, where the great political leaders professed that they would establish peace by overcoming obstacles created by the then so-called enemy groups. But the use of force has only brought out more and more force. Historical evidence points to the fact that things are getting worse and worse through the use of force as a solution. It has not removed the cause of the conflicts. The history of Europe for the last few centuries convinces us that the application of physical force, or force for force, created a vicious circle and brought out more and more venomous tendencies in man. Those who adopted the first method of aggression and physical conquest of individual and collective obstacles have created more and more problems, bringing the world to a frightening state where even thoughtful persons are apprehensive of the complete annihilation of the human race.

CHRIST AND THE CROSS

Jesus, the Christ, by way of the Cross taught the world that aggression is not the method for solving the problems of life or conquering the obstacles. He used the second or spiritual method. We know that when He was being arrested by the Roman soldiers, as we said before, His first disciple, St. Peter, exercised the so-called method of force for force. He drew his sword to rectify the trouble, and Jesus at once reprimanded him and advised him not to give violence for violence.[208] He knew that brute force would not solve the problem. Instead He advocated the spiritual method of overcoming evil by good, which He and His disciples followed. As an incarnation of God, Jesus set an example to the Jews and Gentiles that physical force will not solve the problem of violence. Instead of using physical force for the solution of the problems of life, He manifested spiritual power to conquer evil. When the people brutally insulted Him and crucified Him, He prayed for them, saying: "Father, forgive them; for they know not what they do."[209] Can you find greater manifestation of spiritual power than this? If an ordinary man were about to depart from this world after having been crucified, he would at least mentally curse the people for doing it if he were not able to say anything. Jesus blessed His malefactors who injured, cursed, persecuted, and crucified Him. He not only made this a living principle but He taught His disciples to express the same spirit. St. Peter was also crucified and St. Paul was killed by the enemies of the Messenger of peace and harmony for preaching the highest, the loftiest ideal.

Jesus Himself taught the highest ideals of life to the people at large but they did not understand them because they were living on the animal plane. People who function on this plane cannot absorb the higher principles of life. Go and talk spiritual truths to most people, and they will look at you and think you are an insane person. A spiritual person is regarded as an abnormal person in modern society. Every great spiritual leader has been regarded by many of his contemporaries as an insane or positively harmful person. Can anyone present spiritual truths seriously today? During the war, talk of the gospel of love was discredited. Those who expressed this ideal were condemned. Thousands of people in this country were molested because they believe in the gospel of love. Even recently some were treated as guinea pigs in this country. We know a man who was being treated as a guinea pig in the Massachusetts General Hospital in Boston. He allowed himself to be used for the purpose of determining how malaria can be cured through the use of a certain drug. Did the Government take the responsibility for this man's life? We also know some of the boys who were kept under medical observation during starvation diets to find out whether or not vitamins would revive them at the last stage of life. Some of these men were sent to certain camps (called Civilian Public Service Camps rather than concentration camps). Now why are they treated in this manner? They believe in the gospel of love and fellowship of reconciliation; they believe that hatred cannot be conquered by hatred and that evil cannot be conquered by evil; and they believe that war and the use of the atomic bomb, however glorified by any government, is a curse and a sin against man and God. They believe in the Cross. For their spiritual conviction, about ten thousand persons have had to suffer humiliation in this country. They worked for the government, but their maintenance was provided mostly by the Mennonites, Quakers, and other church organizations. When hostilities ceased, many of these conscientious objectors were retained in the camps even after the service men were allowed to return home. They gave their lives bit by bit for the good of humanity. Some theologians view them as heretics because they still believe in the teachings of Jesus and follow the non-violent method.

So no one should blame Pilate or the Jews very much for crucifying Jesus at that time. The Romans and Jews made mistakes and committed crimes; no one denies that. But are human beings any better today? If Jesus came and declared the same spiritual truths today, He would find that these important military and political leaders of this very Christendom would crucify Him as they crucified bit by bit the ten thousand conscientious objectors. So it is a mistake to condemn a group of people of the first century A. D. because they committed a mistake. The same mistake is being made by people today. Why? Because they think that evil should be conquered by evil. However, some of them will tell us that they do nothing wrong; the evil is all on the other side, namely that of the enemy. They are all saints! Only children could be persuaded to believe that! Atomic bombing is not a saintly act, however it may be glorified. Every sane man thinks it is a crime. Future historians all over the world will record that the leaders who were responsible for such criminal acts are criminals. So Jesus declared that "they that take the sword shall perish with the sword."[210] And

St. Paul said: "Be not overcome of evil, but overcome evil with good."[211]

We know now that the use of the atomic bomb is not stopping anything. The enemies or potential enemies are also preparing atomic bombs and they are also dragooning the scientists. We have heard recent reports that many of the scientists who are responsible for the manufacture of this type of bomb have now denied their responsibility and want to stop its use in the future for destructive purposes. In a recent article, Chancellor Hutchins of the University of Chicago gives many thought provoking and enlightening facts to the public. Some of the nuclear physicisists who were considered responsible for the production of the atomic bomb actually opposed its use for destructive purposes.[212] Chancellor Hutchins and his colleagues in the University of Chicago certainly deserve appreciation; they have followed the spirit of Christianity in their attempt to prevent destruction. We only hope that more and more of these scientists will take a stand on higher religious principles, that political and military leaders will not be able to coerce, tempt, or persuade them to sell their knowledge for the purpose of physical gain and the establishment of power. The more persons there are like Chancellor Hutchins and his colleagues, who will stand firmly on religious principles, the greater spiritual power will be established.

The question will arise: How can we follow the methods of Jesus in this world? Some people will say that He prayed for His enemies, but we are not spiritually evolved like Him; we have our natural tendencies; we cannot conquer our anger when someone acts in an evil manner towards us. Many people think that only Jesus could love His enemies. They believe with Ingersoll that His teachings are obsolete today. Some thinkers say that absolute ethics is not applicable today. Therefore, for all practical purposes, people should follow a practical method and overcome evil by evil. We wonder what these thinkers will say now that the former allies are showing their teeth and threatening the security of the people with the same implements of evil. As in previous periods of history, evil methods are creating more evil. Neither individually nor collectively has this method ever succeeded.

In our individual lives we must learn to control ourselves. Do we not find in family life that those who take up brute force or compulsion suffer the most? Moreover, they do not solve the problem and the result is more and more complications. The same principle is applicable to collective or national life. Take, for instance, the problem of labor and management. We admit that there has been a great deal of injustice on the part of management; no one denies that. We do not believe that even a capitalist would deny it, if he is a thinking man. Some time ago we saw the play, *The Corn is Green,* which depicted the coal mines in England. When we consider the life of those poor miners, we understand what they suffer. At the same time, we must also remember that the methods they are using to try and get better conditions for themselves will not solve the problem. Violence brings out violence. It may be that with this method they will crush the capitalistic system but at the same time they will generate violence in themselves which will create more problems for them.

It reminds us of a very interesting episode in the history of India during the lifetime of Sri Krishna. Two groups of people were fighting for supremacy at that time, and Sri Krishna tried to act as mediator. One group succeeded in gaining supremacy. They became intoxicated by their power and success and created trouble for themselves so that they ultimately destroyed themselves. It was a very sad story. In the same way violence and force is being generated by the unwise advisors of the labor group and it will ultimately create catastrophic trouble. We admit that selfish capitalistic systems produce evil; but if violent methods are being used by labor to help the situation, it will create further problems. Violence has the inherent defect of producing violence.

Take, for instance, the Russian Revolution. We were told by a Russian gentleman that the leaders of the Revolution used to say that it was nothing to sacrifice two million people, and they did it. Is the result beneficial? Are the people now peaceful? Can anyone express his thoughts in that country? The moment a person expresses the slightest opposition to the present policy he no longer exists there. Either he is in Siberia or somewhere unknown to the world. If anyone gives a slap, he will get a slap; if he expresses violence, it will be expressed toward him. Let not any one think that only a few face violence and die in it and that he will escape. If not immediately, it will eventually reach him, and the violence he has generated will destroy him and his followers.

The law of causation or *karma* also indicates that if anyone shows love in exchange for hatred, non-violence for violence, good for evil, or soul force for brute force, he will reap good results. He will generally attract love, non-violence, and soul force to himself. Apart from that, the more he expresses strong and noble qualities, the more he intensifies his own tendencies of doing good.

Jesus shows us how to overcome violence by soul force. What is the nature of soul force? In the first place, in order to manifest it, we do not use physical force to overcome physical force. We must not take any violent step even under provocation nor hate the evil doers, knowing that evil is being done by them because of their ignorance of the higher values of life and because they cannot control their lower nature and impulses of greed, anger, and love of power. In fact, they deserve our positive sympathy. We must not subscribe to the methods of evil nor co-operate with the evil doers. We are to wish only for their good through the spiritual method and overcome evil by love, sympathy, generosity, and nobility. That is the reason Jesus prayed on the Cross: "Father, forgive them; for they know not what they do."[213] He non-co-operated with the evil doers and had nothing to do with their evil actions. He allowed Himself to be crucified without any opposition or violent reaction. Moreover, He expressed soul force in praying for the welfare of His malefactors. This was active, positive manifestation of love and nobility. The man who takes up the spiritual method, the method of soul force, will not stop with non-co-operating with or remaining indifferent to the evil doers but he will positively and aggressively do good to the persons. This is noble revenge, giving blessings for blows rather than blow for blow. It has a wonderful effect on evil persons. If we can patiently and actively pray for their evil propensities and do kind things for their welfare, we will find that their evil propensities will be changed. Some people may say that evil doers do not change; they have tried a few times to return good for evil and it has had no effect. For the sake of argument suppose we accept that some evil doers cannot be changed by love, generosity, and sympathy; even so our spiritual nature is benefited. We are not polluted by evil propensities; thereby we generate tremendous spiritual force.

It has been contended that the activities of police and military forces are necessary for the preservation of society. Our answer is that these activities should be motivated by forgiveness and love with the inspiration of real spiritual force and not by vindictive propensities. It should be emphasized here that the spiritual men, above all, should maintain the spirit of forgiveness and non-violence under all circumstances and thereby lift the police and military forces and the political and economic thinkers to the higher plane of life. Spiritual persons should always be the real guiding forces of a culture, as we mentioned in the previous chapter.

Our master, Swami Brahmananda, told us a story in connection with the conquest of evil by good. A holy man was sitting on the bank of a river performing his daily spiritual practices. Suddenly he saw that a scorpion was being carried away by the current of the river. The poor creature was struggling for its life. Feeling sympathy for it, the holy man wanted to save it and quickly picked it up. No sooner had he done so than the scorpion stung him. The man suffered excruciating pain; however, he placed the scorpion on the ground and withdrew his mind from the pain by thinking of God. After a few minutes he noticed the same scorpion struggling for its life again in the current. He picked it up a second time and was again stung so that he suffered excruciating pain. Nevertheless, the holy man placed it carefully on the ground and continued his spiritual practices. Lo and behold, after a few minutes what did he see but the same scorpion back in the current again struggling for its life! He wondered what he should do. He knew it is the nature of a scorpion to sting and it is the nature of a holy man to do good. He thought to himself: "If he can't change his nature, why should I change mine?" So for the third time he picked the scorpion up and was stung. This time the holy man carried it far away from the river so that it would not fall into the current again.[214] This shows us that a spiritual man must not change his nature even though other people do not and cannot change their evil propensities. A religious man has no choice between brute force and soul force; he has only one path to follow, namely soul force or the path of good. "Then Peter came to him and said, Lord, how oft shall my brother sin against me, and I forgive him? till seven times? Jesus saith unto him, I say not unto thee, Until seven times: but Until seventy times seven."[215]

If we remain pure, loving, and sympathetic to evil doers, this spiritual force will effectively influence the people at large. Let me mention an incident which happened in the life of a great personality, Pavhari Baba, not long ago. This incident is recorded by Swami Vivekananda in a sketch of the life of this saintly man.[216] He had a peculiar hobby of cooking food to give to his friends and the poor. He had a few cooking utensils in his cave for this purpose and he used to obtain the food supplies from a nearby village. One day when he returned from the village, he found that a thief had made a bundle of his utensils and was stealing away with it. When the man saw Pavhari Baba, he dropped the bundle and began to run. Pavhari Baba picked it up, put it on his own shoulder, and ran after him. The faster he ran, the faster ran the thief. Finally, the saint overtook him. He dropped the bundle in front of the thief and with folded hands said: "Take these things, they belong to you." The man was astonished and refused. "No, no! I don't want them. I am sorry I was going to take them." Pavhari Baba insisted. "They belong to you. You must need them otherwise you would not come to get them. Here, you take them." The thief was overcome. He knelt before the saint and burst into tears, exclaiming: "Save me, save me!" This incident changed his life completely. He no longer remained a thief. He renounced the world and became a follower of Pavhari Baba; he became a saintly man himself.

As another instance of soul force, take the life of Chaitanya, an incarnation of God in India. He was molested by two ignoble persons, Jagai and Madhai, who used to villify him and do most deplorable things to Him. One day it so happened that Chaitanya and a number of his followers came out of a house singing the name of God and inspiring the people in the neighborhood. Jagai and Madhai were drunk and had lost their senses; they could not stand the name of God or the devotional atmosphere so they began to throw stones. Chaitanya did not run away even though His face was cut and the blood was flowing. Like Jesus, He went forward with love and embraced them, exclaiming: "Bravo! Well done! Take the name of God." What happened? These ignoble persons were completely transformed.

We know that Sri Ramakrishna was abused, too, by some people; but His love, blessings, and spiritual power transformed them into saintly characters. His disciples received abuse when they first formed as a group. They even had difficulty in finding a house in which to live but finally were able to hire one which was known to be haunted. They lived there quietly, but the children and other people of the neighborhod used to tease and insult them and throw stones at them. They could have disliked the malcreants, but instead their blessings and love transformed the people into their followers and devotees. We heard the story from the persons themselves, who mocked and molested these great disciples of Sri Ramakrishna.

What would most of us do if we were criticized or abused? We would never forget if someone wronged us in any way, no matter how kind they may have been at other times. My master told me one day that if we always do everything good for a person but just once do something wrong, he will forget every good thing we ever did and remember the wrong. On the other hand, if we do all kinds of wrong things all our lives and perform just one noble act, God remembers that and lifts us to a higher plane forgetting all our weaknesses and iniquities.

We humbly submit here that time and again we have seen men of illumination also demonstrate this noble quality of forgetting the iniquities of an individual and lifting him to a higher plane of existence. Because of his awareness of the presence of God, an illumined soul can overlook the weaknesses in a man and see God in him. Jesus completely forgot the iniquities and harmful tendencies of the people who crucified Him.

We can also spread that spiritual force around us, as His disciples and the followers of His disciples did. Do we not know how the early Christians allowed themselves to be devoured by ferocious animals in the Colosseum at Rome? Tremendous spiritual power was generated there. Does anyone think that Christianity became powerful because the Roman Empire became Christianized? The Roman Empire was not the center of power in Christianity; the center of power was in the lives of the people who molded themselves according to the ideals of Jesus. The power of Christianity lies in the Catacombs where the martyrs sacrificed every ounce of their blood for the truth, for God. There lies the strength of Christianity.

So if any man wants to generate strength, he must do it on the spiritual plane, not on the physical plane. According to Buddha: "If some men conquer in battle a thousand times a thousand men, and if another conquer himself, he is the greatest of conquerors."[217] "And he that ruleth himself is better than he that taketh a city."[218] From the Cross we learn that we are to conquer ourselves and not others first. In fact, we cannot conquer anyone if we cannot conquer ourselves. In political and economic domination no one is conquered, the heart and soul of a man under subjugation is extremely indifferent. The gigantic power of imperial Britain conquered and controlled India and other dominions. We know what the Indian people think of British imperialists. We also know how other imperialists in the world have been treated by subject people. There is no love lost between them. There is dislike, almost hatred, for those who use physical force to keep others in subjugation. Therefore, those who use force do not conquer the heart of anyone. This principle functions in individual as well as collective life.

Any man who uses love and sympathy wins the hearts of those with ignoble tendencies, as illustrated by the story of Pavhari Baba and the thief. Do we not know that Jesus changed many individuals in spite of their ignoble tendencies and made them His ardent followers through His love, sympathy, and forgiveness? St. Paul is a great example of remarkable transformation. The early Christians could have expressed hateful feelings to St. Paul; they had sufficient justification to hate him. However they endured his molestation. So we know that the heart of an individual can be won and collective life can be changed through the example of the Cross.

Some thinkers admit that individually people can follow the spirit of the Cross but collectively they cannot do it. They may also say that as persons within a group are not all at the same stage of spiritual development they cannot practice the spirit of the Cross as a group. We admit that the reactions of different individuals to the problems of life are not identical. We have also mentioned that two methods are generally adopted to solve the problems of life — the spiritual and the non-spiritual or soul force and aggressive militant conquest of opposition. It may be argued by many, that the idea of perfectionism is practical in medieval monasteries. Some may also say that the ideals of monks and nuns are not practical in collective life. Our answer is that it is true that an individual can easily reform himself and follow in the footsteps of a great spiritual personality, if he wants to do so; but we admit that it is difficult to change the attitudes and ways of life of a group of persons. However, we firmly believe that the influence of an incarnation can simultaneously change both the thought current of an individual and a group in a given society. As we have already quoted from Sri Ramakrishna, an incarnation is like a ship which carries innumerable persons to the infinite ocean of God.[219] Again, civilizations move in a wave-like motion, as we quoted from Swami Vivekananda.[220] The history of different civilizations reveals that the major trend of a society is changed when an incarnation comes to the world, even though some individuals of that society will remain ignoble. We feel that the spirit of an incarnation inspires a number of persons and they in turn inspire others. In fact, the ideals of an incarnation are unconsciously absorbed by the people in spite of the current trend of thought. So collective life undergoes a gradual process of transformation when it is inspired by the dynamics of individual spiritual power.

It is true that the path of conquest of evil by good is very difficult for an uncontrolled person. It requires courage, moral stamina, and spiritual strength. We may think we have strength when we give blow for blow, but greater strength lies in the conquest of our anger, hatred, animosities, and inordinate affections. Any child can lose his temper and return hatred for hatred, but it requires a spiritual man to overcome hatred and conquer his lower passions. The trouble that we face in the world today is due to the lack of control of the lower passions. Even as Rome was not built in a day, so conquest of lower passions, symbolized by the Cross, is to be achieved bit by bit every day. "And he said to them all, If any man will come after me, let him deny himself, and take up his cross daily, and follow me."[221] We have to struggle intensely with tenacity. We may fail once; we may fail twice; we may fail a hundred times, as Swami Vivekananda tells us; yet, if we are persistent we can conquer the lower, the physical self. When we are established in the conquest, we will find that spiritual force will manifest itself spontaneously. When that is attained, evil has been conquered and the spirit of the Cross will be fulfilled.

---

205. I Cor. 15:34.
206. John 10:17-18.
207. I Cor. 15:41.
208. Matt. 26:52.
209. Luke 23:34.
210. Matt. 26:52.
211. Rom. 12:21.
212. Robert M. Hutchins, "The Bomb Secret is Out!" The American, December, 1947, p. 24.
213. Luke 23:34.
214. **The Eternal Companion** (Hollywood: Vedanta Society of Southern California, 1944), p. 24.
215. Matt. 18:21-22.
216. **Works**, IV, 233-241.
217. **Dhammapada** (Sayings of Buddha) XLVIII:8.
218. Prov. 16:32.
219. **Sayings of Sri Ramakrishna** IV:138.
220. **Works**, IV, 134.
221. Luke 9:23.

CHAPTER VIII

SPIRIT OF EASTER

> Awake to righteousness, and sin not; for some have not the knowledge of God.
>
> . . . .
>
> So also is the resurrection of the dead. It is sown in corruption; it is raised in incorruption:
>
> . . . .
>
> It is sown a natural body; it is raised a spiritual body.[222]

St. Paul, with his spiritual illumination and understanding, explains to us the real spirit of Easter. It is true that Jesus, the Christ, went through indescribable agonies a few days previous to this time, yet He came out victorious. From this occasion, then, there are lessons which are to be learned by every one of the followers of Jesus.

In the first place, we learn that until this corruptible life is changed, there is no possibility of eternal, immortal, incorruptible life. Jesus demonstrated that we must overcome the obstacles, difficulties, and limitations of corruptible life on this plane. Certain of the difficulties of this life are inherent. It goes without saying that as long as this plane of existence is in time, space, and causal relationship, there will be change. Time cannot be stopped. The very nature of time is succession. Consequently, there is inevitable change in everything that exists in the time and space relationship. As such, it will create trouble in life. It is evident in the stages through which we pass from childhood to old age. When we grow from childhood to maturity, the things we adored and loved are no longer objects of enjoyment; we cannot get the same pleasure from them; they are no longer attractive to us. When we go from maturity to old age, we find we are incapable of doing what we wish to do. Changes in mind and body are inevitable. Then there are changes in our friends, relatives, and outside life. If anyone thinks that he can stop these physical changes while living on this plane, he is mistaken. There are persons who aspire to stop them by perpetuating the desirable physical condition and making it more and more enjoyable. Unfortunately, sooner or later they realize that they are trying to do the impossible. Eventually, everyone is taken away from this plane of existence; consequently, they realize that their attempts are failures and are bound to be so because the very nature of the physical world is changeable.

This is also true of mental life. The same kind of experiences do not bring out the same kind of emotional reaction in the same man all of the time. Certain experiences that were extremely enjoyable in the early period of life do not stimulate him later. So man tries to find newer ways of getting pleasure through the same type of experience with new objects. This ever restless tendency to get mental pleasure in new ways shows that he is not satisfied. This very dissatisfaction makes him more restless, and the restlessness itself stimulates his desire for new thrills. Unfortunately, this mental restlessness for more and more and newer and newer thrills affects even his body. In this way the minds of most of us are constantly changing. It is impossible to stop this change in our minds and also in the minds of others who are connected with us. When we cannot change our own individual mind, how can we expect to change the minds of others? The facts of experience will prove to us that change in both mental and physical life is inevitable.

Consequently, we must find the real implications of immortal life. Can we have permanent satisfaction in life, lasting peace and happiness on this plane of existence? Our answer is no, it is impossible. Jesus tells us time and again, and He also demonstrated, that the flesh must be crucified in order to ascend in spirit. Does that mean that we are to crucify ourselves consciously and deliberately by torturing and tormenting the flesh, like ascetics who think that they will thereby have immortal life? There are persons in India and the West who have actually mortified their bodies in the hope of conquest of their physical nature. This is a mistake, and it is not the way in which to conquer our physical, corruptible nature. It can only be overcome by spiritual processes. We must overcome the world with its difficulties and limitations by mental force, not by physical force or torture of the body.

There are many others who try to conquer natural forces by expressing superiority over them and by improving physical conditions. They seem to think that by overcoming the laws of nature through science and other means, they will make their physical life satisfactory. We admit that there is nothing wrong in harnessing and using the forces of nature for comfortable living; in fact, every man is trying to do it in his own way. Uncivilized man is trying to overcome his physical limitations in his own crude way, while civilized man uses scientific precise methods; yet neither has solved the problem of physical change and discomfort. Sooner or later they meet with failure, as the individual and collective history of the world has proven. We do not want to be misunderstood as advocating a pessimistic view of life and unduly stressing otherworldliness. We do not mean to say that man should stop making improvements in physical conditions, nor do we want to imply that scientific improvements are not to be attempted and achieved. What we do mean is that, in spite of these improvements, physical and mental change is inevitable; man does not find a durable life of peace and happiness in these improvements alone or in the conquest of physical nature. The only way he can overcome the limitations in life and the corruptible nature of the body is by attacking the root of the corruption, which is in the mind. As St. Paul says, we must change our corruptible nature. This can be done by changing our consciousness and our reaction to the problems of life with the use of mental force.

The Buddhist teachers tell us that corruption is desire or inordinate longing (*trishna*). According to the Hindu teachers, the cause is more than longing; it is *maya*, a basic ignorance of our true nature. This longing gradually manifests itself outwardly in the form of activities. Swami Vivekananda used to say that if we want to change our lives and action, we must control our thoughts. After all, our thoughts are actually the causes of our activities.

If we can get control over the fine movements, if we

> can get hold of thought at the root, before it has become thought, before it has become action, then it would be possible for us to control the whole. Now, if there is a method by which we can analyze, investigate, understand and finally grapple with those finer powers, the finer causes, then alone is it possible to have control over ourselves, . . .[223]

Similarly the Hebrew proverb runs, "Keep thy heart with all diligence; for out of it are the issues of life."[224] And Jesus said: "There is nothing from without a man, that entering into him can defile him: but the things which come out of him, those are they that defile the man."[225] All the teachers belonging to the different religions are one in their understanding of the cause of our difficulties and solution of our problems, as well as the method of attaining immortal life.

Some people offer a compromise by saying that we can enjoy both the things of this world and spirituality. When there is craving of the flesh and consequent gratification of the finite nature of man, however transitory it may be, awareness of the spirit is dimmed or even destroyed. It is common experience in life that when we remain aware of our physical nature we do not really become aware of our spiritual nature, even though we may have higher flights of intellectualism. It is often argued that even the finite and limited physical expressions are parts of the real, the Absolute. It may be philosophically true that the Absolute is the basis of all existence, but the Absolute is not in the consciousness of a man at the time he is expressing cravings of the flesh. The mind can be interested in only one thing at a time. The great spiritual leaders of the world prove that when they direct their attention to God they have no interest in the things of the world. Even though the world may try to force them to be interested through various means of persuasion and allurement, their minds soar so high that they cannot think of the relative state of existence; they are absorbed in God.

A nephew of Sri Ramakrishna was very devoted to one of his foremost disciples, Swami Brahmananda. He frequently visited the great Swami, who was also fond of him, and always asked his advice for the solution of personal problems. One day when he was there relating his problems concerning personal family disputes and insignificant worldly matters, Swami Brahmananda, who was in a very exalted mood, said to him: "You know, Brother, all my life I have ignored the petty things of this world. I do not know anything except *Brahman* (God). In my old age, how can I persuade myself to take this world seriously as real while it is relative? You are talking of these problems which are existing on the relative plane. How can I bring myself down to this plane and ponder over this while *Brahman* alone is real?" The conflicts and disputes of the world do not exist to the man absorbed in God. The relative vanishes and what remains is nothing but abiding, blissful existence. We see in the life of Sri Ramakrishna that He had to force His mind to the plane of relativity even to talk with and instruct His disciples. So it becomes a serious problem for a God-conscious spiritual man to live in the world as we see it, because the world of confusion and conflict and relativity has its problems by virtue of its very nature and changeability. He has to come into close association with people who are aware of the painful and pleasurable aspects of life; he is on a higher plane while they are on a lower plane. Sometimes they are elated and sometimes they are depressed. The problems are very real to those who are conscious of their suffering and pleasure in the world. On the other hand, the man who lifts himself to the divine plane by conquering the cravings of the flesh does not feel that there are any problems at all. It is amazing to him that people are crying, fighting, quarreling, and destroying one another in their acceptance of the reality of this world and its vicissitudes. In his state of God-consciousness, all the awareness of relative existence and multiplicity vanishes. Consequently, there is no possibility for him to be part of any conflicts or confusion. The awareness of change and the effect thereof vanish from his horizon. This is the state of durable peace and abiding happiness. So it is that Jesus teaches us that we must conquer the flesh in order to be aware of God. It is impossible to be aware of both simultaneously.

Some of the philosophers, like Hegel and others, say that the Absolute is manifested through the world; therefore, we cannot reject anything in the world, although we must see everything in relation to the Absolute. If we want to take God, we have to take every experience, every fact of life along with Him. What is an experience, a fact of life? The experiences we have as children lose their attraction when we grow up a little. The facts of childhood are no longer real; they are mere playthings to the grown-up man. They do not seem to be so effective, so real, so tangible. "When I was a child, I spake as a child, I understood as a child, I thought as a child: but when I became a man, I put away childish things."[226] The grown-up man smiles at himself to think how foolish he was to take the playthings so seriously as things of permanence and to make himself so miserable over the toys and play-facts. As he evolves in spiritual consciousness, the things that he regarded as real facts in life are no longer so serious, pleasurable, or painful. They no longer stimulate the same reactions and they are no longer taken as part of his life. He knows them to be passing phases in the changeable experiences of existence. They are not so important to him as they were when his consciousness functioned on the relative plane. As in the case of Swami Brahmananda, a man of that state of consciousness can hardly force himself to come down to this plane. It is true that so long as a man remains limited to this plane he cannot help but take the things of relative experience seriously. On the other hand, a man of higher consciousness of the unity of existence cannot seriously take these as permanent, nor can he become disturbed over the changeable conditions of life. He is fully awakened to the presence of God everywhere. Although he is not disturbed by the attractive and repulsive states of the relative plane, he is ever ready to be of help to those who are still functioning on that plane. He serves men and women, being aware of the presence of God in them. The man who is aware of relative experiences is compelled to take them seriously according to his own mental status, since he is not aware of the presence of God. But when a man is on the higher plane of existence, he is not even aware of the lower plane. How beautifully St. Paul says: "All flesh is not the same flesh: but there is one kind of flesh of men, another flesh of beasts. . . . There are also celestial bodies, and bodies terrestrial. . ."[227] Those who give value to one forget the other. So the followers of Hegel would be mistaken if they assumed that every experience or every fact of life is equally real, because the concept of reality changes according to the evolution of a man, as Hegel himself taught. To dwell in immediacy, Hegel taught, is the lowest stage of being.

Sri Ramakrishna used to tell the story about the agriculturalist who had a wife and an only child. According to the custom in India, he went out every morning to work in the fields, taking a little food with him. He did not return until afternoon or evening. One day while he was out in the fields, his only son had an attack of cholera and died. Anyone can understand how the mother felt on losing this child without her husband being with her to share in her suffering. She suffered excruciating pain from the loss and no one could console her in her agony. When the husband returned home in the late afternoon, the baby's body was still there. He was stunned and he could not even cry. When he did not cry, his wife became angry and shook him. "Don't you feel the loss of our only child? Don't you even cry?" The man acted as if he were awakened from a slumber. He said: "What? Am I to weep for the loss of this one or for the seven children I lost? Last night I dreamed that I was a king and you were a queen. We had a beautiful palace and there were many people around us. We also had seven children. Then I woke up and the children, kingdom, elephants, palace, and paraphernalia were gone. Everything was very real and I enjoyed it all. Now I find that this one son is dead. I do not know whether to weep for him or my seven sons."

Thus it happens that in our slumber of materialism on the physical plane with its consequent cravings, we forget our real nature. Then we think that this relative experience is vitally important and absolutely real, while, in truth, the only reality is the absolute consciousness which is permanent. All the experiences that the world wants us to take as real have no permanent value at all after we become aware of the incorruptible. The moment higher consciousness is awakened, that very moment the events of relative experiences disappear, even though we were enjoying them and suffering from them in our previous state of consciousness. So how can we take all that we experience in the world as permanent?

We may well ask what the explanation is for the cravings that we have in our hearts. Behind the cravings, behind our material expressions, our aspirations, and our hopes, there is a desire to be permanently happy, to have abiding bliss. All our activities — small and great, private and public — are motivated directly by the basic desire for happiness. Unless a person is mentally deranged, there is no other motivation. If we boil down the various apparent incentives for our activities, we find that they can be traced to the basic desire for happiness, as Spinoza pointed out in his essay *On the Improvement of the Understanding*. In fact, consciously or unconsciously, directly or indirectly, we are expressing this desire in our everyday life. We can safely say that this is the spiritual basis of our life; when we try to be permanently happy, we merely seek that which is equivalent to immortal life. There is no one who does not crave for immortality. It is the inspiration of the poets and the theme of the philosophers; it is the aspiration of the poor man and the rich man. As Professor Brightman says:

> Immortality symbolizes the faith that good purpose never fails to all eternity. The taproot of all human endeavor is in the hope that purpose can achieve values. Those who deny immortality continue to strive largely because they believe that they are laying foundations for the next generation. If courage and meaning are imparted to life by a short look into the future, how much more dignity, hope, and perspective arise from the faith that every life capable of purposive development is eternal.[228]

Everyone is struggling for durable happiness and immortal life; everyone is seeking something permanent, or, to use the Hindu term, eternal bliss. Why do we build a home? It is the desire to have a permanent abode. There is freedom and a sense of permanency in it. Even in little things we find that there is a strong desire for a permanent existence and free life.

Little do we understand that freedom does not lie in expressions of the flesh. Many persons identify freedom with license. They think that when certain desires, aspirations, hopes, and cravings arise, these must be realized no matter what the means are. Then they think they will be free. But do we not learn from the teachings of Christ that only by conquest of the flesh and desires can we enter into a permanent abode and free life? Jesus well knew that "the spirit indeed is willing, but the flesh is weak."[229] Unfortunately, in our ignorance, we catch hold of things that exist temporarily and relatively but we seem to think that they are permanent. This very attitude of mistaking the relative for the permanent makes our human behavior what it is at present. Our emphasis on the relative plane creates problems one after another and then we multiply our bondages. In our mad rush for the fulfillment of our desires, we drive ourselves away from the realm of immortal life of peace and happiness. Jesus demonstrated on Good Friday that we must allow our empirical selves to be crucified in order to conquer the flesh and its cravings. Then alone is there the possibility of changeless immortal life. Jesus proved to us that it is the birthright of everyone and not the exclusive property of any single individual, race, or religious group. It is the basis of our existence. It is the thought, desire, aspiration and ideal of everyone.

It is true that every man has a double nature, physical and spiritual. The physical nature craves for things of this plane of existence as the mind is wholly directed for this purpose. Emotional reactions are influenced by the cravings of the flesh. This also justifies the psychosomatic interpretation of life. Physical expressions, as such, are limited and finite. Nothing different can be expected as the very nature of physical life is limited by time, space, and causation. On the other hand, the spiritual element within us, the divine spark, is illimitable. When we want immortal life, it is really a conscious or unconscious desire to be established in spiritual life. Physical life cannot give us immortal life, as it is by nature finite. Some thinkers seem to feel that they can have physical immortality. However, the very nature of the body presupposes its finiteness. St. Paul makes it clear when he declares: "Now this I say, brethren, that flesh and blood cannot inherit the kingdom of God; neither doth corruption inherit incorruption."[230] The physical body is composed of different component elements. Anything that has components will sooner or later go back to its original state. The spirit of Easter proves that in spite of the mortality of physical nature there remains something in man which is abiding. This abiding element is what St. Paul calls the celestial and spiritual body.

As a great exponent of Jesus, St. Paul makes it clear that we have to be awakened to "righteousness" and have the knowledge of God. Uncontrolled physical craving and the knowledge of God cannot go together. When the craving for physical pleasures dominate the mind, it cannot have simultaneous knowledge of God. The Hindu and Christian views are identical in this respect. Dr. Schweitzer, and such other thinkers, seem to think that a person can know God and at the same time experience what he calls "life and world affirmation."[231] If this were possible, the followers of Jesus, from the great apostles to John Wesley and George Fox, would not have advocated control of the flesh. It is our deliberate opinion that it is absolutely necessary for every person who wants to attain knowledge of God, or that love of God which Jesus describes, to control the flesh. Psychologically speaking, as we explained previously, a mind cannot be interested at the same time in two planes of existence, namely the physical and spiritual. So in order to manifest our spiritual qualities, we must conquer all physical cravings. This does not mean that a spiritual aspirant condemns and destroys the beautiful things of life. He only gives them relative value and prevents his mind from being excited, disturbed, and obsessed by them. When a man has inordinate longing for possessions, accumulations of wealth, and enjoyment of different phases of sense experiences, then alone his mind becomes entangled in them. His mind can hardly rise above these attractions. The major trend of his life remains on the physical plane even though he may have poetic flights and occasional glimpses of higher things. So it is suggested by Jesus Himself and His great followers from time to time that a man has to overcome inordinate cravings of the flesh.

Some Christian devotees argue that if we take that attitude we will negate life and the world. Their point of view is this: This world is created by God; why should not we enjoy the beauty of God's creation? If He did not want us to have satisfaction from physical nature, He would not have made us as we are nor offered to us so many beautiful and enjoyable things. This line of argument seems to be very reasonable from a devotional point of view. They seem to think that those who want to negate the world ("world and life negation") are following negative mysticism. They do not seem to realize that this is not negation of life in the world nor is it negation of the beautiful things that are created by God as objects of the senses. It is only choosing between two interests: the relative and the permanent. Emphasis on the spiritual nature of man and its realization is not negation of life by any means. It is only the fulfillment of life through control of the flesh and its cravings. It is the fulfillment of life through proper emphasis on the true meaning of abiding existence. When a man devotes himself to the realization of his spiritual nature, he only gives emphasis to the highest value of life. Consequently, he shifts the center of his activities from the physical to the spiritual. St. Paul, as a spiritual man, can say that "your body is the temple of the Holy Ghost which is in you."[232] And Jesus spoke of "the temple of his body."[233] Such ideas spiritualize body; they do not materialize spirit. Dr. Schweitzer is thoroughly applying the Christian principle of service and living a life of sacrifice as much as is practical and possible. His noble example is worth imitating, so we feel that this great soul would understand that the conquest of physical craving is only for the renewal of spiritual consciousness in man.

So we have to overcome the causes of unsatisfactory life and its restlessness by changing our thought currents. The world doesn't change; experiences of the world are the same everywhere and at all times. In order to effect a cure, the cause must be removed. In the same way, we must change our corruptible nature, as St. Paul calls it, by transforming it into the celestial or spiritual body. This can be done only by controlling and changing our mental conditions and reactions and not by torturing and tormenting the flesh. The permanent and satisfactory life of peace and happiness that we seek in this world of change is, no doubt, based on our desire for immortality. Yet, in our enthusiasm to attain our objective, we completely ignore the utility of finding a proper method. Permanent peace and happiness, which is equivalent to immortal life, cannot be obtained by corruptible means. In other words, changeable physical and mental conditions cannot give us permanent joy. The corruptible cannot give us the incorruptible unless the very corruptible nature of man, the present state of his life, is changed and transformed. This can only be done by changing the root of corruptibility, as Swami Vivekananda taught and as Jesus held. "If the salt have lost his savour, wherewith shall it be salted?"[234]

This ideal is *not* to be kept apart from everyday life. Many persons think that we may live in a worldly way and if we only believe in certain personalities and go through certain rituals, we are all right. Even some theologians seem to think that if we accept that God historically became human in the form of Jesus, the Christ, then our problems are solved. Thereby we achieve redemption and attain immortal life. According to the Hindu point of view of the teachings of Christ as exemplified by Him, we cannot get immortal, eternal life, merely by acknowledgement of this historical fact or even by the mere acceptance of this personality, for "the devils also believe and tremble."[235] In the Gospel according to St. John it is said: "And the light shineth in darkness; and the darkness comprehended it not."[236] To the Hindu mind, the implication is that comprehension of the light or divinity of Jesus can be attained only when we have the direct awareness or immediate experience of Godhead through the incarnation. When the light comes, ignorance or darkness vanishes. When we really remove darkness, then alone do we have immortal life.

This problem of the flesh is a practical one and a fact of experience. It is not an imaginary or an intellectual problem. Not by changing the concept of life will we be all right nor by going through certain rituals and ceremonies will we be illumined. Our actions are determined by the cravings of the flesh; consequently, we have to change our actions. That is the reason Jesus shows us the way of life.

Jesus and His disciples demonstrated by their lives that a practical change is required. When the Roman soldiers arrested Jesus in the Garden of Gethsemane (we are again using this illustration for emphasis), St. Peter temporarily put on the influence of the flesh and followed what people would call the natural tendency in striking off the ear of one of the soldiers. But later on he understood that he had to change his method of reaction, when Jesus said, "Put up thy sword into the sheath."[237] So Jesus and His followers definitely show us how to live in this world, how to change the thought currents of our lives and actions, and how to react to the real problems of life. These demonstrations show us that we have to change the natural cravings of the flesh. However, it takes considerable time to do this because we have formed certain thought patterns and habits of reaction. Until we become extremely alert and vigilant and tenaciously fight the cravings of the flesh with its natural tendencies, we cannot overcome them so easily. As we have already said, it is graduating from relative to supreme values, from lollipops to bonbons. As Swami Brahmananda declares:

> The mind has to be purged of all attachment; it must be made transparent or it will not be able to catch the reflection of God. True renunciation consists in giving up all attachment for worldly objects to which the mind is bound. When the mind is once

freed from this shackle it will not be affected in the least, even though it is placed in the midst of numberless objects of sense.[238]

This experience is described by St. Paul:

> I knew a man in Christ above fourteen years ago, (whether in the body, I cannot tell; or whether out of the body, I cannot tell: God knoweth;) such an one caught up to the third heaven.
>
> . . . .
>
> How that he was caught up into paradise, and heard unspeakable words.[239]

This is not a question of the acceptance of facts, but it is a question of constant grappling with our own cravings. Consequently, we have to follow systematically a new course of life so that new thought patterns can be established in our consciousness. When that is done by right actions and reactions, then alone there takes place a thorough transformation in the whole of our existence.

Little do we understand that this mind which is now so disturbed and agitated can be made extremely stable and firm. Swami Brahmananda tells us that there is a spiritual mind in everyone in the form of a seed. This has to be developed and nurtured to its full strength in order to understand the very nature of our true Self or God.

> But through *Sadhana* (spiritual practices) a subtle mind opens up—the mind of spirit. That is already in you, but in the form of a germ. In course of time this germ will develop and unfold. The gross mind will lead you to the subtle. The subtle shines forth in the glory of its own self. It is at this stage that you

can have the vision of finer truths. The world with all its diversity will then lose all charm for you. It can delude you no more. Then you will pass your time, day and night, completely lost in the contemplation of God and His glory.[240]

None of us can attain that state of a fully developed spiritual mind unless we go through a series of disciplinary processes. Herein lies the utility of spiritual practices and spiritual living. These two means go together. We are to meditate, pray, and repeat the name of God, at the same time living in a way that all our actions and reactions remind us of the right and higher consciousness of man.

Many people think that disturbing mental conditions will go when they have favorable external conditions. This does not happen because the same mind with its old thought patterns remains. One of the greatest spiritual personalities used to say that even if a person goes to the Himalayas, his mind will go with him. Our impressions and tendencies are still with us even though we may be away from habitation, whether in a convent or a cave. Unless the mind is transformed and its old contents emptied, unless the actions and reactions of the mind are changed, there is no peace. So whether we live in the world, in the busiest city or away from the world in a convent or a monastery, we must change the mental content or thought pattern. The moment our inner nature is thoroughly and completely purified, we can reach that state of illumination "in the twinkling of an eye," as St. Paul says.[241] So spiritual life or the imitation of Christ means the transformation of our mind and its attitudes. This is what the Hindus call *samadhi* or superconscious experience. Inner purification, knowledge of God, or illumination are simultaneous. The moment man's nature is purified, that very moment the Kingdom of God reveals itself, as St. Paul so beautifully declares. When this takes place, we will attain immortality.

Another fact we learn from Easter is that a man can overcome and defy death. How can we do that when we all know that at some time or other this cruel death will come to us? However we may hate it, it is a constant companion, an inevitable fact. If there is anything certain in this life, it is that death is sure to come to every one of us. Sometimes people say that they do not talk or think of it, for what is the use of being a pessimist? The thought of death is not pessimism; it is the understanding of a real fact. It is an expression of realism; it is an understanding of life which has various stages. This body is born and goes through certain changes which lead ultimately to death. But death is not the end of everything. When we are illumined, our ignorance will vanish and there will be no further cause for birth and death. The man who has reached this state of consciousness is the one who can say: "O death, where is thy sting? O grave, where is thy victory?"[242] Death can be defied only when we have that realization of the abiding presence of God in us. So we learn from Jesus at Easter that we can defy death only by realizing the truth. So the Hindu teacher says: "I have realized this Great Being who shines effulgent like the sun beyond all darkness. One passes beyond death only on realizing Him. There is no other way to escape from the cycle of birth and death."[243] And according to Jesus: "He that heareth my word, and believeth on Him that sent me, hath everlasting life, and shall not come into condemnation; but is passed from death unto life."[244]

---

222. I Cor. 15:34, 42, 44.
223. Works, II, 17.
224. Prov. 4:23.
225. Mark 7:15.
226. I Cor. 13:11.
227. Ibid., 15:39-40.
228. Edgar Sheffield Brightman, A Philosophy of Religion (New York: Prentice-Hall, Inc., 1940), p. 409.
229. Matt. 26:41.
230. I Cor. 15:50.
231. Schweitzer, Indian Thought and Its Development, passim.
232. I Cor. 6:19.
233. John 2:21.
234. Matt. 5:13.
235. James 2:19.
236. John 1:5.
237. John 18:11.
238. Spiritual Teachings of Swami Brahmananda, p. 146.
239. II Cor. 12:2, 4.
240. Spiritual Teachings of Swami Brahmananda, p. 126.
241. I Cor. 15:52.
242. Ibid., 15:55.
243. Svetesvatara Upanishad III:8.
244. John 5:24.

CHAPTER IX

TEACHING AND PREACHING

Abide in me, and I in you. As the branch cannot bear fruit of itself, except it abide in the vine; no more can ye, except ye abide in me.

I am the vine, ye are the branches: He that abideth in me and I in him, the same bringeth forth much fruit: for without me, ye can do nothing.

If a man abide not in me, he is cast forth as a branch, and is withered; and men gather them, and cast them into the fire, and they are burned.[245]

. . . .

As the Father hath loved me, so have I loved you: continue ye in my love.

If ye keep my commandments, ye shall abide in my love; even as I have kept my Father's commandments, and abide in his love.[246]

In these few words Jesus points out the real source of power. There are persons who often ask nowadays about the dynamics of religion: "What can religion give us?"

Many persons actually want to know the real power that is behind religion. Why should anyone be interested in religion? Take, for instance, the psychologists and social scientists. They have no interest in it unless it can do something for society. An outstanding psychologist was telling us one day about his attitude toward religion. We asked him directly: "Do you consider religion something useful, or are you interested in it at all?" His answer was direct. "My interest in religion is from the psychological point of view. If it can integrate a personality, then I shall accept it because it is useful."

Many social scientists want to know what religion can do to improve society. They have written many articles and a number of books about the social conditions in our industrial civilization.[247] Elton Mayo of Harvard University, an outstanding thinker, has written books which are widely read.[248] There is in them a considerable number of ideas based on scientific observation which inevitably attracts the mind of the thinking public. Dr. Mayo's works and the investigations of other such thinkers show that the social scientists are frightened by the serious social problems in this industrial civilization. Naturally, some of them ask: "Can religion help us?" In the course of a discussion with us regarding industrial civilization and its problems, the dean of one of the most important universities in the East stated that the Church has failed to solve the complex problems of our age. It goes without saying that many of the outstanding social scientists and teachers of industrial and commercial studies feel the same way. It seems to us that Mr. Ingersoll has not been the only person to make the declaration that Christianity is obsolete and incompatible with industrial civilization. Many social scientists and industrial leaders have directly and indirectly expressed this attitude to us. That is the very reason the books which are being written for the improvement of the social structure and relations between labor and management do not contain statements as to the real value of religion in the solution of the complex problems of the age.

Religion can help society, provided we properly understand it and apply its principles to individual life. It is often said by many thinkers that religion is purely individualistic, that man's religious life and his peace and happiness are for his own personal enjoyment or satisfaction; but what good is there in it for society? During our college days, a prominent English missionary taught us the constitutional history of Europe. He was considered an authority in India by the English professors of European history. On one occasion he was teaching us what they used to call the three R's—Rennaissance, Reformation, and Revolution. When discussing the Reformation, he was extremely enthusiastic in condemning the monastic orders. He told us of the abuses, which we know existed; but he also emphasized that monks and nuns were selfish and that they went away from society to the monasteries and convents to get personal satisfaction in religion; they ran away from the actual problems of life and remained isolated in monastic and conventual life to avoid the various members of society and problems of the world. When I challenged him, he asked at once: "What is the ideal of the Hindu and Buddhist monks?" I explained: "The vow they take is for the good of many and the happiness of many and for realizing God and helping others to realize God. These are the ideas which form part of their vows." The life of St. Francis of Assisi and his followers proved convincingly that monastic life was not a selfish attitude nor was it meant for mere personal satisfaction. It is an undeniable fact that members of various monastic orders in Christian communities prove without the least shade of doubt that even now monks and nuns are following the example of St. Francis and are functioning for the good and happiness of many.

Many persons even question the validity of religious life. Some of them, however, accept the validity of religion from the ethical point of view; that is, it helps society because it inspires men and women with the higher ideals of brotherhood, equality, etc. When we study the lives of great mystics, we find quite different views and expressions of religion from those that have been given by many progressive thinkers.

In the first place, religion must affect the lives of individuals. It is true that religious practices are considerably individualistic, yet the individuals who are transformed by them contribute greatly to society. However, there are certain religious practices which are performed in groups. Singing of hymns, community worship, and prayer are used in all religions. These practices bring different individuals together, creating fellowship and friendliness among those who join in community practices. These practices are indeed very helpful for cultural unification and social improvement. Christians, Hindus, Mohammedans, and Buddhists all share in this view. When we say that religious practices are individualistic, we do not mean thereby that they are likely to make one egocentric or self-centered. We mean that the individuals follow their particular exercises according to their mental constitutions and they grow mentally in God-consciousness in their personal experience. Nevertheless, there are certain practices that can be shared in groups and which are helpful for the various members.

It may be construed that we are overemphasizing individual development without giving any real value to community life. It may also appear that we are coming to the position of the thinkers who consider that individuals will be moral but society will remain immoral. We do not in any way mean to imply that conclusion. What we really want to clarify is that emphasis must be given to individual growth, as the powers, energies, and ways of different individuals vary; therefore their growth in spirituality will also vary. We fully realize that the community life of individual spiritual persons is of great importance. In fact, when an incarnation comes to the world, he gathers around him a number of highly evolved spiritual persons who band together. This is the beginning of what the Christians call the Church, and what the Buddhists and Hindus call *Sangha*. Jesus gathered around Him a band of disciples. The Last Supper is a typical example of the solidification of the spirit of unity. The Christian Church was really established there. The individuals of that group in turn attracted a number of persons to them, and in the course of time their followers attracted innumerable adherents. In this way they gradually established what is known as the Christian community. The different monastic orders, the monastic and lay brothers, and the later brotherhoods among the Christians were all of great importance in fostering the spirit of Jesus. Lay or monastic brotherhood and sisterhood are of great importance in the development of individuals, as they mutually help one another in keeping the religious ideal bright and in disseminating the spirit of the ideal to others.

It should be remembered that Buddha organized such communities by gathering His disciples together. He first inspired them with the ideal of religious development and consecrated service of mankind. Buddhist community life can be regarded as the first organized church or *Sangha* in the history of the world. Throughout the world's history we find that when an incarnation or great spiritual personality draws different persons to him, they grow individually yet live a community life for the good and happiness of many as well as for mutual inspiration and help. From the time of Buddha to Sri Ramakrishna, the great nineteenth century spiritual personality of India, Indian religious teachers have recognized the necessity of community life for the good of the individuals concerned and for society at large. The *Sangha* (Order) of Sri Ramakrishna was also started in the same way as the Buddhist and Christian groups. So we fully recognize the utility of community life, understanding at the same time that people's spiritual growth is individual. As they develop individually, they become powerful agents of community development. Society goes through a change because of the spiritual dynamics of individual personalities. The influence of such integrated personalities is felt as they change the thought current of masses.

So religious dynamics can be found both in the lives of individuals and in the community. St. Francis of Assisi became powerful when he was transformed by his religious experiences. We know that he was the son of a wealthy man and that he was enjoying the world just as any wealthy young man would do. Yet when he had the spiritual experiences after his return from Southern Italy, his life was wholly changed, so much so that he did not find any interest in the worldly pursuits of his colleagues and friends. He translated into action the ideas and ideals which he realized in the course of his spiritual experiences. He felt the oneness of life and existence; consequently, he became the true servant of humanity, nay, of all beings. That is the very reason he could say "Brother Wolf" and "Sister Moon"; he felt the presence of God in all.

The life of St. Paul also demonstrates that after his personal transformation through the power of his dynamic religious experiences he could really be the true servant of man. The Christian Church is deeply indebted to him and his services. There have been many personalities who first had religious realization and then became servants of man. In fact, to make a bold statement, these transformed personalities are the best servants of human society.

As the real dynamics of religion are in the transformation of individual life, we must go through certain disciplinary practices to change not only our ideas but also our emotions. Very few persons realize that the emotions cannot be integrated unless we go through certain disciplinary processes. Some may ask: "Why is this called religion? Let us call it ethics." They may want to call it ethics, but it is necessary to go a little further than that. Ethics, no doubt, teaches us moral principles and moral values. An ethical man must be established in moral principles and live the life of ethical values. Morality is the beginning of religious development, but it is not the end of it. Religion goes a little further than morality. Some people think that certain groups of religious people are non-ethical, but it is far from the truth. If a religion is worth anything it must be based on the higher principles of ethics which make the foundation on which the superstructure of religion is built.

Religion is primarily concerned with awareness of God. We cannot be aware of God if our minds are extremely restless and disturbed by the small petty things of the world. If we are agitated by our emotional urges, by our lower propensities, we cannot become God-conscious. Sri Ramakrishna gives us a beautiful illustration in this connection. If we want to see the reflection of our face in the mirror, the glass must be clean; if it is covered with dust and dirt, we cannot see our image. Similarly, if the lake is full of ripples and waves, we cannot see our face reflected there; but if the water is calm we can see our reflection. Similarly, when our minds are pure, clean, clear, and transparent, then alone can we see the reflection or image of God and feel His presence. "For now we see through a glass, darkly; but then face to face."[249] In order to be aware of God, we must make the mind strong and integrated; otherwise, it is not possible. The primary function of religion is to make us realize God directly or be aware of God immediately. In other words, it must be more than just intellectual conception and mere ethical observances.

When we study the lives of the great spiritual personalities, we find that all of them become aware of God by transforming their minds. So we have to become purely ethical first in order to become aware of God. According to some schools of Vedanta, one has to purify the mind and then the knowledge of the Reality flashes simultaneously. When we are prepared for it, we have the realization automatically; we do not have to go through any ritual or ceremony. Some thinkers emphasize this inner purification so that the knowledge of God will come spontaneously. There are others who perform religious or devotional exercises, worship, and other such practices to make the mind one-pointed and single. The purpose of religious practices is to make the mind concentrated so that it can constantly think of God. For instance, meditation or worship makes our minds single and one-pointed so that the waves of the mind, the different states of the mind, may be kept quiet and directed to the object of meditation—an aspect of God. When a person reaches that state of concentration, he realizes or experiences God.

A person of that experience is a dynamic person. He does not sit passively to enjoy it; he feels an urge to share his knowledge with others. There are, however, those among the illumined souls who have temperaments which are unsuited for various types of social activity. Their states of spiritual realization do not permit them to indulge in external activities. Nevertheless, their thoughts and prayers are constantly directed for the good of society at large. Their very presence inspires people to live an intense spiritual life. These apparently non-active illumined personalities express their love in such a dynamic way that the people who come in contact with them cannot help feeling the intensity of their love. In fact, the great silent personalities do more good to the world than all the activities of the restless so-called social workers with all their activities. Herein lies the utility of religion in society. Swami Turiyananda, one of the great disciples of Sri Ramakrishna, used to tell some of us that when an aspirant goes through intense spiritual practices he feels a spontaneous desire at a certain stage in his evolution in spiritual realizations to share his experiences with others. This urge is to give and give and give all the spiritual treasures that one possesses.

There have been many persons who seem to think that as soon as they get a glimpse of something religious or have a religious idea, they must go out to teach and preach. They take the inspiration from the utterance of Jesus in which He instructs His disciples to go out and preach the Kingdom of God and heal the people. "And, as ye go, preach, saying, The kingdom of heaven is at hand. Heal the sick, cleanse the lepers, raise the dead, cast out devils: freely ye have received, freely give."[250] Many persons forget that Jesus sent His disciples and not just ordinary individuals like any man on the street corner. They were not ordinary in any sense of the term. They were disciples of Jesus, an incarnation of God, and as such they were transformed personalities and illumined souls. Jesus "gave them power"[251] before he asked them to preach. They were fit vehicles to transmit the power of religion to others. What we imply is that religious teaching or preaching can be properly conducted by those who have had religious awakening. We may have intellectual conception; we may indulge in discursive reasoning; we may have theological understanding; yet, if we do not have spiritual power within us, our words will be of very little importance to the people. "... The personality of the man is two-thirds," asserts Swami Vivekananda, "and his intellect, his words, are but one-third. It is the real man, the personality of the man, that runs through us."[252]

We do not minimize the importance of teaching and preaching itself; it is very important in the propagation of religion. Teaching and preaching can be done in two ways. The first is to take responsibility for the students and for their spiritual welfare and illumination. A teacher or preacher of this type necessarily assumes considerable responsibility in order to fulfill that role. When he takes the position of a teacher of religion, he takes a serious step. The man who has that awareness of God, or experience of God, can alone take responsibility for the students. He alone can guide one properly and thoroughly, because a man of God-consciousness can really understand the requirements of the individual. He can feel the nature of the mind; he can understand and actually see the contents of the minds of his friends, students, and disciples; and then he can properly guide and help them. When a man is established in higher realization, his mind becomes completely transparent and free from all preconceived notions and ideas; consequently, he can immediately understand the very nature of his disciples. He can understand the distinct qualities of each particular mind. The relation between such a teacher and student must be extremely harmonious and loving. A teacher goes through the difficulties of imparting knowledge to the student only because of his intense love for him. He must have faith in his student, believing that the student is capable of learning what he has to teach. The teacher through his deep understanding also knows the future possibilities of the student, and his conviction and faith brings out the student's latent possibilities.

A great spiritual personality who is perfectly established in higher realization can transmit knowledge of God to a disciple even if the disciple has not undergone spiritual practices. The disciples of such great teachers can also awaken latent spiritual power and give spiritual realization when they are in that particular mood. Still lesser personalities can help their disciples, too, in awakening spiritual consciousness, provided they, themselves, are established in higher realizations and the students practice according to their advice and directions. Sri Ramakrishna says of teachers:

> He alone is the real teacher who is illuminated by the true knowledge.
>
> . . . .
>
> . . . but all rush to lecture or preach with only a bit of book knowledge in their pocket. Strange indeed. To teach others is the most difficult of tasks. He alone can teach who gets commission from God after attaining Him.
>
> . . . .
>
> To explain God after merely reading the Scriptures is like explaining to another the City of Benares after seeing it only in a map.[253]

St. Paul asks, "Are all teachers?" and clearly expects a negative answer.[254] On the other hand, if anyone takes up the role of teacher without a clear understanding of the psychological requirements of his friends and students, he is likely to confuse and mislead them. "And if the blind lead the blind, both shall fall into the ditch."[255] Individuals have many inherent tendencies which remain in a subtle state in the form of *samskaras.* Swami Vivekananda explains them:

> "Samskara" can be translated very nearly by *inherent tendency.*
>
> . . . .
>
> . . . each action is like the pulsation quivering on the surface of the lake. The vibration dies out and what is left? The Samskaras, the impressions. When a large number of these impressions is left on the mind they coalesce, and become a habit. It is said, 'habit is second nature;' it is first nature also, and the whole nature of man; everything that we are is the result of habit. That gives us consolation, because if it is only habit, we can make and unmake it any time. The *Samskaras* are left by these vibrations passing out of our mind, each one of them leaving its result. Our character is the sum total of these marks, and according as some particular wave prevails one takes that tone.[256]

These *samskaras* or subtle impressions are very powerful even though they may not be known to the person. This is the very reason that many religious leaders who do not have a deeper understanding of human nature cannot really understand the underlying problems of their students. It will not be out of place to remember here that modern psychoanalysts often take the role of teacher of the human mind. The human mind, as we know, has many complex urges in the conscious as well as in the unconscious realm, and these urges often create conflicts and complexes. In order to stabilize the mind, the conflicts must be dissolved. A real spiritual teacher can understand the inherent tendencies, inner conflicts, and subtle impressions of the past in the disciple, as his own mind is illumined and integrated. The psychoanalysts who assume the role of teacher or guide for the integration of the mind, practically (although unconsciously), take the position of a knower of the inner activities of the mind. It has been observed that in spite of their good work, many of them have only an interpretive knowledge of the mind; they do not have direct understanding of the mind of the client. In spite of their good intentions, they will find it very difficult to give stable guidance for the integration of mind and removal of conflict. This is especially important in the person who takes the role of a teacher of religion. If he does not clearly understand the psychological requirements of a student, he cannot properly guide and help the student to grow spiritually. "The things of the spirit of God . . . are spiritually discerned."[257] As a Hindu understands it, spiritual growth depends on the unification and integration of the mind. As we mentioned in Chapter III, Patanjali says: "Yoga is restraining the mind-stuff (Chitta) from taking various forms (Vrittis)."[258] Swami Vivekananda says of this aphorism:

> Then there is the state called Sattva, serenity, calmness, in which the waves cease, and the water of the mind-lake becomes clear. It is not inactive, but rather intensely active. It is the greatest manifestation of power to be calm. It is easy to be active.

> Let the reins go, and the horses will run away with you. Any one can do that, but he who can stop the plunging horses is the strong man. Which requires the greater strength, letting go, or restraining? The calm man is not the man who is dull. You must not mistake Sattva for dullness, or laziness. The calm man is the one who has control over the mind waves. . . . The 'one-pointed' form is when it tries to concentrate and the 'concentrated' form is what brings us to Samadhi.[259]

When a man reaches this state or has deep concentration, he is mentally integrated. He is then capable of helping others to integrate their minds.

Apart from that, there are various predominant characteristics of the individual mind such as the active, meditative, devotional, and intellectual. If the teacher of religion does not understand the predominant characteristics of his student, he cannot help him in his growth. Hindus are convinced that religion is not a superimposition from the outside but it is a process of inner evolution and ultimate realization of God. Therefore, the different students are to be led to the goal by the teacher according to their individual tendencies.

Active persons can reach superconscious realization through the performance of unselfish work without attachment for personal profit and without unhappiness at apparent failure. There is a technique for doing this work.[260] People must forget themselves in the action and also completely forget the result that is going to be achieved. With this method devotional persons constantly remember God in and through their actions, and intellectual persons remember the Absolute and feel oneness in the universe. They try to see the manifestation of God in all and serve them accordingly, with love and devotion. The path of action has no place for restless activity, and those who follow it must always beware of ambition and so-called self-expression, or aggrandizement of the ego. Success in work and action does not mean external achievement; it is rather inner purification and conquest of the lower self; it is subjective rather than objective; it leads its adherents to a peaceful state of mind in the conquest of desire for the fruit of action.

Those who are predominantly meditative by nature should be guided in the methods of concentration and meditation. Hindus realize the utility of the practice of concentration and meditation, and they are entirely convinced that without this one cannot expect to gather mental forces which are dissipated by emotional urges and conflicts. Steady practice relaxes the mind; the restless thoughts become single and one-pointed; and then the nervous system becomes quiet. When concentration is very deep and the mind does not waver but remains focused on the object of thought, a symbol of God, then it becomes meditation. The mind flows continuously to the object without any cessation. There is no succession of thoughts; the mind is unified. The practice of concentration is, no doubt, the kernel of religious development. Without it no one can ever expect to reach the highest state of spiritual realization. It is needed more or less in every path in different ways.

Emotional persons should use their emotions in attaining spiritual realization through the path of love and devotion. As the vast majority of the people in the world are predominantly emotional, it is both convenient and necessary for them to use their emotions for higher spiritual development. All the emotions characteristic in human relationships—mother-child, husband-wife, master-servant, lover-beloved, and friend—can be applied to God according to individual temperaments and requirements. Emotions are great powers, and students should be helped to direct them to an aspect of God suitable to their particular characteristics. Auxiliary methods, such as external and internal (or mental) worship can be used to help the students to think of God. Repetition of the name of God is of immense help in remembering Him. Many great personalities have reached higher mystical experiences through this practice.

Persons of the intellectual type follow the rationalistic method of distinguishing the truth from the untruth and the real from the unreal by using the power of discrimination and analysis. An adamantine will is required for this method, as transitory phenomena and non-essentials have to be negated and rejected in order to understand and know the permanent Reality. The emotions must be controlled and regulated; in fact, no emotional expression should be permitted because any kind of emotional expression presupposes plurality and duality. Followers of this path must constantly think of unity. Anything that arouses the consciousness of multiplicity should be rejected. In order to achieve the consciousness of unity, the power of concentration and will must be developed. The practice of concentration and meditation is very difficult in this path as the mind has to be focused on a non-bodily impersonal aspect of God or the Absolute, which is formless, nameless, and attributeless — Existence-Knowledge-Bliss — Absolute. So this intellectual method is not appropriate for the average man and woman, who is conscious only of forms, names, and attributes on the relative plane of existence.

We realize from the preceding paragraphs that religious training is considerably complicated; it requires not only insight into the tendencies of the student but it also requires tremendous personal development to lead him to the desired goal by his individual method. It also requires tremendous patience and love on the part of the teacher, as the student cannot suddenly make progress due to his old thought patterns and ways of living. That is the very reason the Hindus feel that unless a person is thoroughly qualified he can hardly play the role of a first-class teacher and follow the first method of teaching, as we have already mentioned. Jesus sent His disciples out to teach and preach, as He knew that they were capable of following the first method in assuming reposibility for the spiritual development and ultimate realization of God of their own disciples. He said to them: "As my Father hath sent me, even so send I you."[261]

The second method of teaching and preaching is to share one's own knowledge and understanding with others. In this way, the person is not taking responsibility for the growth and development or for the illumination of any students. It is a kind of recapitulation of what the person has learned, and if anyone is benefited thereby in hearing it, he is welcome to it. It is thinking aloud. As a young man, one of our Swamis was asked by our master, Swami

Brahmananda, to go and teach the people. This young Swami was very humble and, of course, he should have been humble in the presence of such a great teacher. He showed reluctance to assume the role of teacher, but Swami Brahmananda at once answered: "Go and teach what you have learned from us." It is a very significant fact that one can teach in this way, such as: "I learned this from a great personality, and I am telling it to you. It is your task to apply these principles in your life."

There are, however, some persons who are too enthusiastic in converting others or in "saving the souls" of others. As previously mentioned, to save the souls of others is a very important and serious affair in the spiritual field. The personalities who can really do this are few and far between in this world. Those who are enthusiastic to "save the souls" of men are not always actually in a position to do so. What they mean by saving souls is to put a label on the individual, that he is so-and-so and belongs to such and such a group because he has undergone a particular ceremony. Or the moment he joins an institution or an organization he is saved. Would to God it could happen in this way; but, unfortunately, it does not.

About thirty-five years ago, or more, we heard from a friend in India about a number of very humble persons; they were washermen who were converted to Christianity by a very sincere person who believed that by converting them he would rescue their souls. Of course, after these humble persons were converted, they changed their style of dress because they were expecting something to happen to them. When nothing happened, they went to the person who converted them, saying: "What is the matter?

We do not find any change. What shall we do?" He replied: "Well, go and do the same thing that you have being doing." So they had to go back to their washing. Although they were formally and officially converted to Christianity, nothing happened to them, even though they began to use the Western costume. Those people were extremely disturbed because they got nothing out of it and they lost all faith and attraction for the new way of life.

Anyone, even the very sincere person, makes a blunder when he thinks he can rescue the soul of an individual by changing the label of his religion. One can really rescue the soul of a person only when he transforms the personality. In order to do that he must be a dynamic, spiritual person himself. If a person has lower passions or desires, he cannot transmit the knowledge which will transform the people because he does not have it to give.

An awakened soul can kindle spiritual aspiration and potential power of an individual soul by his very presence. We have seen in our humble experiences that a few words from an illumined soul can change a person's whole life. Sometimes this happens by a mere touch. When Swami Vivekananda was living in Madras before coming to this country, many young scholars visited him. One of them liked to argue, and the Swami was very fond of him because of his brilliancy. One day this young professor was delayed in going with his friends to see the Swami and they went along without him. The group assembled and the students were talking with Swami Vivekananda when he suddenly entered into deep silence. While he was in that mood, no one dared to disturb him. Just then the young man arrived and saluted the Swami by touching his feet, according to the Hindu custom. Swami Vivekananda was startled from his absorbed state and exclaimed: "What have you done! Now you will no longer be able to keep your mind on transitory things." It was true that the young man's life was thoroughly changed as a result of touching Swami Vivekananda while he was in that high spiritual mood, and he spent the rest of his life in spiritual practices. There were many such occasions in the presence of Swami Brahmananda and other disciples of Sri Rramakrishna. Many religious people can testify to such facts. The teaching of religion requires no propaganda; it rather becomes contagious when taught by transformed personalities. This is recognized by P. Chenchiah, an Indian Christian leader, who writes:

> Souls who caught the inspiration of a new faith kindled hearts even without conscious effort and these carried the message far and wide. The three Acharyas — Sankara, Ramanuja and Madhwa — spread their creeds all over India without any organised band of preachers. Spiritual contagion — not conscious propaganda — was the real missionary. It was literally true in India that people caught religion as they caught cold.[262]

Another expression of religious dynamics is in society itself. How can society be transformed? Some thinkers seem to believe that society must always remain immoral, as we have already mentioned. It may be true that in certain periods of history society is immoral; yet when an individual is spiritually transformed, his influence affects society tremendously. In fact, the whole ideal of a society is changed. Let us refer to the great mystics of the Middle

Ages in Europe. We all know what the condition of Christianity was during their lifetime. If personalities like St. Francis, St. Anthony, and some others had not come at that period, Christianity would have been practically lost without their influence. John Wesley, the founder of the Methodist Church, really saved England from a social revolution. His influence with that of a few others changed the thought current of the people in England. We also know what the condition of India was at the time Buddha appeared in the sixth century B. C.

In spite of the lofty teachings of the *Upanishads,* India had become extremely devoted to rituals and ceremonies, and the deeper spirit of religion was lost; consequently, society was in a disorganized state. It was Buddha who really changed the outlook of the people. The civilization that flourished after his advent was one of the most glorious periods in the history of India. What were the Jews and Romans just before the advent of Christ? As we have already stated, they were extremely ritualistic and materialistic. Although the Jews thought they were chosen people of God, they had forgotten the spirit of religion. Jesus was just one person; yet, He introduced the dynamics of religion into the lives of the Jews and Gentiles and changed the whole coloring of civilization. It was the influence of Jesus that changed the civilization of Europe and the Western part of Asia.

Nowadays, many of the liberal thinkers, especially reformers inspired by Marxian philosophy, condemn the teachings of religion. They certainly have a right to criticize the abuses of religion but when they generalize and state that the abuses are true religious expressions, then they are mistaken. They learned the glorious ideas of equality, brotherhood, etc., from Jesus and His followers and from earlier prophets, as we expressed in Chapter V. It goes without saying that Europe and America would even now be most uncivilized places if the influence of Jesus had not penetrated into the lives of the people. We find that individuals like Krishna, Buddha, Jesus, and others actually changed the ideal of society and the course of civilization. As the philosopher Höffding said, "Buddha 'softened' Asia, but Jesus taught Europe a great Excelsior."[263]

History shows that after the advent of great spiritual personalities, a civilization reaches its culmination. It develops an all-round culture; and philosophy, literature, art, and music flourish. The influence of Jesus was thoroughly felt in different spheres of life of the early Christians. There is even considerable spiritual awakening when still lesser personalities appear, such as St. Bernard, St. Ignatitus, St. Teresa, and St. John of the Cross, John Wesley, Jacob Boehme, and George Fox. We find that every one of them had tremendous influence in certain areas of their countries. At about the same time, there were a number of similar personalities in different parts of India and every one of them exerted a considerable amount of influence regarding religious methods. Their contributions were as great as those of the medieval Christian mystics. However, in the course of time, the influence of the great spiritual personalities declines; and gradually society becomes immoral. Another dynamic spiritual personality is needed to inspire the people again.

If smaller personalities than the incarnations and the

saints want to do some good to the world, they can do so either by silent spiritual living or by sharing their experiences with others. If anyone feels that he wants to establish a stable society, as the social scientists such as Professor Elton Mayo and others are anxious to do, he must change his personal life. Unless he does so, he cannot help others to do the same. We had the pleasure of discussing this very point with the psychiatrist, Professor Carl Jung of Zurich, and we talked about the utility and effect of meditation in personal and collective life. He seemed to understand its utility and after our discussion he said: "Well, I understand, Swami, that you mean this. If I do not keep my garden clean and orderly I cannot go and tell my neighbor to keep his garden clean and orderly." So it is, that unless we integrate our own minds through spiritual practices, we cannot go and tell others to integrate their minds. If parents lose their tempers every other moment, they cannot tell their children not to lose their tempers. It is a mistake that parents often commit. They want their children to be extremely nice, and it is natural that they would want this, yet if they express lower tendencies and urges they cannot expect their children to be integrated personalities. It is very interesting to note that children learn lying from their parents, although they do not realize this. We happen to know of occasions in which the child answers the telephone when a call comes and the mother instructs the child to say that she is out. This is the beginning of lying. The child learns to lie from the mother; yet when the child lies to the mother, she is extremely annoyed. But you cannot expect him not to lie when he is actually being taught to do it. Many of our shortcomings are transferred to our children thoughtlessly.

So we come to the conclusion that if we want to stabilize the family or society we must express religious dynamics ourselves. If we continue lower habits such as lying or expressing vile tempers, we cannot expect our children or any others to be different. Neither can we expect to find religious idealism in the lives of others unless we ourselves live the life. It is our duty to be inspired by the declaration of Jesus that "ye shall abide in my love." All religions are one in their conviction that the real religious dynamics lies in the transformation of the individual. If only a handful of persons are thoroughly inspired by the ideal and demonstrate it in their lives, society and the world will be changed. This is doubtless what Jesus had in mind when He sent His disciples out to preach. Professor Cadbury writes: "It has been truly said that Jesus believed that character should transform environment, and not vice versa . . ."[264]

---

245. John 15.4-6.
246. Ibid., 15:9-10.
247. Pitirim A. Sorokin, **The Crisis of Our Age and The Reconstruction of Humanity** (Boston: Beacon Press, 1948) are outstanding examples.
248. Elton Mayo, **The Social Problems of an Industrial Civilization** (Boston: Division of Research, Graduate School of Business Administration, Harvard University, 1945); and **The Human Problems of Industrial Civilization** (Boston: Division of Research, Graduate School of Business Administration, Harvard University, 1946).
249. I Cor. 13:12.
250. Matt. 10:7-8; Luke 9:2.
251. Matt. 10:1; Luke 9:1.
252. **Works**, II, 15.
253. **Sayings of Sri Ramakrishna** VIII:205, 210, IX:221.
254. I Cor. 12:29.
255. Matt. 15:14.
256. **Works**, I, 52, 207-208.

257. I Cor. 2:14.
258. Works, I, 200.
259. Ibid., 202-203.
260. Ibid., I, 23-116.
261. John 20:21.
262. P. Chenchiah, "The Church and the Indian Christian," Rethinking Christianity in India (2nd ed.; Madras: A. N. Sudarisanam, 1939), p. 97.
263. Harald Höffding, The Philosophy of Religion (London: Macmillan & Co., Ltd., 1914), p. 304.
264. Henry J. Cadbury, The Peril of Modernizing Jesus (New York: The MacMillan Co., 1937), p. 116.

CHAPTER X

CHRISTIAN MISSIONS

> And, as ye go, preach, saying, The kingdom of heaven is at hand.
>
> Heal the sick, cleanse the lepers, raise the dead, cast out devils: freely ye have received, freely give.[265]
>
> . . . .
>
> And he said unto them, go ye into all the world, and preach the gospel to every creature.[266]

In the light of the previous chapter, the thought of missionary activities will arise in the mind of every thinking person. What should be the place of these activities, according to the Hindu view? There have been many adverse criticisms of Christian missions in India. On the other hand, the Christians seem to be extremely enthusiastic in the propagation of the faith and in "saving souls." It is true that missionary activities in Oriental countries, especially India, have gone through considerable change in the course of the last fifty years; but there still remains a great deal of confusion in the minds of the Hindus and both Eastern and Western Christians. It is high time that the thinking public had a clear understanding of the very nature of Christian missionary activities in the light of the teachings of Jesus.

The above quotations from the teachings of Jesus are the basis of Christian missionary work. Such activities are inspired by one of the noblest sentiments of religious development. As we mentioned in the previous chapter, when a man is inspired by higher spiritual ideals and goes through intense spiritual practices he has a strong desire to share his experiences with others. We made it clear that a kind of missionary work or teaching or preaching forms a part of the spiritual experiences in the lives of many dynamic spiritual personalities. The dynamics of religion is expressed through sharing with others and doing good to them, as Jesus taught when He said "Thou shalt love thy neighbor."[267] This is the tendency of all great spiritual personalities. The great modern spiritual leader, Sri Ramakrishna, and His disciples, such as Swami Vivekananda, Swami Brahmananda, and others, expressed this sentiment in a very emphatic way in their lives, teachings, and activities. Buddha and His disciples expressed this same ideal about six centuries before the advent of Jesus. So it goes without saying that a certain type of missionary activity and teaching of religion is an important part of religious dynamics.

No Hindu of real spiritual culture could gainsay this in the light of the teachings of their spiritual leaders. Until recently, Hinduism has not been a missionary religion like Buddhism, Christianity, and Islam, though the influence of the Hindu religion was spread through personal contact and teaching. It is worthwhile for every missionary worker to note the difference between these three great religious missionary groups. Buddhism is the first religion in the world's history to express missionary zeal and conduct organized missionary activities. There is an interesting phase of these activities in the principles enunciated by the early founders and inspirers. We are told that Asoka, the great Buddhistic emperor of India, advised the missionaries of Buddhism to go and teach the gospel of Buddha based on the fundamental "four noble truths,"[268] as revealed and taught by Buddha. He emphatically told them not to disturb the existing religious concepts of the people and not to create any discord in them but, as fellow workers and ambassadors of Buddha, to spread the message of love and peace as given by Him. As we understand from the declarations of Asoka and from historical evidence, Buddhist missionaries never created or supported any discordant or destructive activities in any society in which they lived or visited.

Next, the great Christian missionary movement, preceded and inspired either by Buddhistic influence or its own dynamics, expressed itself in the form of the Christian mission. Historically, the Mohammedan missionary movement followed that of Christianity.

As we observed in the last chapter, missionary activities can be carried on in two ways: saving the souls of others or sharing with others. Ancient Hinduism and modern Hinduism (known by many Occidental scholars as neo-Hinduism or the Vedanta movement), follows the second method. They do not exactly follow the methods of the Christian missionaries in general. They do not use expressions such as "saving the soul" of man. By advocating the method of sharing spiritual teachings with others, they teach the people who want to be taught. Some Christians also follow this method. It is not incompatible with the spirit of Hindu thought that religious dynamics makes a well-established religious personality strong enough spiritually to transform the personalities of others. According to the Hindus, the *guru* (spiritual teacher), plays a very great part in the life of his disciples. As a spiritual teacher of the highest type he takes the responsibility for the welfare of his disciples; he is supposed to transmit spiritual power to them in the course of teaching them spiritual practices. He is actually helping the personalities to grow in spiritual illumination. So, in that sense, a spiritual teacher can be regarded as a transformer of souls or an illuminer of inner life.

Christian missionary activities have not been conducted in the same way as those of the Hindus in the present era. As we observed in the last chapter, the saving of souls can be done only by illumined personalities of the highest type. The life of Mary Magdalene is an illustration. Many Christian mystics have transformed the personalities of others. Sri Ramakrishna not only influenced but He also transformed many personalities like Mary Magdalene. In our own humble experiences we have seen that His disciples also have done the same. So the saving of souls can be done only by such truly spiritual personalities.

We are firmly convinced that sharing of religious experiences should be the basis of missionary activities of any group. In general, that is the safest attitude. Any Hindu of real spiritual understanding cannot help but support the Christian missionary activities in India on this basis.

Missionary work and conversion go together. So one would naturally ask what the attitude of the Hindus is toward conversion. First, we should have a clear conception of the meaning of conversion. Many theologians seem to think that it necessarily means a change from the sinful state to spiritual understanding and experience. This presupposes that in order to be converted, a person must be sinful. When a Christian converts an individual, he presupposes that the individual is in a sinful state. From St. Paul to the present day missionaries, Christians have indicated that conversion means a transformation from degradation to the saving of souls or illumination. Various writers in Christendom differ in their descriptions of the process of conversion and its total effect on the life of the converted person. It is worth-while also to remember that there are various interpretations of the ceremony as well as the person who is doing the converting. As it is too well known to Christendom what the various theories, attitudes, and practices of conversion are, it is superfluous to elaborate this idea further. We can only mention in a positive way the view of the Hindus.

Most of the writers of the psychology of religion in Western countries seem to feel that awareness of sin is a necessary condition for the experience of conversion. According to Dr. Starbuck:

> The result of an analysis of these different shades of experience coincides with the common designation of this preconversion state in making the *central fact in it all the sense of sin, while the other conditions are various manifestations of this, as determined, first, by differences in temperament, and, second, by whether the ideal life or the sinful life is vivid in consciousness.*

. . . .

Conversion is a process of struggling away from sin, rather than of striving toward righteousness.

. . . .

The sense of sin and depression of feeling are fundamental factors in conversion if not in religious experience in general.[269]

Professor James voices his approval of Dr. Starbuck's opinion and then adds his own point of view:

> To begin with, there are two things in the mind of the candidate for conversion: first, the present incompleteness or wrongness, the 'sin' which he is eager to escape from and second, the positive ideal which he longs to compass. Now with most of us the sense of our present wrongness is a far more distinct piece of our consciousness than is the imagination of any positive ideal we can aim at. In a majority of cases, indeed, the 'sin' almost exclusively engrosses the attention . . .[270]

But Professor Pratt seems to differ from these two prominent thinkers. He writes:

> But in cases of really significant conversion it is rare indeed that the attention of the individual is riveted on his own sinful nature or his gaze turned chiefly upon the past. There are a number of cases of conversion in the New Testament but in not one of them does the sense of sin play an important part. No better record of real conversion is perhaps anywhere to be found than Harold Begbie's "Twice Born Men," and in not a single case there reported is there any-

> thing really comparable to the "conviction period" of theology and psychology![271]

Our point of view is that Professors Starbuck and James are right so far as some individuals are concerned, although we must make it clear that the word "sinfulness" need not necessarily be present in all the cases they mention. Take, for instance, the episode of St. Paul's conversion. On his way to Damascus, he was planning destructive work when suddenly he had that wonderful experience of Jesus which changed his life. This was, indeed, a conversion of the highest type. There have been some such cases in the religious history of the world. Yet the vast majority of people who seek religion do so because of certain limitations, sufferings, or sinfulness; but it will be extremely partial if we generalize that all cases of conversion are based on "sinfulness" of various types. There is a positive attitude on the part of many real devotees belonging to different religious groups who seek God for the bliss of God. It is evident from the above statements that the Hindus in general seek God for various reasons.

According to the Hindu conception, the very process of conversion does not necessarily imply the conciousness of sin and degradation. Various types of persons seek religion and spiritual experiences, as we mentioned in Chapter III. Those who want to know the truth and realize God or who already have that knowledge and only want to love and enjoy Him are by no means in a state of sin or depravity. Sri Ramakrishna heard about God from His parents and relatives in His childhood so He wanted to verify the very existence of God. A child of His age would have no idea of sin, depravity, or limitation;

He wanted to know God positively and in a dynamic way. The history of the world reveals that there are and have been many persons with the desire for knowing, enjoying, and realizing God. So they seek religion and go through what people call conversion or religious experience. It is clear that there are various processes for conversion. The very word "conversion" implies that a devotee gets some thing that he hitherto never experienced. It is also implied that a man is not at present aware of the presence of God; he becomes conscious of Him in the process of conversion. In some cases this conversion may take place spontaneously without outward external help, as we see in the lives of St. Paul and others. But such persons are few and far between in the history of religion. The majority of persons have to go through what the Christians call baptism and confirmation and what the Hindus call initiation. According to some Hindu authorities, initiation is not only important but it is actually essential for a real experience of conversion. Swami Brahmananda says that to attain "calmness of mind and to avert unsteadiness, initiation or help of a guide is necessary. The spiritual path is a most formidable one, strewn with innumerable pitfalls."[272] With initiation a person is able to focus the mind on a suitable spiritual ideal with the help of the *guru*, or spiritual teacher, and to establish a routine of systematic religious practices.

The word "initiation" needs considerable clarification for the Western mind as it is used in connection with social, fraternal, and other such organizations of the West. In a general sense, these organizations use the word to indicate the ceremony of taking a new member into their ranks. Some of the occult and psychic groups also use the word in a slightly different sense to create a certain mystifying and hazy effect in the minds of the newcomers. For this reason it is important that we make the meaning of initiation clear, according to the Hindu view. As we have already quoted from the teachings of Swami Brahmananda, initiation is absolutely necessary for the spiritual development of the initiate. At the time of initiation, the teacher awakens the spiritual consciousness of the disciple who commits himself wholly to the guidance of the teacher and to God. Commitment and self-surrender are necessary qualifications for the transmittal of power by the teacher and the awakening of spiritual consciousness in the disciple. We can say that this occasion is the beginning of spiritual life. The Hindus regard it as the second or spiritual birth of an individual. Jesus refers to this when He says: "Verily, verily, I say unto thee, Except a man be born again, he cannot see the kingdom of God. . . . That which is born of the flesh is flesh; and that which is born of the Spirit is spirit."[273] The ideas of Jesus and the Hindus can be equated.

It would be wise at this point to clarify the experience of conversion in order to understand the implications of the Hindu conception. Hindus take conversion very seriously, and we are sure that many serious Christians do the same. However, the Hindu view is that affiliation with any religious group does not change the level of religion; whether the label is changed or not, it is an inner transformation; it is a new experience which alters the outlook and ways of life of the person who has been converted. For the sake of proper understanding of the Hindu view of conversion, we are equating this term with initiation, making its significance different from the process of baptism and confirmation. Certain ceremonies are also observed by the Hindus which are similar to baptism; but the conversion experience discussed by Professors James, Starbuck, and Pratt is much deeper than ordinary people consider it. To these outstanding psychologists of religion, the conversion experience is an outstanding event in the course of spiritual growth. According to the Hindu viewpoint, if we equate conversion with initiation, this is indeed the beginning of real spiritual awakening and spiritual experience.

In some cases and to some extent, conversion may be sudden; it also may be a gradual process. We happen to know that when some persons are initiated they undergo a radical change and have definite spiritual experiences which make them directly and immediately aware of the presence of God. We must, however, admit that such cases are rare. The vast majority of the cases go through the gradual process of spiritual development and transformation. Even when they are initiated and converted, they have to go through the process of spiritual practices and gradually attain the ultimate goal of conversion. Although the process is gradual, the converted person feels that something is taking place in his life. The effect is observed in the person according to his predominant tendencies and individual characteristics. If the person has been previously disrupted and disorganized and has lukewarm enthusiasm for spiritual development, then the process of change will be slow even though he may be converted or initiated by a tremendously powerful spiritual personality. If the individual possesses strong disrupting tendencies in the form of subtle impressions (*Samskaras*) in the unconscious mind, it requires time to overcome and change them. A great religious teacher does not usually expect or desire to transform the personality suddenly, because this may create certain unfavorable reactions. According to Swami Brahmananda:

> A wise guide can give an upward lift to the struggling mind, even when it is not mature. Such help also has its dangers. If repeated too often, a greater struggle and a deeper despair may result.[274]

Cases have been known where a "convert" seeks a new conversion annually. Swami Brahmananda used to tell us that such reactions should be avoided. He would always emphasize steady and gradual development of the personality instead of radical and sudden change with the possibilities of a set-back caused by the reactions. It is our deliberate understanding that in the long run the gradual process is more effective, unless a person is converted by a tremendously powerful illumined soul. We must admit that such personalities are very, very rare.

The qualifications of the individual who initiates or converts in the highest sense of the term should be reviewed here. According to the Hindu view, great emphasis is given to the qualifications of the teacher and spiritual guide. "A teacher must be well established in God. He must also be acquainted with the spirit of the scriptures and understand the nature and requirements of the disciple."[275] Suffice it to say that emphasis is given not to the office or religious affiliation but to the personality. If the transformed person or illumined soul gives initiation or converts anyone, there will be an inevitable change in the make-up of the converted individual.

It is often observed that the Hindu teacher prepares and cultivates the soil of the disciple before he sows the seed of the spiritual plant. In other words, a Hindu teacher gives a certain amount of preliminary training so that the disciple can absorb and assimilate later definite spiritual instructions and the transmission of spiritual understanding and experience. This preparation is not mere intellectual or scholastic training. It should be clearly understood that this training is part of initiation or conversion through certain forms of spiritual discipline. A disciple can then develop gradually and ultimately realize the culmination of spiritual development.[276] It should be noted that sometimes a sudden emotional experience is attained during some emotional religious expressions in the form of mass or group movements, such as evangelical activities. It is quite conceivable that in hearing a persuasive evangelical speaker, there arises a kind of emotional excitement even in a so-called "sinful" or weak person. When he hears the appeal from an emotional evangelical leader to "save his soul," a person gets a kind of emotional excitement. But the short-sighted evangelical leader and the so-called converted person become extremely enthusiastic to say the least. It is observed that within a brief time most of these exciting cases do not stand the test of life. Swami Vivekananda describes this type of activity in Hindu and Christian groups as temporary emotional spiritual experiences. He also says that invariably these cases show various reactions. He is of the opinion that, even though some of these people get a certain amount of spiritual exaltation, in the long run they have serious set-backs in normal life. It is also observed that many of them show considerable emotional disruption even after evangelical activities. Professor McVicker Hunt, formerly of Brown University, studied a number of so-called evangelical conversions. His scientific observations tally with the remarks of the illustrious Swami. He says:

> Near this same community . . . emotional revivals were frequently conducted. *We* and certain others attended regularly, entering violently into the experience of conversion. *We* reported that on one evening he and *Ho* "went forward" four times, crying each time, until they were finally informed that once each evening was sufficient. After such experiences the boys present promised each other to give up their perversions. Only a little later, however, . . . these resolves were shattered. Every broken resolve resulted in feelings of guilt which increased with time so that in later adolescence the boys were almost continuously miserable.[277].

So we suggest that the temporary evangelical conversion experience should be supported by regular ethical and psychological training. This should also be followed by systematic spiritual practices in order to change the tendencies, or *Samskaras,* of the subconscious mind in the form of previous impressions.[278] It is definitely observed that such conversion experiences must be strengthened by spiritual discipline and exercises. This is the very reason that the great Christian mystics and Hindu teachers advocate the necessity of religious practices so much. According to St. Augustine:

> For the effect following upon prayer will be excellent in proportion to the fervour of the desire which precedes its utterance. And therefore, what else is intended by the words of the apostle: "Pray without ceasing," than, "Desire without intermission, from Him who alone can give it, a happy life, which no life can be but that which is eternal?" This, therefore, let us desire continually from the Lord our God; and thus let us pray continually.[279]

We find in Theologia Germanica:

> Yet there be certain means thereunto, [to be possessed by the Spirit of God] as the saying is, "To learn an art which thou knowest not, four things are needful." . . . The fourth is to put thy own hand to the work, and practice it with all industry.[280]

St. Thomas Aquinas writes:

> It is therefore evident by way of induction that man's ultimate happiness consists solely in the contemplation of God.[281]

And in her writings St. Teresa says:

> I may speak of that which I know by experience; and so, I say, let him never cease from prayer who has once begun it, be his life ever so wicked; for prayer is the way to amend it, and without prayer such amendment will be much more difficult. . . . And as to him who has not begun to pray, I implore him by the love of our Lord not to deprive himself of so great a good.[282]

Sri Ramakrishna says:

> The practice of meditation on God will create a

> tendency of mind to think of Him spontaneously even at the last moment.
>
> . . . .
>
> Meditate upon God, the sole Existence, Knowledge and Bliss Eternal, and you also shall have bliss.
>
> Mind is like the flame of a lamp. When the wind of desire blows, it is restless; when there is no wind, it is steady. The latter is the state of mind in Yoga. Ordinarily the mind is scattered, one portion here, another portion there. It is necessary to collect the scattered mind and direct it towards one point.[283]

Swami Vivekananda speaks of its utility:

> The greatest help to spiritual life is meditation (Dhyana). In meditation we divest ourselves of all material conditions and feel our divine nature.[284]

And again he declares:

> Meditation is the one thing. Meditate! The greatest thing is meditation. It is the nearest approach to spiritual life—the mind meditating. It is the one moment in our daily life that we are not at all material,—the Soul thinking of Itself, free from all matter,—this marvelous touch of the Soul![285]

We make bold to say that without systematic spiritual exercises the emotions are not integrated; consequently, real spiritual experiences, which are the objective of so-called conversion, cannot be attained.

Professor Pitirim A. Sorokin has a great deal to say about personal development in his recent book, *The Reconstruction of Humanity*.

It will not be out of place to mention that many of the Christian preachers do not seem to be very conscious of the necessity of spiritual practices. They seem to think that when a person has gone through formal ritualistic conversion, his religious life is satisfied. Some of the leaders even go so far as to say that spiritual practices are not needed. It is the grace of God and awareness of the historical manifestation of God, in the form of Jesus, that does the job. Soren Kierkegaard is a strong advocate of this viewpoint. Many of his admirers and followers in Europe and America openly and privately support this viewpoint; at least they do not seem to advocate the necessity of spiritual practices, as did the great Christian mystics from St. Paul to John Wesley and George Fox. On the other hand, Hindu teachers feel that without spiritual practices after so-called conversion or initiation, the personality of an individual is not integrated. Some Christian theologians also make it clear that in spite of intellectual flashes and theological flights a man can remain emotionally unintegrated. As we previously mentioned, Karl Barth seems to advocate methods that are against the teachings of Christ in what is regarded as the gospel of love by many devout Christians.

We note with deep appreciation what Professor Northrop has to say:

> Religious reform is essential because the traditional forms of education, political oratory, literature, and religious ceremonies have conditioned the attitudes, feelings, preferences, and spontaneous reactions of men to the old ideology. Consequently, even if one's scientific and philosophic intelligence puts old doctrine behind one, one's emotions, feelings, and habits, and even one's conscience carry them on. It is pre-

cisely for this reason that religious conversion, as well as education, is necessary in society. The old man must be made new.[286]

Hindu teachers and some of the Christian leaders, will agree that the experience of conversion must be followed with definite spiritual practices to integrate and harmonize emotions and ideals. Sri Ramakrishna says that inner and outer life must be harmonious in a spiritual personality. A spiritual teacher who wants to change the life of others and to save the souls of others must save his own soul first. In other words, he must be thoroughly established in God-consciousness by purifying and unifying his own emotions. If the emotions and ideals do not act in harmony and are not synthesized then a teacher cannot really convert a person nor can he inspire and transform an individual. That is the very reason we said in the previous chapter that teaching and preaching must be supported by a dynamic personality. The personality must first grow in the individual and then alone can one have an effective experience of conversion.

It is but natural that the Christian missionaries would like to understand the attitude of the Hindus toward the Christian mission and its various activities. It will be wise for us to remember the conclusions of Chapter I. For clarification and emphasis, we have indulged in repetition.

Insofar as a Hindu takes Jesus as the embodiment of divine love in human form, he worships Jesus as veritable God. Therefore, he understands something of the real spirit of Christianity. So it is obvious that the relationship between Hindus and Christians ought to be harmonious and extremely friendly. Yet in these days of national awakening in India, there have been many questions in the minds of Western Christians as to whether or not they will be welcome in India when India becomes independent. Some of the nationalistic Indian Christians seem to express considerable dissatisfaction toward the Western Christian Church. From a survey of the relation of Christians and Hindus in India, it becomes clear that there are certain reasons for this attitude of dissatisfaction.

According to tradition, St. Thomas began the Christian missionary movement in India when he went there with a number of his followers in the early Christian era. Hindus in general and rulers in particular gave shelter to these religious guests and helped them in their own religious culture. The Hindus were so friendly that they not only allowed the Christians to worship God in their own way but they also co-operated with them and helped them to spread their religious convictions to the people of India. The Christians on the Malabar coast of Southern India will testify how well they have been treated for centuries by the rulers and common people in India. Later on, Portuguese, French, English, and American Christians were also welcomed and accepted as guests of India. They were not only encouraged to worship in their own ways but they were also allowed to convert the Hindus without any hindrance whatsoever. Moreover, they were not molested or insulted even when they condemned and criticized the views and practices of the Hindus. Often these criticisms bespoke of utter misunderstanding and confusion of even the Hindu philosophical and psychological concepts. Although many statements were made carelessly, unjustly, and superficially, no aggressive steps were taken against the Christians for the most part. Answers were in the form of a smile and indifference, as the people knew that many of these missionaries uttered sentiments without understanding them. That is the very reason that Christian missions had few adherents among the scholars and higher classes of the Hindus, even though they accept Christ as an incarnation of God.[287]

So naturally the question arises as to why even the Indian Christians seem to be antagonistic to Western Christians; although we must admit that the Hindus in general do not yet show any animosity toward Western Christians or to Indian Christians. This change of attitude, suspicion, and, to some extent, antagonism were created because of some unfortunate historical evidences. It is well known to everyone in Christendom that during the days of British imperialism the Christian missionaries had to make certain declarations, which directly or indirectly made them support that imperialism. One of the outstanding Christians and a great educator, Dr. Kumarappa, an Indian Christian, expressed this explicitly in *Harpers Magazine* about twenty years ago. He told the Western public that the Oriental people have justification for this suspicion of Western Christian activities in Oriental countries, that the missionary activities of Western Christians of late were conducted either before or after political conquest in the Orient, or they were preceded or followed by commercial conquest. It might have been accidental; nevertheless, the Orientals became suspicious. Dr. Kumarappa gives a clear idea of the problem:

> Rightly or wrongly, the East has come to think of Christianity as part of the political game of the West. In religion it talks of "going about doing good"; in politics this takes the form of "ruling others for their good."
>
> . . . .
>
> Before the Christians went to Africa the Africans had lands but no Bibles; now they have Bibles but no lands. . . . Hence the East concludes that the political method of the West is first to send missionaries, then traders, and then gunboats to deprive the helpless peoples of their lands and to take possession of their natural resources.
>
> Is it any wonder if, with such knowledge of Western penetration, the East becomes distrustful of the professed philanthropy of the Christians, turns hostile to a religion which has let itself be used by foreign powers for political expansion, and grows more and more suspicious of the real mission of the missionary?[288]

We were told that Dr. E. Stanley Jones, the great Western Christian missionary to India, advised a recent conference of missionaries to quit India if they are not sympathetic toward the national aspirations of the Indians. We do know that many of the Western Christians have not been sympathetic to the national cause of India, although many others have been. The advice of Dr. Jones explicitly makes it clear that he is fully aware of the mentality of many of the Western Christians in

India. Bishop Frederick Fisher was another Christian leader who recognized the validity of this viewpoint. When he expressed sympathetic understanding of the Hindus and their aspirations, he was advised to leave India. Many other such American Christian leaders were compelled to leave the country because of their sympathetic attitude. We do not mean that the support of the national cause is an indication of the validity of the Christian missionary activity. But we want to make it clear that the Indians had reason to think that many Christian missionaries, directly or indirectly, supported various types of imperialism. No Indian can minimize the services of Christian missionaries in the field of education, medicine, and agriculture. Many noble souls inspired by the spirit of the Good Samaritan have devoted their lives and time for suffering humanity in India for years and years. The noble spirit of such Christian leaders is greatly appreciated and will continue to be appreciated by the Hindus. The pioneering work in spreading the system of Western education was done by many Christian missionaries. Many of the Western countries contributed enormously to medical and educational institutions in India. The Report of the Laymen's Commission gives us a clear understanding of what was done by Christian missionaries in the field of social service.[289]

However, as we happen to know the Hindu mind, we make bold to say that the Hindus can never have any antagonism toward the devotees of Christ, whether they are Oriental or Occidental, because of their very attitude toward incarnations since time immemorial. Sri Ramakrishna, the great modern spiritual leader, used to say that religious devotees are in a class of their own; they are not limited to any particular race or nationality. In other words, the worshippers of God—whether they take Christ, Krishna, or Buddha for their ideal—belong to the same group. From ancient times up to the days of Sri Ramakrishna, all the great teachers of India have emphasized this fact. Having been born and brought up in India, we are fully aware of the Hindu mentality and attitude toward those in other religions. So we would like to make it very clear that Christians in general have nothing to be concerned about. No Hindu with any understanding of religion will have any suspicious or unpleasant feeling or attitude toward real Christians, the devotees of Christ. The Christian Church should always express the teachings of Christ and uphold His spirit; then there will be no question of any unpleasant relationship between the Christians and Hindus or any other groups. The spirit of loving God and neighbor taught by Jesus will always establish brotherhood, if Christians remember this. A Hindu understands that true Christianity has no connection whatsoever with imperialism of either political or economic types even though it has been used by some for these purposes, as we have seen in previous chapters.

It is refreshing to note that Professor J. J. Kumarappa not only expressed this viewpoint, as mentioned previously, but Eddy Asirvatham, A. N. Sudarisanam, and a number of others also clearly expressed this same idea. Imperialism of any type is based on selfishness, greed, and love of power and it flourished by exploitation of dominated people. It is indeed encouraging to note what these Indian Christians themselves are saying. We quote from the manuscript of Professor Eddy Asirvatham:

> The Christian Scriptures clearly say that God has not left Himself without witnesses at any time or in any generation. Yet this outstanding Christian theologian and missionary wants to confine the revelation of an all-loving and merciful God to the four corners of the religion into which he happens to have been born.
>
> . . . .
>
> Christianity can make no headway in India unless we bring an understanding mind and a sympathetic approach to bear upon our study of non-Christian faiths, without surrendering at the same time the core of our religion which is the personality and the ever-living spirit of our Master, Jesus Christ.[290]

It must be admitted, however, that some Christians, both Western and Indian, have not cared in the past to understand the religious ideals of the Hindus. But as we have been watching the national movements of Indian Christians, we are convinced that they are fully aware of Indian culture and its contribution to the world civilization. This understanding of the Indian and some of the Western Christians has completely removed any doubts that might have been in the minds of some observers. We are sure that this very understanding and appreciation of Hindu ideals in religion on the part of Western Christians will strengthen the bond between these two religious groups.

The Christian missionary movement in India has undergone different phases of change. In the earlier days, the missionaries regarded Christianity as the only true religion which could lead one to God by proclaiming the redemption of the human soul through the intercession of Jesus, the Christ. Hinduism and other religions were considered to be false. There has been a gradual change in this point of view in the last twenty-five years, and the missionaries have come to regard Christianity as perfect, while Hinduism was thought of as imperfect. We must admit that this latter point of view has been accepted and expressed by only certain types of persons. A further change in attitude, led by liberal thinkers like Dr. Farquhar, Dr. Miller, Dr. Hogg, and Dr. E. Stanley Jones determines that Christianity is the ultimate goal of religion and Hinduism is in the process of reaching that goal. In other words, even the most liberal thinkers in the missionary field seem to think Christianity is the last word in religion.

It is interesting to note what Dr. Hogg has to say regarding this topic in his recent book, *The Christian Message to the Hindu.* Dr. Hogg is a great soul with a very noble purpose. We deeply appreciate his services for the cause of mankind. He gives recognition to the Hindu religious attitude of thousands of years. His appreciation of the Ramakrishna Mission is indeed very good. However, a man of his good will and experience in India should have understood the true spirit of Indian religion much better. We wonder how he can interpret some of the experiences of Jesus and His disciples in the episode of Transfiguration, or the spiritual experiences of St. Paul, St. Francis, and St. Teresa when he rejects, however courteously, the Hindu idea of the realization of

God. He writes: "Typically it [the Hindu religious spirit] has longed and sought to *see* God, to win and maintain a vividly immediate and engrossing realisation of the Divine Being."[291] Is this not also the spirit of all the Christian mystics, whether they follow the path of negation or affirmation, as Dr. Rufus Jones shows in his *Studies of Mystic Religion* and *The Luminous Trail*? Jesus says, according to the Gospel of St. John: "And the glory which thou [my Father] gavest me I have given them; that they may be one, even as we are one."[292] Again, Dr. Hogg further tells his readers:

> Whatever of the Divine Reality they may have beheld more overwhelmingly than many of us have done, it has not been granted them to recognize in Jesus 'The Word made flesh,' and through His crucifixion to feel the utter devastatingness of God's judgment upon guilt and sin, and in His resurrection to know themselves claimed for a Cause in the following of an invincible Leader.[293]

Many of his supposed points of difference are due to his own interpretation of the Hindu view. For instance, he says: ". . . the Hindu mind has never made 'righteousness' or 'holiness' central to its conception of God."[294] He did not consider at all the prerequisites of real spiritual life, as discussed by the Hindus themselves. These are the basic principles for ethical training of the mind so that the mind can conceive of God. Hindus in expressing their ideas in Sanskrit or other languages do not use the word "holiness." However, *sat-chit-ananda* (existence, knowledge, bliss), *satyam* (truth), *sundaram* (beautiful), are attributes of value and imply an ethical devotion which is overlooked by Dr. Hogg. We wonder why he is so insistent on establishing an absolute difference in the conceptions of the incarnation of God according to Hindu and Christian views. To quote Dr. Hogg:

> The Hindu *avatar* is a temporary intervention of the Divine which is made in a guise that is a disguise, and which is intrinsically repeatable in other disguises. The Incarnate Christ, on the other hand, is a unique intervention determinative once for all of the course of world-history, and effected in a guise which is an unsurpassable revelation, within the temporal and concrete, of the character and purpose of God.[295]

Cannot missionary activities be conducted by preaching the personality of Jesus, as Professor Asirvatham so appropriately mentioned?[296] Would such preaching require all the assertions made by Dr. Hogg?

It seems to a Hindu mind that this very attitude is a narrow view of God, who is regarded as the Infinite. A story by Sri Ramakrishna illustrates the Hindu point of view. Two people fell into a violent dispute as to the color of a chameleon. One said it was red; another claimed it was blue. Being unable to settle the argument, they consulted the man who lived under the tree where the disputed chameleon was found. The man told each of them that he was right, for he knew that the chameleon constantly changes its color, while at different times it has no color. So it would be seen differently by different persons.[297] Hindus say that every incarnation is unique in the expression of divine glory. Nevertheless, they are manifestations of the same divine Being. It is very refreshing to read what a great Christian missionary, Dr. Justin Abbott, has to say in this connection.

> Probably the chief cause for the misunderstanding of Hindu Theology by the West, is that the word, "Polytheism," as understood in the West carries the same idea as Hindu Polytheism. But Polytheism as understood in the West is entirely different from Hindu Polytheism. Polytheism in the West is simply plurality of gods. Hindu Polytheism is God-Supreme, manifesting Himself in many forms of divine beings. . . . Thus, rightly considered, Hindu Theology is as Monotheistic as Christianity and Islamism. . . . It is a Polytheism based on the strictest Monotheism.[298]

Mr. P. Chenchiah, an Indian Christian scholar, also expresses a similar viewpoint. He writes:

> Higher Hinduism has moved away from the religion of sacrifices from the days of the Upanishads. It has not only moved away from sacrifice as a religious act but has ceased long ago to express its vital concepts in terms thereof. The exposition of Jesus as a propitiation does not evoke any response. As for sin, saviour and salvation — all the major religions of the world are full of it. Whatever excuse there was before the days of comparative religious study for holding that a saviour and salvation are peculiar to Christianity, we can no longer continue in the error.[299]

A distinction is often made by many Christian missionary leaders that Christianity is a revealed religion because of the miracles performed by its Founder and His disciples, but other religions are natural and without the element of the supernatural. A study of Hinduism and other mystic religions will reveal that this viewpoint is untenable, as there have been many saints and incarnations in these religions who have had similar types of experiences and realizations of God. We are happy that many Indian Christian leaders feel the same way. P. Chenchiah writes that:

> There was a type of convert in the past who hated Hinduism and surrendered himself wholeheartedly to what he supposed to be Christianity. The convert of today regards Hinduism as his spiritual mother who has nurtured him in a sense of spiritual values in the past. He discovers the supreme value of Christ, not in spite of Hinduism but because Hinduism has taught him to discern spiritual greatness.[300]

Another Indian Christian, V. Chakkarai, states that: "We must, therefore, candidly recognize the manifest fact that Hinduism does provide the spiritual nourishment that Hindus demand."[301] It is very interesting to note what a great Christian scholar in Germany says. Dr. Otto is not only a great Christian scholar, but also a great scholar of Oriental religions, especially Hinduism. He studied Hindu philosophy and religion directly in India. He says: "Whether the flower of mysticism blooms in India or in China, in Persia or on the Rhine and in Erfurt, its fruit is one."[302] Miss Margaret Noble, a great scholar of Indian culture, has a deep understanding of India and the West, as she was born and brought up in England and afterwards lived in India. She (Sister Nivedita) says:

> The Christian ideal might be demonstrated successfully in India now, as it was in Italy in the days of St. Francis by the Begging Friars, for India has retained the ideal of such life even more completely than Italy ever had it. To the individual Christian, therefore, who is willing to accept the charge laid upon him, the way is clear. Let him go forth to the gentle East, strong in his mission, filled with burning renunciation, as 'a lamb amongst wolves.'[303]

An Indian Catholic scholar, Anthony Elenjimiptam, gives us definite material for thought. It is evident that he appreciates deeply the contribution of Hinduism.

> Now I am fully convinced that the Christian religion, which claims to be catholic, can really be catholic and grow more and more in catholicity, if it is wise and humble enough to look critically and dispassionately to the cultural heritage of Indian Catholicism, which is all-inclusive, all-embracing, all-enfolding.[304]

Professor W. E. Hocking makes it very clear that Hinduism, especially the Ramakrishna-Vedanta movement, can contribute considerably to Christianity in order for it to be effective and appreciated by non-Christian religions.

> When two religions are present in the same region each tends to adopt from the other whatever seems to be peculiarly expressive in its language or significant in its ways. Whether inadvertently or by a

> less conscious kind of approbation, there is mutual teaching and learning.[305]

Professor E. S. Brightman and others, too, in America, do not hesitate to appreciate the religious contributions of the Hindus to world culture. In his introduction to the admirable translation of *Stotramala*, Dr. Justin Abbott, an American Unitarian Missionary, expresses deep appreciation of the Hindu saints and philosophy of religion and its contribution to the world. He says: "The West has need to beg the pardon of India for its misconception of Hindu religious thought, . . ."[306] The late Dr. Thomas J. Sunderland and the late Bishop Frederick Fisher, formerly of Calcutta, were great admirers of Hindu life and culture. Dr. Sunderland's book, *India in Bondage*, shows how appreciative he was.[307] There are a number of books written by other modern missionaries which include appreciation of Hindu views of religion. Dr. E. Stanley Jones is also trying to establish better understanding between Indian and American cultural groups. As an evidence of his deeper appreciation of Hindu religious methods, he conducts *ashramas* (religious retreats).

It is very important to note that the Indian Christians have become considerably conscious of their national culture. The quotations that are given here in this chapter from the great Indian Christian leaders indicate very definitely that they do not only understand the spirit of Hinduism but they also appreciate the contribution of Hindu culture to the world at large. If we are allowed to make a prediction, we must say that this spirit will grow immensely as time goes on. The Christian Churches in

India will absorb some of the Indian ways of life. Dr. Stanley Jones has already introduced the *ashrama* in India and America. Many of the Christian leaders, Indian as well as Western, realize that Christianity should be preached to the Indians in their own cultural background. Some have formed the *Christa-sevadal* which considerably follows the ways of the Indian religious leaders. This brotherhood and such other movements are extremely encouraging for better understanding between the Christian and Hindu groups. As we have already said, the missionary movement has gone through definite changes. As time goes on, there will be more such absorptions and mutual assimilation. It will not be out of place to say that the Hindu missionary movement in the West will also have a similar attitude, as we have already noticed that the Hindu missionary leaders of the Ramakrishna Order follow the style and ways of living in the Western countries to a considerable extent. They understand the deeper side of Christian cultures (idealistic religious culture) and realize the utility of the scientific attitude and its contribution to the betterment of everyday life. They also appreciate what the modern, pragmatic, scientific West can contribute to India. It is but fitting that the Christian and Hindu missionaries should mutually understand the spirit of each other.

A question may arise in the minds of many persons in this connection: When Hinduism becomes a more aggressive missionary movement, will there be a conflict between this and the missionary movement of the Christians? As it is known, the Vedanta movement in America is conducted by the monks of the Ramakrishna Order of India. These religious leaders are often questioned about the nature of their activities; they are asked if they are not following practically the same method of converting Christians to the Hindu faith as the Christians themselves follow. It is frequently assumed that the very presence of the Swamis of the Ramakrishna Order in Europe and North and South America, lands of the Christians, definitely indicates a challenge to the aggressive Christian movement in the East. It is suspected that perhaps they will also become aggressive missionaries when India becomes fully independent and has a place in the family of nations.

Our answer to this is that the very foundation of Hindu philosophical and religious thought can never allow a Hindu missionary to become a party to any type of religious bias or fanatical zeal. Even in the Vedic scriptures, which date back to antiquity (at least to four thousand B. C.), we find that "Truth is one; men call it by various names."[308] Time and again, this idea was vigorously and dynamically declared by a number of successive teachers. In the *Bhagavad-Gita*, Sri Krishna popularized this viewpoint at least as early as one thousand B. C. In the modern age, Sri Ramakrishna has demonstrated this truth in His life by following different religious methods prescribed by the Christians, Buddhists, Mohammedans, Hindus, and others for reaching the same state of God-consciousness. The very life of Sri Ramakrishna is an interpretation and validification of that ancient Vedic teaching that "Truth is one." It will not be out of place to note that because of this spirit of universality of religion in principle and practice the

Hindus not only welcomed Christian guests into their midst but also gave shelter to the Jews and Zoroastrians when they had to leave their homelands, as according to tradition, St. Thomas had to do. Later on, when the Mohammedans settled in India, the Hindus and Mohammedans generally lived together mutually contributing to each other and developing new groups. Many Mohammedan saints had Hindu followers as the Hindu saints had Mohammedan followers. This shows that the genius of Hindu philosophy and religion has the inherent possibility of creating harmony with other religious groups within India and outside its borders.

Buddhist missionaries were sent out of India to teach the Gospel of Buddha and share it with the existing religious groups of the day, as we have previously mentioned in an earlier chapter. This is the spirit of the Indian missionary movement. Swami Vivekananda is the first great Hindu missionary to come out of India with the dynamic message of the harmony and universality of religion. In his first address to the Parliament of Religions, which assembled in Chicago in 1893 for the first time in the history of the world and where different religious leaders presented their views, the illustrious Swami declared:

> To the Hindu, then, the whole world of religions is only a travelling, a coming up, of different men and women, through various conditions and circumstances, to the same goal.
>
> . . . .
>
> It will be a religion which will have no place for persecution or intolerance in its policy, which will

> recognise divinity in every man and woman, and whose whole scope, whose whole force, will be centered in aiding humanity to realise its own true, divine nature.[309]

These utterances of the Swami are the guiding principle of the followers of this great movement.

The missionary movement of the Hindus is not to condemn, criticize, or look down upon other religious groups and their practices, however different they may be, as the representatives of this movement know that these religious practices and ideals are also leading people to the same goal. This may lead to the challenge: Why, then, do the so-called Hindu missionaries, liberal or conservative, come to the land of the Christians where the people are following Jewish and Christian ideals? Our answer is that, for good or bad, the Indians have for centuries and centuries cultivated the techniques of religious practices and have developed a comprehensive psychology of the highest type based on all functions of the human mind — unconscious, conscious, and superconscious. Just as physical and social scientists share their knowledge from the United States and Germany to Russia, India, and China, so the representatives of the Hindu religion want to share their spiritual treasures with other groups. It will not be out of place to mention that for centuries the people of some religions unfortunately were looked down upon and treated unsympathetically by well-meaning and devoted followers of another religion. As we said in Chapter I, it was the privilege of the Hindus to discover that God incarnates at different times in different forms to inspire mankind and lead them to divine realization in mystic and practical life. So it is but fitting that the representatives of Hinduism would come out to share the principle of harmony in religion and show that the different religious groups can work and live together and practice their respective religious exercises without striking any discordant note.

Science has brought the nations of the world close together. It is almost unbelievable that one can have a trip around the world in a few hours. It is equally inconceivable that a business man can go from New York to Bombay, stop over in New Delhi for a few days and come back within a week. For good or bad, the different groups with different religious and cultural backgrounds and aesthetic sensibilities are brought together. So the people have to learn to live with different types of persons with different backgrounds, even from a selfish point of view of self-preservation and psychological stability. As we have observed in a small family, the persons who do not know how to harmonize themselves with various members of the same family are perfectly miserable, living a life of unhappiness and isolation. This is also true in the family of nations. It is a mistake to think that all nations will be alike and have the same cultural pattern in the aesthetic sense, or that the members of the same family will express themselves in an identical manner. Therefore, we must find a means of harmonizing the different ways of life.

Professor F. S. C. Northrop has something very constructive to say in his great work, *The Meeting of East and West*:

> It appears, therefore, when the paradoxically confusing and tragic conflicts of the world are analyzed one by one and then traced to the basic philosophical problem underlying them, and when this problem of the relation between immediately apprehended and theoretically inferred factors in things is then solved by replacing the traditional three-termed relation of appearance by the two-termed relation of epistemic correlation, that a realistically grounded, scientifically verifiable idea of the good for man and his world is provided in which the unique achievements of both the East and the West are united and the traditional incompatible and conflicting partial values of the different parts of the West are first reconstructed and then reconciled, so that *each* is seen to have something unique to contribute and *all* are reformed so as to supplement and reinforce instead of combat and destroy each other.[310]

The real representatives of Hinduism, Christianity, and other religions can exchange ideas and ideals and live a life of personal integration. This very method will act as direct and indirect dissemination of religious living. This friendship of the devotees of God belonging to different religions will have a tremendous influence in society. We have seen in India that Hindu and Mohammedan devotees not only appreciated one another but also respected one another's personalities and ways of living. In fact, they are the people who established peaceful living in Indian society by their own personal examples. This very idea is the basis of a harmonious, universal society of mankind. The more man goes toward God, the greater power he will have for living in a co-operative and co-ordinated social organization. In spite of present-day disputes in India, which are created by non-religious persons — political leaders using religion as a cloak — there will be a harmonious society when people understand the basic principles of religion and try to live according to them.

From a sociological point of view, it is very important that the different cultural patterns developed by certain religious groups be known by others. The presence of the Hindu missionaries in America will definitely bring to light in American society that the Hindus have certain cultural patterns based on religious idealism which has been developed for centuries.

> This [growing influence of Oriental culture and religion on Western life] cannot fail to have the most profound effect on the development of our culture, and in many directions its influence is already apparent. So far, however, it has made little impression on Church Christianity, where it is regarded as a dangerous and competitive tendency. This is a symptom of the interior weakness and uncertainty of Church religion, for in the great ages of Christian thought theology has always been able to embrace and absorb alien systems much to its own enrichment.[311]

The family of nations can establish harmony in spite of divergent thought patterns and aesthetic sensibilities, if we know that other cultures produce men and women of integration and spiritual realization. As the Christian missionaries in India should remember that they are ambassadors of Christian culture to India, so would the Indians like to see the best manifestation of Christian culture in them.

Conversely, the Christian nations, like America, would also evaluate the facts of the Hindu religion in the personalities who come here as ambassadors from India, in the form of a missionary movement. We feel that for the greater good of the world civilization and consciousness of one world, the mutual exchange of ideas and ideals through integrated spiritual personalities is absolutely necessary. Hence, Hindus should welcome Christian missionaries and Christians should welcome Hindu missionaries as co-workers and co-builders of a harmonious civilization. Even from an economic and political point of view, such commingling of noble representatives of different cultures will be extremely helpful for durable peace in this conflicting world. We make bold to say that the missionary activities of all religious groups in the future should be inspired to work for the common good of mankind, harmonious living, and the realization of God in individual ways with acceptance of other viewpoints as valid and true, and as Swami Vivekananda says: "For the happiness of many and for the good of many."

---

265. Matt. 10:7-8; Luke 9:2.
266. Mark 16:15.
267. Matt. 22:39; Mark 12:31; Luke 10:27.
268. **Dhammapada** (Sayings of Buddha) XII:10-13.
269. Edwin Diller Starbuck, **The Psychology of Religion** (New York: Charles Scribner's Sons, 1899), pp. 58, 64, 67.

CHRISTIAN MISSIONS

270. William James, **The Varieties of Religious Experience** (New York: Longmans, Green Ñ Co., 1929), p. 209.
271. James Bisset Pratt, **The Religious Consciousness** (New York: The Macmillan Co., 1945), p. 155.
272. **Spiritual Teachings of Swami Brahmananda**, p. 102.
273. John 3:3 and 6.
274. **Spiritual Teachings of Swami Brahmananda**, p. 104.
275. **Upanishads.**
276. Swami Akhilananda, **Hindu Psychology** (New York: Harper & Bros., 1946), pp. 191-195.
277. J. McV. Hunt, "An Instance of the Social Origin of Conflict Resulting in Psychoses," **The American Journal of Orthopsychiatry**, VIII (January, 1938), p. 159.
278. Swami Akhilananda, **Hindu Psychology**, chaps. VI and XI.
279. A Select Library of Nicene and Post-Nicene Fathers of the Christian Church, Vol. I, **The Confessions and Letters of St. Augustin**, ed. Philip Schaff, D. D., LL.D. (Buffalo: The Christian Literature Co., 1886), Letter CXXX, chap. IX.
280. **Theologia Germanica**, trans. Susanna Winkworth (London: Macmillan & Co., 1874), pp. 74-75.
281. **Basic Writings of St. Thomas Aquinas**, II, ed. Anton C. Pegis (New York: Random House Inc., 1945), p. 60.
282. **The Life of St. Teresa of Jesus**, p. 59.
283. **The Gospel of Ramakrishna**, revised by Swami Abhedananda, pp. 48, 190, 275.
284. **Works**, II, 37.
285. Ibid, V. 180.
286. F. S. C. Northrop, **The Meeting of the East and West** (New York: The MacMillan Co., 1946), p. 482.
287. Swami Abhedananda, **Why a Hindu Accepts Christ and Rejects Churchianity.**
288. John Jesudason Cornelius (Now J. J. Kumarappa), "An Oriental Looks at Christian Missions," **Harpers Magazine**, 154 (April 1927), pp. 599-600.
289. Laymen's Foreign Mission Inquiry, Chairman William E. Hocking, **Rethinking Missions** (New York: Harper & Bros., 1932), **passim.**
290. Eddy Asirvatham, **Christianity in the Indian Crucible**, chap. II Manuscript to be published.
291. A. G. Hogg, **The Christian Message to the Hindu** (London: S.C.M. Press, 1947), p. 31.
292. John 17:22.
293. Hogg, **op. cit.**, pp. 32-33.
294. Ibid., p. 34.
295. Ibid., p. 35.
296. **Supra**, p. 267.
297. **Sayings of Sri Ramakrishna**, XXXVIII:721.
298. Justin E. Abbot, **Stotramala**, The Poet-Saints of Maharashtra, (Poona: Scottish Mission Industries Co., Ltd., 1929), pp. xii-xiii.
299. P. Chenchiah, "Jesus and Non-Christian Faith," **Rethinking Christianity in India** (2nd ed.; Madras: A. N. Sudarisanam, 1939), p. 60.
300. Ibid., p. 51.
301. V. Chakkarai, "The Relations Between Christianity and Non-Christian Faiths," **Rethinking Christianity in India**, p. 71.

302. Rudolph Otto, **Mysticism East and West** (New York: The Macmillan Co., 1932) p. xv.
303. Margaret E. Noble, **Lambs Among Wolves** (Calcutta: Udbodhan Office, 1928), p. 31.
304. Anthony Elenjimiptam, "Catholicity of Sri Ramakrishna," **Prabudha Bharata**, Vol. 52, October, 1947.
305. Hocking, **Living Religions and a World Faith**, p. 177.
306. Abbott, **Stotramala**, p. xiii.
307. Thomas Jobey Sunderland, **India in Bondage** (New York: Lewis Coperland Co., 1932).
308. **Rig-Veda.**
309. **Works**, I, pp. 16, 17.
310. Northrop, **The Meeting of the East and West**, p. 478.
311. Alan W. Watts, **Behold the Spirit** (New York: Pantheon Books Inc., 1947), pp. 58-59.

BIBLIOGRAPHY

Books

Abbot, Justin E. **Stotramala.** The Poet-Saints of Maharashtra. Poona: Scottish Mission Industries Co., Ltd., 1929.

Abhedananda, Swami. **How to be a Yogi.** San Francisco: The Vedanta Ashrama, 1902.

————.**Why a Hindu Accepts Christ and Rejects Churchianity.**

Akhilananda, Swami. **Hindu Psychology.** New York: Harper & Bros., 1946.

A Select Library of Nicene and Post-Nicene Fathers of the Christian Church. Vol. I. **The Confessions and Letters of St. Agustin.** Edited by Philip Schaff, D. D., LL. D. Buffalo: The Christian Literature Co., 1886.

Asirvatham, Eddy. **Christianity in the Indian Crucible** (Manuscript to be published).

————. "India." **Christianity Today.** Edited by Henry Smith Leiper. New York: Morehouse-Gorham Co., 1947.

————. "Problems of the Christian Church in India." **Christian World Mission.** Edited by William K. Anderson. Nashville: Commission on Ministerial Training, The Methodist Church, 1946.

Barth, Karl. **This Christian Cause.** New York: The MacMillan Co., 1941.

Basic Writings of St. Thomas Aquinas. Vol. II. Edited by Anton C. Pegis. New York: Random House, Inc., 1945.

Baumann, Julius. **The Character of Jesus.** 1908.

Binet-Senglé, Charles. **The Insanity of Jesus.** 3rd ed., ed., Vols. I, II; 1st ed., Vols. III, IV. Paris, 1911.

Brightman, Edgar Sheffield. **A Philosophy of Religion.** New York: Prentice-Hall, Inc., 1940.

Bundy, Walter E. **The Psychic Health of Jesus.** New York: The MacMillan Co., 1922.

Cadbury, Henry J. **The Peril of Modernizing Jesus.** New York: The MacMillan Co., 1937.

Chakkarai, V. "The Relations between Christianity and Non-Christian Faiths." **Rethinking Christianity in India.** 2nd ed. Madras: A. N. Sudarisanam, 1939.

Chenchiah, P. "Jesus and Non-Christian Faiths." **Rethinking Christianity in India.** 2nd. ed. Madras: A. N. Sudarisanam, 1939.

————. "The Church and the Indian Christian." **Rethinking Christianity in India.** 2nd ed. Madras: A. N. Sudarisanam, 1939.

Dhammapada (Sayings of Buddha).

Dostoevski, Fedor. **The Brothers Karamazov.** Translated by Constance Garnett. Part two, Book V. New York: Random House, 1933.

Encyclopedia of Religion and Ethics. Vol. IX, Edited by James Hastings. New York: Charles Scribner's Sons, 1917.

Hirsch, William. **Conclusions of a Psychiatrist.** New York, 1912.

Hocking, William Ernest. **Living Religions and a World Faith.** New York: The MacMillan Co., 1940.

Hogg, A. G. **The Christian Message to the Hindu.** London: S. C. M. Press, 1947.

Holtzman, H. J. **The Messianic Consciousness of Jesus.** 1907.

Holtzmann, Oskar. **Was Jesus an Ecstatic?** 1903.

Hough, Lynn Harold. **The Meaning of Human Experience.** New York: Longman's, Green & Co., 1929.

Ignatius, St. **Spiritual Exercises.**

James, William. **The Varieties of Religious Experiences.** New York: Longmans, Green & Co., 1929.

Kempis, Thomas á. **The Following of Christ.** New York: Catholic Publishing Co.

Kumarappa, J. J. **Practice and Precepts of Jesus.** Ahmedabad: Navajivan Publishing House, 1945.

Lawrence, Brother. **The Practice of the Presence of God.** New York: Fleming H. Revell Co., 1895.

Laymen's Foreign Mission Inquiry. Chairman William E. Hocking. **Rethinking Missions.** New York: Harper & Bros., 1932.

Loosten, George de (Dr. Georg Lomer) **Jesus Christ from the Standpoint of Psychiatry.** Bamberg, 1905.

Mayo, Elton. **The Social Problems of an Industrial Civilization.** Boston: Division of Research, Graduate School of Business Administration, Harvard University, 1945.

New Testament. **Holy Bible.** Matthew, Mark, Luke, John, Acts of the Apostles, Romans, I Corinthians, II Corinthians, Philippians, and James.

Niebuhr, Reinhold. **Christianity and Power Politics.** New York: Charles Scribner's Sons, 1940.

Noble, Margaret E., **Lambs Among Wolves.** Calcutta: Udbodhan Office, 1928.

F. S. C. Northrop, **The Meeting of East and West.** New York: The MacMillan Co., 1946.

Old Testament. **Holy Bible.** Proverbs.

Otto, Rudolph. **India's Religion of Grace and Christianity Compared and Contrasted.** Translated by Frank High Foster, D. D. New York: The MacMillan Co., 1930.

————. **Mysticism East and West.** New York: The MacMillan Co., 1932.

Pantanjali. **Yoga Aphorisms.**

Pratt, James Bissett. **The Religious Consciousness.** New York: The MacMillan Co., 1945.

Rasmussen, Emil. **Jesus, A Comparative Study in Psychopathology.** Leipzig, 1905.

Rig-Veda.

Ronaldshay, Earl of. **The Heart of Aryavarta.** London: Constable & Co., Ltd., 1925.

Saradananda, Swami. **Sri Sri Ramakrishna Lilaprasanga.** Vol II. Calcutta: Udbodhan Office.

Sayings of Sri Ramakrishna. Mylapore, Madras: Sri Ramakrishna

Math, 1925.
Schweitzer, Albert. **Indian Thought and Its Development.** New York: Henry Holt & Co., 1936.
————. **Out of My Life and Thought.** Translated by C. T. Campion, M. A. New York: Henry Holt & Co., 1933.
————. **The Psychiatric Study of Jesus.** Boston: The Beacon Press, 1948.
Sorokin, Pitirim A. **The Crisis of Our Age.** New York: E. P. Dutton & Co., Inc., 1942.
————. **The Reconstruction of Humanity.** Boston: Beacon Press, 1948.
Spiritual **Teachings of Swami Brahmananda.** 2nd ed. Mylapore, Madras: Sri Ramakrishna Math, 1933.
Srimad-Bhagavad-Gita. Translated by Swami Swarupananda. 5th ed. Mayavati, Almora, Himalayas: Advaita Ashrama, 1933.
Srimad-Bhagavad-Gita.
Srimad Bhagavatam, The Wisdom of God. Translated by Swami Prabhavananda. New York: G. P. Putnam's Sons, 1943.
Starbuck, Edwin Diller. **The Psychology of Religion.** New York: Charles Scribner's Sons, 1899.
Strauss, David Friedrich. **The Life of Jesus Revised for the German People.** 1865.
Sunderland, Thomas Jobey. **India in Bondage.** New York: Lewis Coperland Co., 1932.
Tawney, R. H. **Religion and the Rise of Capitalism.** New York: Harcourt Brace & Co., Inc., 1947.
Teachings of Swami Shivananda. Calcutta: Udbodhan office.
Temple, William, **Mens Creatrix.** London: MacMillan & Co., Ltd., 1917.
Teresa, St. **Way of Perfection.** London: Thomas Baker, 1935.
The **Complete Works of Swami Vivekananda.** Mayavati, Almora, Himalayas: Advaita Ashrama. Vols. I-VII.
The **Eternal Companion.** Hollywood: Vedanta Society of Southern California, 1944.
The **Gospel of Ramakrishna.** Revised by Swami Abhedananda. New York: The Vedanta Society, 1947.
The Gospel of Sri Ramakrishna. Translated by Swami Nikhilananda. New York: Ramakrishna-Vivekananda Center, 1942.
The Life of St. Teresa of Jesus. Translated by David Lewis. London: Thomas Baker, 1924.
Theologia Germanica. Translated by Susanna Winkworth. London: MacMillan & Co., 1874.
Upanishads. **Katha Upanishad; Svetesvatara Upanishad.** Vol. III; **Taittiriya Upanishad.** Vol. VII.
Urwick, Edward J. **The Message of Plato.** London: Methuen Co., 1920.
Watts, Alan W. **Behold the Spirit.** New York: Pantheon Books, Inc., 1947.

Public Documents

Evidence before Parliament. Com., 1853.

Articles

Brightman, Edgar Sheffield. "The Neo-Orthodox Trend," **The Journal of Bible and Religion,** Vol. XIV (August, 1946).

Cornelius, John Jesudason (J. J. Kumarappa). "An Oriental Looks at Christian Missions," **Harper's Magazine**, April, 1927.

Elenjimiptam, Anthony. "Catholicity of Sri Ramakrishna," **Prabuddha Bharata,** Vol. 52 (October, 1947).

Evening Bulletin (Providence), December 24, 1935.

Hunt, J. McV. "An Instance of the Social Origin of Conflict Resulting in Psychoses," **The American Journal of Orthopsychiatry,** Vol. VIII (January, 1938).

Hutchins, Robert M. "The Bomb Secret is Out!" **The American,** Dember, **1947.**

Johnson, Paul E. "Is Christianity Imperialistic?" **Aryan Path,** Vol. 8, No. 5 (May, 1937).

Knudson, Albert C. "The Theology of Crisis," **The Sixth Biennial Meeting of the Conference of Theological Seminaries and Colleges in the United States and Canada,** Bulletin 6, September, **1928.**

INDEX

Abbot, Justin, 271, 274
Abhedananda, Swami, 97
Asirvatham, Eddy, 120, 171, 177, 266, 267
Aurelius, Marcus, 22, 47

Barth, Karl, 51, 164, 165, 260
Bhagavad-Gita, 64, 67, 78, 87, 93, 133, 276
Bhagavatam, 88
Bhakti Yoga, 91
Bliss, 207, 208, 213, 251
Boehme, Jacob, 124, 126, 241
Brahmananda, Swami, 38, 39, 53, 190, 203, 205, 214, 215, 237, 239, 246, 252, 253, 255
Brightman, Edgar S., 49, 165, 208, 274
Buddha, 20, 36, 38, 62, 79, 136, 137, 144, 145, 224, 240, 241, 246, 247, 266, 277

Cadbury, Henry, 165, 243
Chaitanya, 192
Chakkarai, V., 272
Chenchiah, P., 239, 272
Christian Century, 170
Church, The, 122, 177, 220, 223, 225, 262
Cicero, 22
Confucius, 136
Conversion, 237, 248-257, 259-261

Devotional exercises; *see* Spiritual practices

Elenjimiptam, Anthony, 273
Emerson, 39
Epictetus, 22

Farquhar, 268
Fisher, Bishop Frederick, 265, 274
Fox, George, 48, 120, 124, 126, 210, 241, 260
Freud, 19

Gandhi, Mahatma, 171, 175
Guru; see Spiritual teacher

Hatha Yoga, 94
Hegel, 204, 206
Hocking, William E., 165, 174, 273
Höffding, 241
Hogg, 268-270
Holmes, John Haynes, 171
Hough, 50
Humanists, 32, 67, 68, 131
Hunt, McVicker, 257
Hutchins, Chancellor, 186

Immortality, 208, 212, 217
Immortal life, 207, 209, 212, 213
Imperialism, 22, 162, 263, 265, 266
Ingersoll, 138, 220

INDEX

Initiation, 252-254, 256, 260

James, 250, 251, 254
Jnana Yoga, 95
Jones, E. Stanley, 162, 171, 264, 268, 274, 275
Jones, Rufus M., 165, 269
Johnson, Paul E., 161
Jung, Carl, 242

Karma, (law of cause and effect), 39, 188
Karma Yoga, 92, 93
Katha Upanishad, 74
Keith, Sir Arthur, 63
Kempis, Thomas A, 54, 62
Kierkegaard, Soren, 260
Knudson, 51
Krishna, Sri, 20, 21, 32, 38, 39, 41, 67, 73, 78, 79, 85, 87, 93, 101, 144, 145, 188, 241, 266, 276
Kumarappa, J. C., 165, 171
Kumarappa, J. J., 171, 263, 264, 266

Laotze, 136
Lawrence, Brother, 124, 144
Lawrence, Bishop W. Appleton, 165

Macaulay, Lord, 158
Madhwa, 239
Marx, Karl, 137
Marxian philosophy, 240
Marxists, 131
Mayo, Elton, 220, 242
Miller, 268
Mind, states of, 112
Monotheism, 271

Narada, 103
Negative mysticism, 55, 56, 211
Neo-Calvinists, 48
Niebuhr, Reinhold, 122, 138, 162, 163, 165, 166
Noble, Margaret, 272
Northrop, F.S.C., 260, 279

Otto, Rudolph, 40, 272

Pantajali, 73, 75, 78, 83, 232
Plato, 47
Plotinus, 47, 119
Polytheism, 271
Powers
- occult, 85-87, 94
- psychic, 81, 83-85, 94

Pratt, 250, 254
Psychiatrists, 18, 19
Psychoanalysts, 37, 231, 232
Psychologists, 35, 254
- materialistic, 54

Raja Yoga, 94
Ramakrishna, Sri, 20, 23, 25, 34, 36, 38, 41, 66, 73, 78-80, 104, 114, 124, 137, 144-146, 193, 196, 203, 206, 224, 228, 230, 246, 248, 251, 258, 261, 265, 266, 270, 276
Ramakrishna Mission, 268
Ramakrishna Order, 224, 275
Ramanuja, Ramanujacharya, 103, 239
Religious
- dynamics, 225
- experiences; *see* Spiritual experiences
- exercises; *see* Spiritual practices
- practices; *see* Spiritual practices

Ronaldshay, Earl of, 130, 131

St. Anthony, 124, 134, 240

INDEX

St. Augustine, 66, 258
St. Bernard, 126, 241
St. Francis, 115, 134, 176, 177, 222, 225, 240, 268, 273
St. John of the Cross, 53, 241
St. Ignatius, 120, 126, 241
St. Paul, 24, 50, 68, 76, 81, 110, 168, 180, 183, 186, 195, 198, 201, 205, 210, 212, 215-217, 225, 230, 249, 251, 252, 260, 268
St. Teresa, 53, 120, 124, 126, 241, 258, 268
St. Thérèse (Little Flower), 124
St. Thomas, 262, 277
St. Thomas Aquinas, 258
Samadhi; see Superconscious realization
Samskaras (inherent tendencies), 231, 255, 257
Sangha (religious order), 223, 224
Sankara, 239
Schweitzer, Albert, 18, 19, 31, 49, 55, 210, 212
Seneca, 22
Socrates, 47
Sorokin, Pitirim A., 47, 59, 141, 259
Spinoza, 207
Spiritual
  exercises; *see* spiritual practices
  experiences, 54, 57, 126, 225, 246, 251, 256, 259, 268; *see also* Spiritual realization and Superconscious realization
  practices, 26, 40, 51, 52, 66, 70, 84, 96, 97, 100-102, 107, 108, 111-113, 116-121, 123, 125, 126, 148, 215, 216, 222, 227, 228, 239, 248, 254, 257, 259-261, 278
  realization, 80, 83, 85, 227, 234; *see also* Spiritual experiences and Superconscious realization
  teacher, 229, 230, 232, 233, 236, 248, 252, 255, 261
Starbuck, 249, 250, 251, 254
Sudarisanam, A. N., 266
Sunderland, Thos. J., 274
Superconscious
  realization, 53, 84, 216, 233; *see also* Spiritual experiences and Spiritual realization
  state, 28

Tawney, R. H., 135, 143, 166
Temple, Archbishop William, 156-160
Theologia Germanica, 258
Theologians, 54, 260
  crisis, 50
  neo-orthodox, 48-50, 167-169
Turiyananda, Swami, 228

Upanishads, 240

Vivekananda, Swami, 17, 35, 36, 42, 43, 53, 64, 67, 69, 74, 77, 85, 89, 93, 97, 103, 105, 106, 113-115, 172, 191, 192, 196, 213, 229, 231, 232, 238, 239, 246, 256, 259, 277, 282

Wesley, John, 48, 120, 126, 210, 240, 241, 260

Yoga, 65, 67, 70, 72-82, 85, 87, 91-97, 215, 232, 259; *see also* *Bhakti Yoga* and *Karma Yoga*